Published 2021
Printed in the United States of America
Print ISBN: 978-1-64742-104-5
E-ISBN: 978-1-64742-105-2
Library of Congress Control Number: 2021904801

For information, address:
She Writes Press
1569 Solano Ave #546
Berkeley, CA 94707

Interior designs by Tabitha Lahr

She Writes Press is a division of SparkPoint Studio, LLC.

REBELLION, 1967

1967

A Memoir

JANET LUONGO

SHE WRITES PRESS

Dad in WWII, Mom as a Powers model, their wedding,
and our family of five in 1950.

Our grandmother, Nanny, with Grandpa Hugo, Dad, Mom,
and sisters Maureen, Barbara, and me.

I dedicate this story to
My gifted but hurt parents and sisters
My grandmother, Nanny, who watched over us.
Jim, my husband, for all his love and support
People, especially girls, who face daunting obstacles.

Janet in Grandpa Hugo's garden, age two and fourteen.

FOREWORD

There was a child went forth every day,
And the first object he looked upon and received with wonder or
* pity or love or dread, that object he became,*
And that object became part of him for the day or a certain
* part of the day . . .*
or for many years or stretching cycles of years.
—From *Leaves of Grass* by Walt Whitman.

first heard this Whitman poem as a choral reading orches-
trated by a dark-haired woman with lips lined in red. The
detail of her red lips helped me remember how the voices rolled
over me in waves—men together, women together, the solos, the
children, then everyone in unison. Each wave of sound aroused
different feelings, and words like "stretching cycles of years"
opened my eyes to see the world as a great spinning wonder.

An impressionable grade school student, I sat with my parents
and sisters for Sunday worship that our Unitarian congregation
held in the Hollis Cinema while waiting for our modern church
to be erected. Nationwide, Unitarians soon merged with Universalists. This band of free thinkers was considered quite odd
by the Catholic children in our neighborhood of Queens Village,
New York. I learned that being different was okay.

Whitman's poems created excitement about the open road. I loved exploring beyond my neighborhood on my blue bicycle with my best friend Meryl Lee, both of us skinny and smart, playing and laughing until we wet our pants. Inspired those years by the adventures of Nancy Drew, problem-solver, I developed an unrelenting desire to write a book myself.

Like Whitman's child who "became" the objects looked upon, I closely observed, absorbed sensations, and acted on emotions stirred by brokenness in society, my family, and my heart. At age fifteen in 1964, I stood up before our UU congregation in our new boxy modern church to deliver a monologue, "Who Am I?" This memoir explores that same question.

————

I tell my story from the point of view of my younger self, who reveals her inner desires as she moves through pluralistic New York City in the 1960s. I now trust that all the experiences—ecstatic love and dreadful fear—taught me what I needed to know about myself, my family, and my country.

This memoir has truly been a life-long project that began over fifty years ago with journal entries the year I came of age. Reading the entries a dozen years later, I pieced together a first draft, but hid it under my bed until my son was grown. I pulled it out to review ten years ago. Each sketchy recollection opened portals to an abundance of vivid memories that I shaped into a narrative, hoping it would read like a novel, and thereby provide an equally vivid experience for you, the reader, all the while remaining true to facts, impressions, and the essence of emotional truth.

I capitalize Black and White people because I consider them both socially constructed racial identities. The summer after the racial justice demonstrations of 2020, several organizations and newspapers, such as the Washington Post, began to capitalize Black. I follow the recommendation of The National

Association of Black Journalists: "Whenever a color is used to appropriately describe race then it should be capitalized, including White and Brown."

There are no angels or villains among the characters with whom I engaged—Black, Brown, White, and multiracial people of varying ethnicity. All of us are like children who go forth, curious to explore the world. As we stumble, climb, and break through protective barriers, there's no way to escape mistakes. The key is to get back up, honestly assess and act on what we learned, and graciously forgive ourselves. For all the people in my story, I feel compassion.

Mom with her sister Pauline, 1933

CONTENTS

PART I: SPRING AND SUMMER, 1966

Duffy family, 1965

Chapter 1
MOM

Arriving home from school, I opened the door and stopped dead at what I saw: Mom on the sofa, a man kissing her on the mouth—a white-haired man. Their heads lifted. I had never seen the man in my life. I passed to the kitchenette and found my younger sister Maureen, who shrugged and looked at me with a tight mouth. Dad had only been gone a couple months.

Maureen, Mom, and I were all who remained living in our apartment. My older sister Barbara had broken away from the family first, about a year ago, vowing she'd never let our alcoholic father slap her again. When she turned eighteen, she ran away to marry a man twice her age, a handsome French nightclub singer with a shrunken liver. Dad moved out soon after I turned seventeen in March. In April, Mom flew to Tijuana, Mexico, and returned with divorce papers and a couple bottles of Kahlua. After years of fighting and talking about it, at last their divorce was final, and Mom was free.

We three women agreed we'd pitch in with chores and anything it took to survive and thrive. I worked a part time job after school, and Maureen, just sixteen, babysat. Mom, still beautiful at thirty-nine, had a glamorous fashion job in Manhattan. We figured she'd date and play the field until she found a good man. Eventually. This was only May. *What's the hurry?*

Maureen and I huddled in the kitchenette at the narrow table between the fridge and a window covered with blinds, holding our breath, straining to hear what was going on between Mom and the old guy. Maureen surprised me by blurting out, "I miss Dad." We talked about good times with him, like when he rowed his three girls out on a lake to fish but we'd caught nothing but old boots. And Jones Beach, when he'd held me safe in the deep water beyond the breakers. We'd never forget him taking us to the mouth of the Hudson River, where we gaped at the Statue of Liberty. Maureen and I didn't talk about the long years of his heart-wrenching fights with Mom—followed by breaking up and making up, only for the cycle to start again—which made the long-dreaded divorce feel almost like relief.

But soon after the divorce, I heard Mom crying in the shower. It broke my heart the way she called out Dad's name, "Eddy, Eddy!" I knew her elopement story: She'd loved Dad so much that despite her parents' disapproval, she ran away with him when she was eighteen. I thought, the way she cried, her love for him hadn't fully died.

Yet here she sat, cuddling with this stranger. Maureen took Velveeta cheese from the refrigerator and whispered, "What does Mom see in this dull guy?" I sure didn't know. Dad, with his black curly hair and roaring laugh, had an Irish wildness about him. I didn't get either why Barbara had married a man of forty. I said, "What's this attraction to old men? I myself like boys my own age."

Maureen nodded and swung her long silky hair that I envied (I'd inherited Dad's unruly curls). She liked my boyfriend, a senior like me about to graduate Jamaica High School, class of 1966. I'd noticed him in the school hall when spring fever hit. I flirted with him and found out he'd recently moved to America from Argentina with his family of Armenian descent. His teammates on the track team couldn't pronounce his name, Ambakum, so instead they playfully called him "Va-Va-Voom."

He asked me to swim with him one weekday night at our high school pool, which surprised me because, first, the idea of the pool was new and cool, and second, playing instead of doing homework had never entered my bookworm head. But I agreed, allowing myself some fun. I'd already been accepted to college and didn't have to worry.

Maureen slowly spread rubbery orange cheese on Ritz crackers. From the living room we heard the romantic crooning of Frank Sinatra—too smooth for me. I favored the raspy twangs of Bob Dylan. Mom probably dropped the album on the turntable to mask noise from Hillside Avenue but sounds of cars honking and the vibrations of subway trains underground still reached our apartment on the eleventh floor.

I poured boiling water over Lipton tea bags in acrylic cups. We sat and listened. Mom, our sole parent now, needed to be closely watched. We recalled Mom had mentioned a man from the Unitarian church network she said she knew for years. Was the guy smooching with her that guy? Already they acted too close for comfort.

I tilted a box of sugar over a teaspoon. We watched, but no sugar came out. I pulled back the spoon, and just then a pile of sugar dumped into the pot, making us burst out laughing. I burned with the urgent need to urinate and charged to the bathroom past the triple bunk in our bedroom. I just made it. I sat back in relief and noted that our bathroom seemed emptier since Barbara had cleared out all her makeup when she moved out.

Barbara rented a house nearby with her husband, and they'd allowed Ambakum and me to spend time alone there in private. There he gave me his high school ring, and we became lovers. One evening in bed, Ambakum said, "I worry things will change when you start college." But I assured him he had nothing to worry about—I wasn't going away, though that had been my dream. Back in third grade the principal placed me on the fast track to college before I even knew what college meant, and teachers presented college as such a lofty goal that I imagined it as a magic paradise where I'd be free and happy ever after.

My parents used to note that Dad's brother, George, who landed a great job at IBM soon after earning a bachelor's degree, was the only one in the family (so far) to graduate college. Dad took a course here and there, but duties forced him to quit. It was Mom who earned a degree.

Mom started at the Fashion Institute of Technology the fall I started ninth grade, and two years later her associate degree led to an art job. My parents assumed I'd fulfill my dream of going off to college, perhaps Ivy League. But when the time came, the divorce sapped their attention, and they couldn't afford to send me anywhere.

Luckily, I had a backup, the esteemed City University of New York, which charged no tuition for residents of the city with high grades. CUNY had a branch in our borough, and Dad, when he still lived at home, proposed the Queens campus, just a short bus ride away, where many of my school classmates would attend. So convenient! But this was in total conflict with my dream of adventure. I chose a campus in Manhattan: City College. There I felt sure I'd discover new cool friends and study what I liked: poetry and art.

Sure, I'd still have to live at home, but Jamaica had some benefits. I'd be near what I loved: my sisters, a few close friends, my part time job, my Hollis Unitarian church, and most of all, Ambakum, who kept me laughing. I washed my hands in the bathroom sink, looked in the mirror, and told myself, "Hey, you'll soon be a college girl in New York City, and you're gonna have a blast."

Heading back to the kitchen I saw Mom waiting for me and noticed the man had left. Maureen flashed me a look of chagrin. Mom gathered herself and in a dreamy voice, she said, "Doug proposed to me, and I accepted."

———————

Two months later, I awakened in Doug's big house in New Jersey under rustling trees. A late August rain tapped my window, and the moist air made my skin tingle. I felt safe being inside, lying on the satiny sheet on my soft, wide bed. I could feel the heat already rising, and I slipped my hand over my breast in the way that Ambakum had touched me after sneaking into my bed when he visited over the summer. That was one perk of having my own room. Across the hall, Maureen had her own room now, too. Mom and her new husband, Doug, slept upstairs.

I thought Mom might like the security that Doug promised, but this dull suburb in New Jersey bored me silly. How I missed New York City! From our former apartment in Jamaica, I'd been able to hop right on the subway for Manhattan, which surged with color, energy, and life. I'd loved it since childhood, ever since our parents introduced my sisters and me to the astounding free culture available in New York. Mom loved art, so off we went to art museums. Dad loved history, so he steered us to sites like the Statue of Liberty. Each hoped to pass on their passions, and it worked. I got hooked on both art and history.

By age thirteen I traveled by subway to Manhattan with classmates to window shop on Fifth Avenue. At fourteen I tagged along with Barbara to Unitarian youth meetings. In high school, I had three close Jewish girlfriends. Penny took me to political lectures, Annie to a Chuck Berry concert, and Vera to the opera. I explored Harlem with my Black friend, Rudy. Sometimes I traveled alone. For only fifteen cents each way, I could take the subway anywhere in the city I wanted to go. Even if I stopped for an egg salad sandwich and a cup of coffee, the whole day still cost under a buck.

One Saturday a month, I looked forward to regional Unitarian youth meetings at Community Church in Manhattan. Afterwards, a bunch of us climbed onto a bus going down Fifth

Avenue for a trip to Greenwich Village where the beatniks and folksingers hung out. Once, we recognized Pete Seeger carrying his banjo and felt thrilled he actually spoke to us. At times we came upon rallies for peace or civil rights. Sounds of Negro spirituals, or refrains from "We Shall Overcome," drew us to gatherings where I swayed, sang, and sometimes wept. Often anti-protesters showed up, spouting wildly different opinions ranging from extreme liberal to extreme conservative. Our Unitarian Universalist faith encouraged "a free search for truth," and, curious, I picked up literature from all sides.

Here in New Brunswick, everyone seemed to look the same, speak the same, and think the same. I felt stuck, because I couldn't go anywhere without being driven. I yearned for my boyfriend, my friends, my freedom, and exciting places to go. The saving grace here was the quiet that allowed me to do what I loved—to read and to paint.

A small work in progress, smelling of wet oil paint, leaned against the wall on top of my bookcase: a realistic rendering of an apple tree. With a background of field and sky, I made the tree appear normal in every way—the shape, color, and size—but it was actually *far* from normal. My subject: a tiny, pruned bonsai tree.

I thought it seemed weird that Doug's hobby was stunting the growth of young trees, but a bonsai tree proved easy to paint, and I invited Maureen to paint with me this day, hoping she'd mope less about missing her friends.

I stuck my foot out from under the sheet, almost ready to emerge from this cocoon. I glanced at my bookshelf, the books I'd finished, like *Jane Eyre*, and books I had to start, like *Candide*—both on the required summer reading list sent from City College when I'd been accepted.

I felt pissed off that Mom hadn't considered that moving me to New Jersey would make the City University of *New York* out of reach. At first, I flat out refused to move. Doug jumped to figure out how to eliminate any obstacle to his marrying Mom. He concocted a commuting plan: I'd take a bus to the train, the train to the city, and the subway to college. And to get back and forth from the bus? He'd buy me a motor scooter.

A motor scooter! I almost died laughing. But Ambakum loved the idea and tagged along with me when Doug and Mom took me to the dealer. The salesman gave standard instruction on how to drive the scooter, and I mounted it. He said to think of it like a bicycle. I'd loved the bike I rode as a kid, but this was nothing like a bike. This thing weighed a ton, you had to turn it on and fiddle with something called a throttle. Trying it out, with the salesman yelling and rushing after me, I almost crashed the scooter before we even left the parking lot. But Ambakum jumped on and caught on quickly. He said, "I'll teach you how to drive it." So, because *Ambakum* drove the scooter well, Doug bought it for *me*. Didn't make sense, but I went along.

With the whole summer before us, the scooter added an extra attraction for Ambakum to visit me. (The primary attraction: making secret love with me at night in my room.) During the day, he was supposed to teach me how to drive the scooter, but usually, I just plopped on the back and let him scoot me around the groomed streets and lush lawns of Doug's neighborhood.

When summer's end drew near, with college just around the corner, Mom said, "Janet, let's see how well you mastered the scooter."

I flushed and admitted I'd made no progress since I nearly crashed it.

"Then," she said carefully, "Doug's plan to get you to the city from here doesn't make much sense."

I waited, letting that fact sink in. Commuting by scooter, bus, train, and subway—and back—would take four hours a day. That plan never did make any sense. I faced the reality that the college experience I'd worked for and dreamed about for most of my life was not happening. Over the next few days, I didn't talk or eat, which pushed Mom into panic. To keep his new bride happy, Doug came up with Plan B: I'd attend nearby Rutgers University.

What? How? I knew Rutgers was lovely—Ambakum and I had scooted by the campus—and it had a good reputation. Doug said that with my grades, I'd surely be accepted, maybe even get a scholarship. He added, "If not, I'll cover the tuition." His generosity astounded me, and I was afraid to hope. With the term starting soon, Doug quickly got his friends in the admission office to arrange an interview.

My stomach jumped at the thought of my interview at Rutgers the next week. I threw off the sheets and flipped around, and, with feet planted on the pillow, I looked out the window upside down. I saw rain clouds. But the sun was shining somewhere. I said to myself, "You're gonna dazzle them on your interview."

Suddenly, I heard Mom shouting from the hall to Maureen and me. "Wake up girls! Pack your bags. We're going to New York!"

———————

I jumped out of bed. Mom said we were going to her mother's house, right away. I called to her, "What's happening? Is Nanny okay?" Mom assured me Nanny was fine but said nothing else. I reminded Mom of my interview at Rutgers on Monday. "We're going just for the weekend, right?" But Mom was out of earshot. I threw on my shorts and a T-shirt, grabbed a book and my journal, and stuffed underwear and a change of clothes into my suitcase. I grabbed donuts from Doug's kitchen for me and my bleary-eyed sister, and we jumped into Mom's Buick, just before drops pelted the windshield. Wipers scraped back and forth as we raced to our grandmother's house past the stinking petroleum pits that lined the Jersey Turnpike.

Maureen sang along with the Beatles song, "Yesterday,"

playing on the radio. I asked Mom why we had to go, but she wouldn't answer. I picked up my book, my usual source of escape. I read everywhere—car, bus, subway, even in elevators. I'd grabbed a naturalist's book, *The Immense Journey* by Loren Eisley, and quickly got lost in a moving passage about floating in a shallow and lonely river.

On the Verrazano Bridge over the Hudson River, Maureen poked me. We leaned forward to catch sight of the Statue of Liberty holding up her torch. Whenever we passed her, we'd remember the poem that Emma Lazarus wrote for her. Dad had taught us, and we liked to recite the famous lines, ending with, "yearning to be free." An hour and a half later, Mom stopped the car in front of Nanny's stone house in a lily-white neighborhood of Queens—the farthest possible edge of New York City. The story went that when Grandpa bought it in the roaring twenties, farmers' fields surrounded the house. Where cows once grazed in green pastures, convenience stores now sold cartons of pasteurized and homogenized milk.

I avoided puddles as I dashed to shelter on the porch, tapped on the glass door, and, wet and sticky, waited on the doorstep. Through the glass I watched Nanny, looking like her regular heavy-bosomed self, lumbering down from the upstairs apartment, her face lighting up when she saw me. "Hello, Darling." As the door cracked open, the aroma of Hungarian beef goulash filled my nostrils. Nanny wiped the wet off us with her cotton apron, pointed Mom to the back, and invited Maureen upstairs with her. I followed Mom through the living room, where sheets covered the sofas and chairs, and all the drapes were drawn. Mom shivered. "This place has been like a morgue since Pauline died in the Depression."

———

Mom had long ago told the story of when she, an eight-year-old child called Francie, contracted scarlet fever. She recovered. Soon her younger sister Pauline flared up with fever, and the doctor treated her for scarlet fever also, saying she'd caught it from Frances. Three days later Pauline died.

The doctor's diagnosis proved wrong. Pauline's appendix burst, and she died of poisoning. Nanny suffered a shock from which she never recovered. Mom described how she was left alone to deal with the death of her sister. At the funeral, Nanny wailed uncontrollably at the burial site and tried to throw herself onto the coffin. Grief twisted Nanny's mind, rendering her unable to love her surviving daughter, Francie. Mom suffered great loneliness and was never the same either. When she developed into a pretty girl who attracted boys and reveled in the attention of an Irish lad four years her senior, her parents sent her off to an all-girls Catholic boarding school. Immediately after graduating, she married the lad, my dad, Ed Duffy, and within five years they had three girls.

In Nanny's back hall where a phone sat on a table, Mom turned in to the master bedroom and tossed her suitcase on the bed. I stood in her doorway.

"Mom, this is a *really* bad time for a trip. Rutgers—"

Without looking at me, she held her hand up to cut me off. For years, all through the divorce, she'd confided in me every little idea that popped into her head. Now, not a word. She pulled out a pair of heels. *Heels?* For a weekend at Nanny's house?

"Mom, I need to know. How long are we staying?"

"We'll talk later."

"Fine." I dumped my bags in the back room facing the yard. The house was very familiar to me because once—when we were still a family of five—we'd moved in here to live with Nanny and stayed a couple years.

Four years before, in 1962, Grandpa Hugo died suddenly. Our parents told us that Nanny was not able to live on her own. Though she'd lived in America for forty years, she'd never learned to read or write English or to balance a checkbook. So, our family was going to sacrifice our home to help Nanny. Later, I learned the real reason we moved. It was a first step in Mom's plan to become independent of Dad. She said she couldn't depend on him becoming sober because he was a "periodic alcoholic." That made sense from what I'd observed in my childhood: Dad could be sober for a month or two, but then he'd reach for a drink, get drunk, fight with Mom, threaten divorce, and leave us. After a while he'd return, they'd make up, and he'd be fine for a while until the cycle repeated. Until one time they didn't make up. Mom woke up. "I have to face the real possibility that one day he might not come back," she said when I was about twelve. *Then how would we live?* I thought.

She reluctantly faced the fact that she had to get a job, one that paid enough to support herself and her girls. For that she needed an education. She secretly applied to the Fashion Institute of Technology, and once she was accepted, in the spring of 1962, she revealed her plan to Dad. A good guy when sober, ashamed of being an alcoholic, he understood her worry about a breakup. I overheard him telling Mom, "But we just don't have the money for the tuition."

Then, that summer, when Grandpa died, Nanny and my parents decided that merging our two households into one would save money and allow Mom to earn her associate degree. Mom said, "Nanny will be home for you kids after school, and she'll make you dinner. You in turn can help her with companionship."

I thought, *Wow, both Nanny and Mom can't be on their own because they lack education. That's not gonna be you. In the fall, you'll be a sophomore in high school. Keep your nose to the grindstone and get into the best college you can—your path to a good job and independence.*

I felt proud that Mom pursued her dream of becoming a fashion illustrator. Grandpa Hugo would also have been proud. He'd worked as an artist, too: a master colorist doing photogravure for the *New York Herald Tribune*. Grandpa did so well that he purchased a lake house in the Catskills, where my sisters and I spent our summers as children. In addition, he could afford to buy this stone residence in Queens where Nanny now lived alone.

I looked out the back window at drizzle soaking the weeds where Grandpa had once created a garden. Years ago, it had bloomed with ornamental plants and maiden grass that reminded him of his native Austria. The backyard was tiny, but Grandpa had made it seem huge to us girls by creating winding paths lined with sheltering trees. I remembered following Barbara's pudgy legs, Maureen in her baby shoes toddling after us. I remembered chasing Mommy round and round the magical maze that never ended, until we caught her, and she fell down in the maiden grass, laughing.

———

A chair scraped on the floor in the hall and startled me. I heard Mom dial the phone, speak quietly, and hang up quickly. I heard the sounds of unzipping bags and hangers clanging coming from the adjacent room, the one she'd shared with Dad for the two years we lived here. As soon as Mom graduated from the Fashion Institute of Technology, she landed an art job in Manhattan, just as she hoped. Our family moved out of Nanny's house and rented an apartment in Jamaica.

Now we were back at Nanny's. *But for how long?*

Mom called to me from the front door. "Janet, I'm going out." I dashed to get some answers but caught only a peek at her pretty summer dress as she clicked down the stoop in her heels, skirting puddles. Over a bare shoulder she blew back a kiss. "I won't be too long." The scent of Mom's perfume lingered in the humid air.

Soon the aroma of Nanny's Hungarian goulash lured me to the basement kitchen. Maureen also thundered down the stairs, her brow scrunched up, asking, "Where did Mommy go?" I answered that I hoped she was going to see her therapist.

———

Mom had been seeing an elderly psychologist, Dr. Steiner, for several years. My sisters and I had met with her, too, so she could get a sense of our family dynamics. She had made the trip to Mom's wedding to Doug to celebrate her patient's promising new start—a sparkling bride in a gold sheath and a diamond necklace. Nanny shared a few words in German with Dr. Steiner, but I doubted Nanny would have been so friendly if she knew the doctor was Jewish.

Nanny had said at the wedding reception that Doug was "a good man," then added, "The first husband was a no-good Irishman." She didn't like the Irish, and didn't care for frivolous Frenchmen either, not even Barbara's husband Maurice. If Nanny knew Doug was a Unitarian Universalist, the same "godless" religion that Dad raised us, she may not have called Doug "a good man." Nanny apparently approved only of White Catholics originating in countries from the former Austro-Hungarian Empire and Germany, the Axis that fought against us in World War II.

In a corner of the basement, I saw Nanny's old sewing machine, and thought, *For all her prejudices, Nanny completely devoted herself to my sisters and me.* Every new school year, she bought us new clothes and mended our old clothes by adjusting hems according to the latest fashion. She walked to our house every morning with fresh-baked rolls and buns and watched us when our parents partied. I thought, *How could she be such a mysterious mix of love and hate?*

The yellow transistor radio emitted static, and Maureen clicked it off. She stated, "It's Friday night, and I'm going out," and she set off to catch the bus to see her close friend Aviva in Jamaica.

I wanted to go to Jamaica, too, to see Ambakum. I missed his green eyes and sweet smell, but mostly I missed the way he made me laugh. His hilarious slips—calling a man's goatee a "tee goat," and the public library the "pubic" library—delighted me. My heart pounding, I moved upstairs to dial him. Ambakum's frail mother conveyed that he wasn't home. Disheartened, I phoned my girlfriends starting with Vera, my best friend in senior year. I hadn't seen her in months and missed her sorely. Her Hungarian mother told me, "No, darling, Verushka has already left for Vassar." I tried Annie, always a delight, but she'd gone off to New York University. My good friend Penny didn't answer, and I figured she was probably out organizing for the homeless.

I then tried Rudy, a boy I'd befriended in homeroom last year; his sister took a message. Feeling lonely, I retreated to my room to read.

A door slammed. "Janet, I'm back," Mom called. She leaned against the doorway of my room, flushed and looking pleased.

"Got your business done?" I asked. She nodded. "So now we're free to go home to Jersey?"

Her expression changed from dreamy to disturbed. "Oh, no. Can't." Worried, I reminded her about my interview at Rutgers on Monday. Her pretty face looked pushed and pulled by emotions. In a shaky voice, she said, "Janet, I'm sorry. We're not going back."

"But . . ."

"Home is here for us now."

"At Nanny's?" Maybe I hadn't heard right.

She explained, with finality, "It's over with Doug."

Over? It had only started! My head pounded. Mom sat on my bed and said she was sorry about Rutgers. My throat tightened and out came a whine. "Mom, you can't keep changing everything!" She tried to hug me, but I pulled away. "Look Mom, you went to college. Now it's *my* turn."

"Of course, it is, darling. You *will* go to college."

"I'm confused. Rutgers is out, so you mean City College? From all the way out here?" I threw myself face down on my pillow and punched it.

My mother descended to the kitchen. My ears tuned in to her every move: her footsteps coming back up the stairs, a muffled phone call, rustling in her room, an exhale, a sigh so deep I felt my own chest rise and fall. The scratch of a match. She called my name in a whisper, "Janet?"

At the threshold of her room, the orange tip of her cigarette floating in the darkness helped me discern her figure in a chair by the double bed—the same bed where years before Nanny and Grandpa had slept under a crucifix and where they'd laid out the tiny, embalmed body of their daughter, Pauline. A chilly gloom seemed to hang in the air. When our whole family had lived here, I'd heard through thin walls Mom rocking with Dad on that bed.

"Come sit with me," Mom said, indicating a chair set in front of her. I took a few steps in. The floor seemed sticky under my bare feet, and my nostrils filled with smoke and a musty scent— Mom wore a new perfume.

I sank into the chair and clutched the carved wooden arms. Mom sat in the shadows, sucking on her cigarette. The smoke irritated my eyes. I rubbed them and said, "So . . .?"

"Doug is begging me to come back to him."

A twist I did not expect. My future was in Mom's hands, and I felt helpless. I thought, *Live here, there, I don't really care. I just want to know where so I can deal with it.* I looked at the crumpled pack of Virginia Slims on the bed and asked with as much neutrality as I could muster, "So are you going to go back with him?"

She said no. "Doug was a jack rabbit."

The last thing I wanted to hear about was my mother's sex life, but she leaned in. "The marriage was never . . . consummated. That means no sex. I mean, we had sex but—"

"Mom!" I put my hands over my ears. She stopped talking. In a few moments, I asked, "So you'll divorce Doug, too?"

Mom said, "Yes. But not exactly. It won't count as a divorce by law, I found out." It seemed she'd gone to see a lawyer. "If the marriage wasn't consummated, I can get an annulment." She added, "That means it doesn't count."

I bit my lip. She could change a word but not the fact that she left a husband for the second time in six months. She repeated that we'd be staying with Nanny, for the moment. Moment to moment! That's how she operated. No plans, just impulses. I crossed my arms.

"What's the matter? I thought you'd be happy we're back in New York."

"Very happy. But we can't live here—it's too far from City College." Mom fell back in her chair. I didn't want to hurt her; but I demanded she consider my needs too. I said, "From Jamaica, it would have been closer."

Mom brightened. "Janet, would you like to move back there?"

She knocked me over. *Sure!* I thought. *From Jamaica, reaching City College would a drag, but possible; Maureen could continue at Jamaica High.* "Can we?"

"Janet, yes. We can move back. Maybe in our old building on the edge of Jamaica Estates, a short walk to the subway."

"Really?" I expected her to announce we could afford it because she'd landed a new job. I'd try to get my mural painting job back. I said, "The three of us will pitch in for the rent."

"That's sweet," Mom said. "But here's the good news." I cocked my head. "Your father said he'll cover the rent."

What? *Dad?* Then I got it. That's where she'd been. She'd gone to see *him*. I felt dizzy, trapped on a merry-go-round and I couldn't escape. Mom was saying I was sensible, a good judge of character, wise beyond my years. Dozens of times over the last few years, she'd asked me to prop her up, judge my *father*, and tell *my mother* what to do. It seemed like a role reversal and caused me to feel queasy.

She reached for my hand. I wiggled them away from her. My fingers felt cold though the evening was warm. What was wrong with me? I loved Mom very much, and yet, my heart felt shielded in ice. She revealed, "Tonight your father asked me to remarry him." Whop! Another dizzy turn on the merry-go-round. "Should I give him another chance?"

I tried to get my bearings. Did "a chance" mean Dad would move back in with us? I realized it didn't matter what I said. She did what she wanted anyway. Mom played with her hair, bounced her legs, and said, "No other man has ever attracted me like your father."

I felt sick and bolted up. I thought, *I have to get out of here.* I dashed out the side door. In the misty night, I crossed the avenue to the playground and twirled on the swings. I felt drawn to walk to our old family home on Gettysburg Street, a block away, and I plopped on the curb to stare at it. I conjured memories of Dad when he was young and handsome, perched on a ladder painting the shingles or mowing the little patch of grass on our front lawn. He was proud of this single-family home he'd managed to purchase using the GI Bill. He'd bathed my sisters and me when we were small enough to all fit in one tub. Afterwards he'd cook hamburgers, and our family all watched the *Jackie Gleason Show* or *Twilight Zone* together.

Then noise filled my mind—noise of the parties Dad and Mom threw and the awful fights that followed, so loud they woke up my sisters and me. Dad said Mom had to stop flirting, and Mom said Dad had to stop drinking. We girls cringed listening to them yell, curse, and taunt each other. One night we heard them downstairs dividing up the property—Dad would keep his Chevrolet, but Mom could keep the house. Barbara and Maureen and I worried about who we would live with and who would get to keep our cat, Beauty.

Years later, the first year we lived in our Jamaica apartment, Dad went often to meetings of Alcoholics Anonymous and tried to stay sober by following "steps." He said the step that encouraged him to accept a higher power was hard for him because he didn't believe in God. At least, not the way "God" was presented in the Catholic Church, which he'd left because he felt that priests obsessed about sins, especially sex, and laid on guilt. He decided to raise his daughters without guilt.

In the spring of that year, 1965, Dad botched up an attempt to follow another step, the one about taking moral inventory and making amends to everyone he'd hurt. Mom, so upset by his revelations, promptly regurgitated them all to my sisters and me. She said that Dad's way of doing that "step" was to list every misdeed and infidelity and to confess it all to her during one long, horrible night.

I don't know what Dad expected Mom to do, but she kicked him the hell out. When they got to the making-up stage and Dad came home, he surmised that his three daughters knew all the details about his confession. He must have been very ashamed. That's the only way I can explain what he did to us next.

One evening soon after, Dad told my sisters and me to wait in our bedroom. Then he called us out to the dining room one by one, Barbara first. I heard him berating her, then a slap, then crying.

He'd hit Barbara before. When she was twelve, he learned she'd played hooky with an older boy and gave her a beating; I hid in a corner and wept as I heard the blows and Barbara's cries. That horrible incident was a departure from his libertarian parenting style.

Dad had never hit me, or even berated me, and I knew I'd done nothing wrong, so when he called me to the dining room and told me to sit down across from him, I wasn't afraid. He told me I had to obey my mother and clean my room. I said, "I will." I was about to rise when he whacked me across the face, knocking me off the chair. Shocked at the pain, I too started crying and ran back to the bedroom. I warned Maureen not to go when he called, but she did. And the same thing happened to her. The three of us, our cheeks stinging and red with slap marks, locked ourselves in our bathroom, holding each other and bawling.

A couple months later, in June, Barbara moved out. Dad left the following year. At the time of the divorce, I felt torn up with a brew of sadness, anger, love—but part of me celebrated the decision, an implied promise that we wouldn't be subjected anymore to the roller coaster of our parents' passions.

I myself had a decision to make. Sitting on the curb lost in memories, I hadn't noticed the weather changing. A fog had rolled in. Emotionally drained, I headed back to Nanny's house to sleep.

Mom greeted me in the hall to ask if we could talk more. I told her I felt too tired, but she insisted. "Tell me, don't you think people can change?"

"Yes. But Mom, tell me one thing," I said. "Has Dad stopped drinking?"

"He says so."

I shrugged. How many times had he told her that?

Her look softened. "Your father wants to come back. He wants another chance to be your dad."

"Oh, please. Stop. Don't bring us into it, Mom. He knows you told us every rotten thing he did. He's so ashamed he can hardly look at me. Do you really think he can just stroll back into our family like nothing happened and be our *daddy* again?"

Swinging her foot, she said, "All I know is I miss him."

Frustrated, I tried to appeal to her vanity. "Look, Mom, you easily attract men. You're sure to find a good man. Just wait, meet some new people."

"I don't want to date," she said. "Because I love your father and want to remarry him." Like air seeping out of a balloon, she released a long breath. "And I don't want to live on my own."

I stood up and said with certainty, "But I do want to live on my own."

PART II:
FALL, 1966

Maureen

Chapter 2
MAUREEN

Professor Berkowitz handed back our essays late Friday afternoon as she strolled past lines of desks. When she came to me, she said, "Let's talk after class."

I gazed out the window beyond the stone buildings to the waving trees and sunny skies, eager to start my weekend. But I felt curious. Dr. Berkowitz had praised my previous essay and maybe now wanted the deep discussion I'd yearned for at college. I'd worked hard on the essay topic, "Something True," clacking away until midnight on my yellow Samsonite typewriter, a surprise gift from Dad when I enrolled at City College.

In Berkowitz's office, in her cubicle stinking of mimeograph ink, we sat facing each other. From a pile of papers around her black typewriter, she pulled out my essay and peered at me over spectacles. "Very well written, just what I expected from my top student," she said. "Your content is imaginative. But therein lies the problem. The assignment was not fiction, but something *true* about your life."

"It is true."

Looking unconvinced, she read from my paper: "'Some people have summer affairs. My mother had a summer marriage.'"

"True."

She read: "'My mother ended that to move back with my father. I'm living on my own now in my own apartment.'"

Again true.

She lowered my paper. Eyebrows pinched, she said, "But you're only a freshman, eighteen—"

"No. I'm seventeen. I skipped a grade."

"Janet," she said decisively, "a seventeen-year-old can't get a lease."

I told her my father had signed the lease.

"Tell me there's truth in your next lines: 'I live in the same building as my parents, but in a separate apartment—they live on the seventh floor, and I live on the second floor.'"

I nodded.

She flopped back, and said, "Honestly, it sounded like an adolescent fantasy. But I see now, you have, indeed, fulfilled the assignment." She changed the grade on top to an A, then looked at me with sympathy. "May I ask how that . . . arrangement . . . came about?"

I answered that I didn't want to live with my parents. "I told them, 'If I'm mature enough to go to college, I'm mature enough to have my own apartment.'"

She asked how I felt about living alone.

I said I wasn't alone, I lived with my sister.

She looked relieved and said, "Oh, your older sister."

"No, younger. Maureen is sixteen."

She looked concerned and asked how a sixteen-year-old got in the picture. I said Maureen was fed up with our parents, too, and talked back a lot, so Dad and Mom hatched the idea of the two apartments.

"Because the girl talked back? Then every teenager in the country would be tossed out of their homes!" She said she'd never heard of anything like this. "Is it even *legal*?"

I began to tremble. Dr. Berkowitz asked softly if I felt okay with all this. I told her it was my idea to move out.

"Oy. You feel you got what you asked for?"

I felt confused. I couldn't answer. Dr. Berkowitz crossed her skinny legs under her long skirt, smiled, and shared a personal story. "Once, like you, I told my parents I was going to run away. I declared I had everything I needed—except . . . a bell on my bike!"

I smiled.

"I was a child, about ten years old. I told them I wanted to leave home. But, Janet, my parents didn't pack me a suitcase."

She seemed to find my situation peculiar. I thought, *I guess it is.*

———

I walked downhill from campus, thinking about my professor's question: Did I get what I asked for? Overall, not really. Registering so late I got stuck with dull courses, like Calculus and Urban Planning. In French Literature, I liked studying *Candide*, but the professor's dry and contemptuous manner turned me off. My favorite, Berkowitz's English class, challenged me less than my Advanced Placement class in high school.

My original urge had been to get away from my parents' chaos and to move closer to City College. Mom and Dad had checked out rooms with me in Manhattan, until Maureen announced she'd rather live with me than them. Our parents quickly concocted the two-apartment arrangement in Jamaica. That part worked out—I felt more distant from chaos. But, sadly, I was still very distant from college. Round trip, it took me four subway rides, three hours underground and a hike uphill, often carrying a heavy book bag on my shoulders.

Sure, at first, having my own apartment did feel like a fantasy, as Dr. Berkowitz imagined, and Maureen's best friends celebrated on their first visit. They represented the melting pot of New York City: Aviva and Ruthie were Jewish; Natasha, Russian Orthodox; and Rosita, the love child of a German woman and a Black GI. They all told us they envied that we could come and go as we pleased. Aviva, a lively girl with thick blonde hair, said, "How cool! I'm so jealous. You're free." True, freedom was the best part. No one to tell us not to tack pictures to the walls or play our favorite music as loud as we wanted.

Another day, Penny, a best friend, visited with a surprise gift—a kitten! Maureen and I named her "Felice," which means Lucky. She made our studio a home.

I'd met Penny in 1963, in tenth grade history class, attracted by her hair highlighted with a copper rinse and her intense curiosity, and we became fast friends. We ate together every day in the cafeteria and talked about books. She was reading *It Can't Happen Here*, by Sinclair Lewis, a satire written while Hitler and fascism was rising in Europe. She said the author wrote about a demagogue who stoked fear, got elected president of the United States and imposed totalitarian rule—the point being, yes, it can happen here.

Like me, Penny followed current affairs. We pored over the *New York Times* that I lugged around, a subscription from my father who hooked me on discussing current events. The spring before we met, Penny and I both followed Dr. Martin Luther King Jr. and felt horrified when Bull O'Connor set dogs on King's fellow activists in Birmingham, Alabama. We both admired President Kennedy's strong defense of the civil rights protests as moral, legal, and constitutional. In late August, Dr. King led the March on Washington for Jobs and Freedom in Washington, D.C., and we both regretted not hearing live Dr. King's remarkable speech, "I Have a Dream." In mid-September white supremacists bombed the 16th Street Baptist Church in Birmingham. Penny and I cried when we saw the school photographs of the smiling faces of the four innocent Black girls killed in that bombing.

In my apartment I played for Penny albums by Joan Baez I purchased soon after her performance at the March on Washington. Her high voice, sad but sweet, soothed me. I'd memorized the words to "Kumbaya." Penny picked up Felice and commented on my painting, "Flopsy and Mopsy," two grey wool bunnies leaning against a bottle of whisky. She said, "Sweetie, are those dolls supposed to represent you and Maureen?"

"Yep."

Penny knew about Dad's boozing. When things blew up at home in junior year, her family invited me to live with them in their modest apartment. I didn't move then, but Penny said she was not surprised that our family had separated.

"Here," she said and handed me a recently published book, *Rush to Judgment*, by Mark Lane.

The book threw my mind back again a few years to 1963. Penny and I were studying side by side in history class when a buzz in the hall disturbed us. Our teacher opened the door and news flooded in like sewage: "President John F. Kennedy has been shot," she said. No one moved. *Shot. But still alive?* I grasped at the hope.

Later at home, I heard TV anchor Walter Cronkite announce our Kennedy's death. A numbing grief took hold. Like people across our nation and world, I sat in disbelief, riveted to the TV. A few days afterwards, watching police transport Lee Harvey Oswald, the suspected assassin, I jumped seeing Oswald grimace in pain and grip his stomach. Jack Ruby had shot him point blank. The murder, live on TV, immediately following the murder of a beloved president, shattered my sense of innocence.

Back at school, I moped around, devoid of motivation to study. Penny quoted a line spoken at JFK's funeral: "Those who cannot learn from history are doomed to repeat it." She coaxed me back to my homework and routines, but my trust remained unrestored.

A couple months later, in January, Penny said, "You know the official conclusion that Oswald was the lone assassin?" I nodded. "Well, there are some who question that story, like Mark Lane." She told me his credentials: A representative in the New York State Assembly and a lawyer for civil rights cases, he'd dared to join a Freedom Ride in the South. One evening after school, Penny and I took a trip to Manhattan to hear him speak. We descended to a dark basement where Mark Lane, wearing a suit and black-rimmed glasses, projected images that challenged the Warren Commission's conclusion about Kennedy's death.

I took the book, *Rush to Judgment*. The idea that adults in positions of trust might not tell the whole truth gave me a sick feeling. Penny left, saying, "We have to think for ourselves."

———————

I ached to be alone with Ambakum. Our apartment offered us privacy, and we'd no longer have to sneak off someplace to strip off our clothes and explore each other. Seeing his fresh face at the door lit up my mood. He looked around, curious. "Just one room? And your bed—so little?" But then he pulled me to him. "Your heart, my heart, close again," he said, acting happy as a puppy.

I wished I could be so happy. The deal our parents gave us: They paid for rent ($110 a month) and food (about a dollar a day for each of us). But Maureen and I had to pay for any extra expenses, such as subway fare, shoes, books, records, movies, snacks, or anything fun. Maureen looked for babysitting jobs, and I hoped my former boss would hire me back. Chores like cleaning and laundry were nothing new for Maureen and me, though we did have to cook more. Shopping was tough because we had to lug heavy bags from the grocery store many long blocks.

Ambakum made jokes and acted as playful as ever, but I didn't find him as funny as I had before. He couldn't stay over with Maureen there. He said, "You must take break, go for fun."

The next day, Saturday, we took the subway to Central Park, where we meandered along winding paths, surrounded by steel skyscrapers. Finding a clear blue lake, Ambakum said, "Boats! Let's rent." While we sat on a bench waiting for a boat, he put his hand on my tummy, which startled me, causing me to recall my panic in the middle of the summer when my period was late.

I'd felt sick with worry. If I got pregnant so young, what would happen to my dreams of college, a good job, and independence? When Ambakum visited me in Jersey, I warned him I could be pregnant and waited for his shocked reaction. But he was happy! He asked me to marry him and said he wanted lots of children with me. Not exactly what I pictured for my life just then. I wasn't ready to think of him as my *husband*, forever. A week later I called him with the news that my period had finally arrived. While I felt relief, he sounded disappointed. He said, "No matter. We keep going with our plan to marry." I told him there was no need.

A boat turned up. He eagerly pulled on the oars and I leaned back, looking up at the trees and clouds in the sky above us. He shouted, "I love you!" I jerked up and rocked the boat. He said more softly, "We should marry. That way, you get pregnant, no worries. Janet, you are the girl for me. I want family with you. Two children. Or more. What do you say, more is merry?"

Marriage, children did not seem at all merry to me then. "Ambakum," I said. "Think. I'm in college, and you're living at home. And we have no jobs."

"We could live with my parents." I froze. They lived in a one-bedroom apartment near downtown Jamaica. The idea horrified me.

On the way home in a packed subway car, Ambakum and I hung onto straps to keep our balance. While he remained happy-go-lucky, I couldn't rise to his level of lightheartedness. I tightened with confusion. Ambakum was the first boy I'd loved and made love to. Last summer, riding on the scooter with my arms around his beautiful body, I shouted my love out loud. Now I felt uncertain. Studying my expression, he asked what was wrong. I couldn't say.

He continued to press me, until I finally mustered the courage to say, "You know, marriage is a big decision. Marriages can fail. I know. To make sure we're right for each other . . . maybe we should . . . see other people?"

He looked stunned. He said, "No. I hate that, you dating other guys."

As dear as he was, I spoke firmly. "I can't be your sweetheart anymore."

His mouth fell open, and he slumped onto a vacant seat. With a choked voice, he said, "You never will find a boy who loves you more than me." Then, right there in the subway, he folded onto himself, head to his knees. Giant tears dropped off his face.

Part of me wanted to embrace him, breathe in his sweet smell, erase the pain, and tell him, "I'm so sorry." But another part of me smelled the fresh air of new freedom.

Chapter 3
BILL, RUDY, AND STAN

I needed more than a dollar a day and had to get serious about money. On Saturday around dusk, which was descending earlier and leaving me yearning for more brightness, I hightailed it over to Bill's to get my job back. He worked in a loft over the Hollis Cinema, which showed artful and sexy foreign films. The previous fall, the beginning of my senior year, he'd hosted a hootenanny fundraiser for our nearby church that I'd attended with Mom. We shared our love of art, and Bill surprised me by saying, "You know, I could use an assistant." I began working for him after school. Painting murals—the coolest job ever!

Calling me "Duffy," he told me my duties were to pack up, set up, clean up. One Saturday, carrying portfolios and sketch books, we traveled to Manhattan to meet a businessman about a commission. On the bus, Bill paid our fares—thirty cents in coins—then squeezed his body next to mine on the seat. People glared. Because of the paint stains on our jeans? Bill laughed, "Duffy, they're just not used to seeing a skinny little White girl with a fat old Black man." He said to let them stare; they've got to *see* integration before they accept it.

Mr. Middlemarch did hire Bill to paint a mural of an old English scene of gentlemen on a fox hunt and a portrait of himself

and his wife. From the Jamaica Public Library, I borrowed reproductions of Gainsborough and other European painters that Bill
used for reference in creating the first versions of the scene and
the portrait. On a glorious fall day, we packed Bill's rickety car,
headed out to the Middlemarch estate in Olde Westbury, Long
Island, and clanked past the sturdy trees with golden leaves that
lined a driveway that seemed miles long.

Bill directed me to apply gesso on a wall in the mansion,
while he tuned in to classical music on the radio he carried everywhere. He fiddled with his portrait of Mrs. Middlemarch, who
had performed in nightclubs, to make her look aristocratic. He
told me that her husband, rich in new money, wanted his new
estate in Olde Westbury to look like he descended from landed
gentry. I found the idea phony and funny.

Bill took out a sketch of the fox hunt scene and said he'd
create a "cartoon," which I thought meant a comic. He laughed
and explained a *cartoon* is the word for an outline that Renaissance masters used. I took our endeavor more seriously.

———————

Now, almost a year later, climbing peeling wooden stairs to Bill's
loft, I heard familiar classical music and smiled. Bill threw open
the door. Balancing a palette in one hand, he beamed, "Hey,
Duffy!" I wrapped my arms around his huge waist. He hadn't
thought he'd see me again, but said he was glad I'd landed back
in Jamaica and was attending City College. He asked, "Are the
students tearing the place apart?"

I laughed and said, "We just want a voice. Last week I
jumped into a pit with protesters." He asked why. I said, "To
stop bulldozing trees for a parking lot." I told him I had my own
apartment and needed work.

"It happens that—" He stood up. "Remember the English
fox hunt?" He ducked into his cluttered office, retrieved a magazine, and opened a page showing Middlemarch and his wife

posing in front of our mural. In *Better Homes and Gardens*, a national magazine!

"Bill, you'll be famous!"

Bill told me the owner of Squires restaurant phoned him after seeing the magazine spread. He wanted a mural of Old English gentry that fit his brand. "Gentleman and their wives in elegant clothing, at leisure, strolling through town." The Post-Impressionist, Seurat, came to mind. Bill said, "It's possible he'd hire us for his whole *chain* of Squires."

He called me his apprentice, and my imagination transported me to the Italian Renaissance, the age of Leonardo da Vinci and Michelangelo, who broke out of the dark ages and revived classic ideals of art, science, and democracy.

Bill did get the Squires commission, saying it was "the break we needed."

———

That night, celebrating over spaghetti, Maureen and I talked about re-igniting our friendships. I hadn't yet heard back from Rudy, a slim boy with cropped hair and skin the color of cocoa. The year before, on our way home from school, we'd sometimes bop down the hill together, sharing our aspirations. I called again, and Rudy himself answered. Hearing his warm baritone voice made me smile, and I caught the next bus to downtown Jamaica to meet him. A downpour forced the bus to slog through puddles as big as a pond.

———

Sitting by the pond on our way home from school the previous spring, Rudy's eyes had landed squarely at the "Equal" button pinned to my jacket—simply a white equal sign in a black circle. He said, "Do you really think it's true?"

"What?"

"That Blacks and Whites are equal?"

How could Rudy question that? Astonished, I sputtered that equality was a "self-evident" truth, as Thomas Jefferson put it.

He looked away and said, "You know, in all my years in school we've never studied an accomplished Black person, not one." I pondered, but only came up with Frederick Douglass. Rudy looked unconvinced, saying that great man got merely a lousy footnote, only because of his influence on Lincoln. "Besides," he said, "if we study only *one* Black person, maybe no one else is worth studying."

I realized something. "Except for a poem or two by Emily Dickinson, women are left out of the curriculum, too," I said. "You don't ask if women are equal to men."

"That's because they're *not* equal," he joked. I poked him, but it wasn't a good joke. As a female, I fiercely wanted to be free and equal.

One Saturday soon afterwards, Rudy accompanied me and my Unitarian youth group to Harlem to tutor junior high kids. When he walked me home, my dad invited him in for a Coke. Dad loved discussing issues, and he asked us about Harlem. I said, "The kids wanted to go to the Metropolitan Museum."

Dad thought it was good the kids got out of their neighborhood. He talked about his experience in Bedford Stuyvesant, a slum in Brooklyn. "I saw schools so overcrowded and rundown, it's no wonder people can't read." He agreed that Negroes deserved "a fair shake."

I watched Rudy's face as Dad shared his observations: landlords there don't maintain buildings; men who can't find employment hang out on the streets; despair leads some to drugs and alcohol. Ignorance prevails. Dad described an incident. "A girl got hit by a car. She wasn't badly hurt, but, still, I had to write the police report."

At the word, "police," Rudy bit his lip.

Dad went on relating how the girl's mother pronounced her daughter's name, something that sounded like "*Famali* Jones."

Dad said, "I asked her to spell her child's first name as I wrote. She spelled out: 'F-E-M-A-L-E.' I told her that spells, 'female.' The mother answered, 'Whichever way you say it, officer, *Female Jones* is the name the hospital gave my baby. Written on the birth papers." Dad told us he'd been floored.

Rudy, holding his body stiff, nodded politely and stood to leave. I followed him outside. He said, "Is your father a cop?" I told him he was now a lieutenant in Bedford Stuyvesant in Brooklyn." Rudy chided me, "Why didn't you tell me your father was a cop?"

"Oh. You can see he's liberal. I wasn't hiding it. I just didn't think his job mattered."

He looked at me in wide-eyed disbelief. I then learned how "police," even the word, could trigger visceral fear in Black men. "Of course, you're right," I said. "I'm so sorry. I should have told you before."

The bus wheezed into the terminal and braked, rain pounding down. I spotted Rudy beaming and holding an umbrella up, and I ducked underneath. He said, "Let's get dry in a coffee shop."

I took his arm, noticing he seemed thinner and walked with a limp. I asked, "Is your leg okay?"

"Yeah," he said. "I'm glad you're back in Jamaica." He told me he did exciting work in Jamaica with a community activist named Stan. He supported Dr. Martin Luther King Jr. for pushing President Johnson to get the Voting Rights Act passed and to launch the Great Society and War on Poverty. "LBJ sends officials up from Washington," Rudy said. "They're hot on pumping money into the ghetto. Stan got a gang of us together. We try to get funds for youth education, even art programs. Stan is far out. You'd like him. You could —"

A cop in rain gear stood in front of us. His feet planted wide, he glowered and smacked his night stick in his gloved hand. Rudy whispered, "Let's drop arms." Though afraid, I held on tighter, in defiance. Tense, we walked gingerly past the cop. He followed us. Rudy and I ran and ducked into the first coffee shop, slid into a booth, and caught our breath.

"What just happened?" I said. "That cop scaring us! His job is to keep us safe."

"Your father taught you that?" Rudy asked. I answered yes. A smile flickered on his lips, and I asked what he was thinking. "Janet, every TV show—Western, crime, even the news—teaches us that cops are good guys going after bad guys." I waited for his point. He said, "That cop saw me as a bad guy."

"Outrageous."

He shrugged. "Don't worry. I'm used to cops assuming I'm a criminal."

I said, "Rudy, you're one of the most gentle people I know."

He stood to go to his apartment to keep his appointment with Stan. He insisted I meet him.

———

Upstairs in Rudy's ten-story, brick apartment building, Rudy made Nescafe coffee. He said his sister was avoiding me. "Because I'm White?" My question hung like the white blinds on the window, closed slats blocking the darkness.

Rudy said, "She didn't like my having a Jewish girlfriend last summer." He switched to talking about attending Queens College. It wouldn't be until January—if he got into the SEEK program for minorities. "It's tough," he said. "Word is the scouts are looking for 'sparkle.'"

I laughed and said, "You're deep, you're curious. You write poems. You're passionate about civil rights. I'd definitely call that *sparkle*."

But he didn't cheer up. He said he desperately needed the student deferment. "The military is on my tail. Recruiters say I need to fight for freedom for America, meaning, *White* America.

They need us Black boys to be grunts on the front line. But you know I can't pick up a gun and shoot poor peasants who never hurt me or attacked my country."

"I agree the Vietnam war is horribly immoral."

He said, "I've been called for a physical." I gasped. He said, "But they don't take you if you're underweight."

Oh, I thought, *that's why he's so thin.*

"If starvation doesn't work, I'll try . . ." Rudy lifted his pants leg to show his ankle. He pulled back a bandage to expose raw red skin and a raging wound oozing with pus. I covered my mouth to keep from gagging. Rudy picked up a carving knife from the drain. "When the draft board called me for a physical, I cut my ankle. Every day I pour dirty dishwater over it to infect it."

"Rudy, you could lose your foot!"

"I don't have enough money to pay a psychiatrist to say I'm crazy. I can't get to Canada, and I don't want to go to jail." I felt sickened by the predicament guys in my generation had to deal with, especially young Black men like Rudy. He said, "I know I could lose my foot, but I gotta stand up for myself. I'll fight for freedom—not in some hellish jungle, but right here at home in South Jamaica, where I don't have to kill or maim anyone."

"But Rudy, you're maiming yourself."

Rudy's face showed some hope when he said Stan had written a recommendation for college that would help him get a student deferment. A buzzer sounded. Rudy brightened and yelled, "It's Stan!" Via intercom, Rudy invited Stan up and jumped to the door to wait. "Stan makes us feel like we belong. We call ourselves 'Stan's Gang.' He wakes us up to the power we have to free ourselves. You'll see."

Stan appeared. He looked at me and his eyes flashed, as if surprised to find Rudy with . . . a White girl? Likewise, I didn't expect him to be as striking as a movie star—with tight curls falling over his forehead, he looked like a Black Tony Curtis. Seeming to be in his thirties, he stood straight, dressed in casual slacks and an orange sweater that stretched over his broad chest.

Rudy told Stan a bit about me, and Stan's eyebrows lifted. He said, "Miss Duffy, pleased to meet you," in a formal but charming way. "Our community can use the talents of an artist and college student like you." We all sat on stools, and Stan asked why I felt committed to civil rights.

"Reverend Dr. Martin Luther King Jr." He asked to hear more. I took a breath, and my mind flew back three years to watching on TV the March on Washington, D.C. I related how at age fourteen I felt mesmerized by King's passionate speech, "I Have a Dream," and my blood pumped through me so fiercely I wished I could jump out of my skin and fly bodily to D.C.

Feeling Stan's smiling brown eyes upon me, I again noticed my blood pumping. He said softly, "So you like brother Martin's dream for his sons, to be judged 'not by the color of their skin but by the content of their character?'" I nodded. He said, "Then you probably don't want to miss our next community meeting."

I felt drawn in, but in over my head. I stuttered that I had to study. Out of habit, I reached out to shake hands. Stan hesitated, then met my grasp. A jolt. I felt engulfed in the warm energy that emanated from him. "I understand," he said. His eyes locked with mine. "Can we count on you to come to Jamaica on Friday?"

No words, not even air, came out of my throat.

On Friday evening, so warm we wore merely T-shirts and jeans, Rudy and I headed through Jamaica while trains rattled above us on the elevated lines. We hurried to connect with Stan and his gang at the Community Center. On the street thick with smells of hot dogs and pretzels and sounds of James Brown's "I Got You" blasting from a Sam Goody's store, we jostled past people, White and Black, in work clothes or decked out ready to party.

My family had shopped for bargain clothes every fall in Jamaica, but we never dared step a foot off the main street into "bad" neighborhoods. Once such neighborhood, South Jamaica, was where Rudy now pointed, saying, "Later, we go down there to Stan's place." Looking at the shabby buildings as another train rumbled by, it struck me: *Damn*. South Jamaica, literally, is on *the other side of the tracks*.

We entered the Community Center, and for the first time I found myself one of the few White faces in a sea of Black faces. At my church and school, Black people were the "minority." *Here, the minority is me*, I thought. I felt self-conscious, along with the shy White guy up front aiming a whirring overhead projector to a screen filling up with acronyms: HARYOU, OEO, EOA.

"Alphabet soup," whispered a man in my ear. I turned to see Stan smiling, his cheeks as round as peaches, and felt myself tremble. He said, "Miss Duffy, glad you came with Rudy." I saw Arthur, who I already knew through Rudy, carrying *The Fire Next Time*, by James Baldwin. I never saw him without a book.

To the young people clamoring around him, Stan called, "Meet Duffy." *Duffy* would become my nickname with them, as it was with Bill. A skinny guy, Josiah, avoided me, but a stocky guy burst out, "Hi, Duffy! I'm Socrates!" He pumped my hand up and down, making me laugh.

I said, "I love your name, Socrates."

"Call me Soc."

His rose-colored glasses matched his personality. I said, "Soc, I love your glasses, too." He pulled them off and his bright eyes lit up his big square face.

Stan introduced a Black girl with straightened hair wearing a snug dress, Vicky, who took minutes, and a petite White girl, Susan, who typed them. I recognized Susan from school and offered to help type. The friendly vibes of Stan's gang put me at ease.

A teen at Freedom Place, Jamaica

The speaker tapped the microphone, introduced himself as an official messenger from President Lyndon B. Johnson. He said President John Kennedy had pledged a "War on Poverty" that LBJ vowed to honor. A Black preacher shouted, "With pressure from brother Martin," and the crowd applauded.

Statistics flashed on the screen: Before LBJ took office, one in five people lived in poverty in America. "Shame!" shouted people around me. I wasn't used to audiences calling out. The speaker promised the president would relieve, cure, and prevent all aspects of poverty. He listed the array of programs of the Great Society: Head Start, Medicare and Medicaid, Food Stamps, VISTA, Job Corps, Legal Aid, Community Service Block Grants, and Neighborhood Youth Corps. The audience called out approval, and I joined them.

People stood to give testimony. A father: "My sons now gets job training after school, instead of hanging out. I worry less." A grandmother: "I praise the Lord I can see a doctor." A mother: "I go to work with peace of mind, because my children are safe in preschool, and my baby is getting milk." The stories disturbed me. I had never once had to worry about seeing a doctor or being fed.

The official declared, "You, the local community, know better than anyone else what you need." He urged us to create new programs and apply for funds now. Shyness gone, he proclaimed, "Power is in your hands."

Cheers followed, and I clapped and shouted with everyone else. I thought, *Here I am, witnessing history in the making.* For the first time in months, I felt fully awake.

Stan's gang streamed outside where stars brightened the sky, all of us feeling energized by the vision: America free of poverty and racism. Some of us squeezed into Stan's white Impala to head to Freedom Place, the "headquarters" in South Jamaica. We bumped over the railroad tracks and pulled up to a pizza parlor in a strip mall. The scene outside the car window was not the neat Queens Village where I grew up; not the tree-lined hills of Hollis where I worshipped; not the gorgeous homes on curving roads in Jamaica Estates behind my apartment building. Not even the elegant wrought-iron rails on stoops I'd seen on old brownstones in Harlem.

Driving deeper into South Jamaica, we passed old factories with windows smashed or replaced with boards vandalized with curse words. I saw makeshift shacks with corrugated iron roofs and pictured families, wet and cold, huddling in storms. Vacant lots, stripped of trees, were dumps for trash and broken bottles. All looked like black and white photos of cities in war-torn Europe.

My attention turned to giant billboards: a beautiful Black woman with streaming straight hair advertising a hair relaxer stood opposite a billboard of a handsome Black man in a suit, enjoying a Kool cigarette. I whispered to Rudy, "You know, I never saw Black faces on billboards."

Rudy said, "Likewise, I never saw Black faces on ads *outside* Black neighborhoods. In mainstream magazines, on TV—everything's all about White people, isn't it?"

Socrates chimed in. "We folks get the message: 'White's the way we supposed to be.'" I felt uncomfortable absorbing that hard truth: the world I lived in excluded Black people like they didn't exist.

Stan parked in a lot in front of a boxy stucco structure, which served as Stan's business office during the week and Freedom Place on Fridays. Rudy frowned when he spotted a guy in a dark navy pea coat sucking on a cigarette. Rudy challenged him, "Clarence! Where you been, man?"

"Just one step ahead of the cops." He darted an unfriendly look at me, flicked his cigarette butt, and stepped inside with Rudy. I followed Vicky and Susan. They handed me pages to type before they squeezed into a cubicle, and Stan took me to an old black typewriter in the back room where Clarence slumped in a folding chair that Rudy set up.

I tried to ignore Clarence, glanced at Vicky's notes, and asked Stan the meaning of an acronym. Stan raised his eyebrows and commented I had the vocabulary of a college girl. Clarence snorted. Arthur and Socrates entered the room, as Stan explained EOA stands for Economic Opportunity Act.

"The keystone of the War on Poverty," Rudy said.

Arthur added in his sad way, "A war in which Johnson's foot soldiers snoop around our neighborhoods, pretending to search for 'pockets of poverty.'"

"Well, sure enough," Socrates piped in. "Here we is, a pocket of poor folks." His droopy eyes peered over his rosy shades. "How come nobody done notice us all this time?"

Clarence lurched out of his chair, startling me. Pacing, he said, "Brothers got no jobs, got stinking schools and cockroaches. Niggers are invisible. Until last year. Watts. A White cop busted brother Frye and all hell broke loose. The cops' reaction: bust more heads."

Wondering if Dad had ever *busted heads*, my intestines twisted. He had once described a night when his beat covered South Jamaica, finding himself alone in a crowded hall. A fight broke out; people started yelling and pushing. He knew if the crowd turned on him, he'd be "a goner." He told me, "I simply issued commands, ordered people, 'Stop, stand back, move away!' No one was more surprised than me," he said, "when the crowd obeyed—that's the power of the uniform."

Clarence blabbed on about the Los Angeles Watts riots in 1965, when thirty-four died. He said, "Two months ago, in Chicago's West Side, it's fuckin' hot, kids open fire hydrants, cops chase down one guy who yells the pigs are tryin' to kill him. Stores looted, brothers and cops shot, a pregnant girl killed. Total dead: two. LA beat Chicago."

Rudy said, "Keeping score, man? You make race riots sound like a sport."

"Or a war." Arthur said riots had erupted that past summer in cities all over the country—even in New Brunswick, New Jersey, while I was trapped in a suburban cocoon.

Clarence said, "Why only Black folks supposed to be non-violent, when violence is all we get?" Arthur nodded, and Stan said it was a valid question. But when Clarence added, "Burnin' and looting is fighting back," Stan intervened.

He said, looking stern, "When you damage your own neighborhood, son, you're not fighting back. You're giving up." I breathed easier. Stan said, "Violence is not what we promote here. Cool down."

"Cool down," Clarence repeated, mocking Stan. Clarence barreled on, "Brothers ain't cooling down. They ain't taking no shit no more."

Shoulders thrown back, Stan faced Clarence and said, "It sounds like violence excites you."

"Man, just sayin' glad us niggers fighting back against those fuckin' racist cops—"

Stan got in Clarence's face. "Leave your street talk on the street or hit the street yourself."

I hoped this wouldn't turn into a brawl like the one my father had defused. But Clarence stormed out of the room. I tuned my ears to the door and when I heard it slam shut, my spine relaxed a few vertebrae.

The door opened again. I gasped. But it was only the pizza deliveryman. Stan offered me the first slice. The smell of the pepperoni and cheese tempted me, but my stomach felt too tight to eat. Stan told me he was sorry about Clarence. He said he acted tough, but underneath was consumed by fear. I tried to understand, but thought, *How can I possibly grasp what a young Black male faces in his life?*

I asked, "Do you have anything for me to work on?"

Stan passed me a gray piece of paper, which he'd just got from a local woman. She'd made some errors but had carefully hand-printed this letter: *There is a woman with six children the landlord are trying to evicted her from her home. The house was badly wired also the pluming. She had no place to go. Is there a housing law which prevents landlord from evicted this family out in the street?*

I'd never known a family thrown out of their home. My sister and I were relocated a few times, but not thrown out. Stan handed me the phone book where he'd circled agencies that might help. Since the woman didn't list a phone number, I wrote her back. I said to Stan, "This kind of poverty should not exist in America. It's invisible. Schools need to teach the truth."

Stan said, "Duffy, on the streets of the ghetto, you'll learn more about real life in America than you'll ever learn in the halls of college."

———————

On campus the next week, tall Gothic buildings towering around me, I recalled that as a tuition-free college, City College of New York was termed the Harvard of the poor. Shepherd Hall resembled a cathedral, but the rocky, rough-hewn walls indicated a rebellion against tradition. I hurried to the library's art section, borrowed reproductions from nineteenth century masters, and brought them to Squires on Lexington Avenue. I found the restaurant under renovation, workers gone, and Bill in his paint-splattered overalls set up and ready to go.

I spread out the prints of pale gentlemen in top hats escorting fair ladies in bonnets along orderly city boulevards, and into my mind popped images of the gray shacks and littered streets of South Jamaica. "Hey, Bill, do you ever work for the cause?"

He shared a story of a friend who was protesting discrimination at a construction company and had asked him to help. "He told me to lay down in front of a truck, saying no truck could get past my Black ass." I fell over laughing. Bill said, "Anybody can lie down, Duffy. But not everybody can paint. My cause is art."

"Yes. But what about the cause of *freedom*?"

"Every day I paint I'm working for freedom." Bill told me that as a young man he'd loved art, but never learned about one Black artist in school, so he let art go. Until he felt called. He got free of a dull job and an unhappy marriage and taught himself to paint. He joked he had to honor his calling, even though it would be scary to be "the first Black artist in history."

I laughed and admired his personal courage. "But now we have the chance to free everyone, to create a 'Great Society.'"

Bill smiled. "Duffy, look at the two of us. We're doing what we love, which makes us free." He said that just by working together making art, we were doing something. "We're creating a *great society* right here. Now let's go make some art."

On a makeshift table—cardboard placed over two saw-horses—Bill rolled out a six-foot scroll, transforming the messy workspace into an artists' studio and lighting up my imagination. This detailed pencil cartoon of an English town had to be copied to the wall. My job. I shrank.

He held up an object that looked like a rolling cutter. "Do you think you can learn to use this tool?" I nodded, though unsure. The small silver wheel looked prickly. Bill demonstrated following the pencil lines with the cutter. "Concentrate."

I rolled the wheel and perforated the huge white cartoon. Then we each took an end, climbed up ladders, and, carefully balancing ourselves, taped it to the primed wall.

He next demonstrated another Renaissance technique. He picked up a cheesecloth pouch the size of an apple, pulled the drawstrings tight, and smacked the pouch—puff, puff—against the cartoon. It looked like fun. "The dust goes through the holes to the wall and forms an outline on the mural." He called the process "flocking." Bill handed me the pouch packed with blue chalk. "Ready?"

I worked yard by yard. Delighted, I pictured Michelangelo's apprentices on scaffolding preparing the Sistine Chapel. During the hours I flocked, my nostrils breathed in the dry smell of chalk, and the air filled with the magic of sparkling light blue particles. Pulling the cartoon down from the white wall, we saw before us the whole town outlined in baby blue. Like ghosts, people rode in horse-drawn carriages; gentlemen stopped to converse; ladies strolled with children into candy shops.

"You did it, Duffy!" Bill said. "Soon color will bring the town to life, make it look real."

"No," I said, thinking of the grey ghetto. "In reality, there's a lot of ugliness."

"All the more reason for artists to paint beauty."

That sounded profound, and I wanted to believe it. I said, "But aren't we ignoring destruction, the riots, the ugly war, the hatred going on?"

"No. As artists, we defeat destruction with the opposite: creation. Art is the opposite of war. We counter the ugly by expressing beauty."

———————

Returning later that week, I saw that Bill had fleshed out in color a few figures—a gentleman helping an elderly lady across a cobblestone street. He said, "I like painting people living a slower and gentler life."

I thought right away of "Willoughby," an episode broadcast years ago in Rod Serling's TV show, *Twilight Zone*. Bill didn't have a TV, so I told him the story: A contemporary businessman commuted to a big city. Stressed by greedy bosses and his wife's demand for money, he often dozed on the train. Every night, the conductor announced a stop called "Willoughby," and he'd see out the window a delightful nineteenth-century town similar to the one Bill and I were creating. One evening during a swirling snowstorm, the conductor woke the man by shouting, "Willoughby! Next stop Willoughby!" The business-man rose with delirious excitement and jumped off the train to his death.

Though Bill didn't care for the ending, we began calling our mural "Willoughby." The subject of our mural still bothered me. I said, "Isn't it celebrating a privileged life enjoyed only by decked-out rich people."

Bill laughed. "Not all rich people are bad." I knew that was true. Like not all poor people, or all White people or all Black people were bad. Stereotypes were wrong. Bill said, "Think of it this way: We show people being kind. We're not celebrating wealth, but a vision of harmony."

His words turned me around. I said, "I can get into that—portraying kindness."

"Good. Remember, Duffy, we need to hold the vision."

———————

On Sunday a local doctor was offering free health exams for poor folks at Freedom Place, and Rudy passed on Stan's request for my assistance. I readily showed up, and Stan said he hoped to bring in the locals. I asked why the doctor wasn't giving the exams at the hospital. Stan said, "These folks, even if half dead, would rather suffer from disease than venture into that scary, spanking white hospital building."

Rudy said everyone in the neighborhood trusted Stan, so the doctor asked Stan to host the clinic. Vicky had hung posters at the shelter, unemployment center, and welfare office, and Soc posted two at Lou's Liquor store.

Stan announced the doctor had arrived. A man with a mustache appeared, wearing spectacles, a raincoat, and furry Russian-style hat. I caught myself surprised that this Black man was a doctor, realizing that for my whole life the only doctors I met, or saw on TV, were White men. Stan introduced us to one of the first Black neurosurgeons in America and the new director of Interfaith Hospital in Jamaica. "Today he's here to help the helpless. Welcome Dr. Matthew."

"Thank you. Call me Doc."

"What's up, Doc?" Socrates cracked, and we all laughed.

Doc thanked us for reaching out to folks who struggle with alcoholism, "a disease and a slow killer." I'd heard similar words at an AA meeting I'd attended with Dad and hoped Dad would sober up before it was too late.

Doc said, "If the ghetto folk won't go to the hospital, the hospital will come to the ghetto." We cheered. He removed his hat, exposing his shiny head, bald on top with tufts of dark hair on the temples.

"This dude is like Howdy Doody," Soc whispered. Funny. But I elbowed him to cut the jokes. Soc and Rudy put up chairs and screens; I set up the registration table; Vicky and Susan made sandwiches; and Doc stood ready in a white medical coat. But no one showed up, and we worried the bologna sandwiches would dry up. Stan ducked out.

After an hour Doc challenged us to sympathize with the men's reluctance. "If you hadn't bathed or changed your underwear in two months, would you be eager to strip down?"

Stan popped in the door, saying, "The guys are coming." Doc asked how he attracted them. He said, "I just put the word out they get it free."

Doc asked, "They didn't know the exam is free?"

"Not the exam, the wine."

The gang laughed while Stan stacked large Gallo wine bottles on the table, and we went out to welcome the men. Most stood across the parking lot, eyes squinting; others took cautious steps toward us, and some leaned against the stucco building. I smelled the stink of alcohol and couldn't help being repelled, but Stan greeted each man by name. Still, no one dared to come inside. The day was damp and unseasonably cold for October, and even in my fleece-lined jacket I shivered.

I asked Stan how the men, with no jackets at all, could stand the cold?

"With that much alcohol in you, you become oblivious," he said. "They're a hardy bunch—they can endure temperatures and conditions way beyond my tolerance."

Finally, a man with a nasty cut on his forehead asked Stan, "True you got free wine?"

Stan said, "Fred, ever know me to tell you a lie?"

The men chuckled and mumbled, "Stan, no, he tells no lies." Fred stepped inside. Two followed him. Vicky lifted her nose in reaction to body odor. Susan steered them to the food. They ignored the bologna but reached immediately for the wine. Vicky pulled the Gallo bottle back. She told them *after* the exam, they'd get a cup of wine.

Fred grumbled that he didn't want no damn exam and turned right around, his buddies ready to follow. But he couldn't get past Stan, who said, "Come on now, Fred. You got a nasty cut, there. Doc will fix you right up. Go with Duffy here, she'll get you started."

I smiled at Fred and held his arm as he stumbled up the step to the back room. We sat down at the table, and I picked up an intake form. "Okay, I got your first name, Fred. What's your last name?"

"Don't like givin' out no *in-fo-ma-tion*."

"I hate official forms, too, but only Doc will see this—not the government."

"Not the *po-lice* neither?"

"Definitely not the police."

He told me I was pretty. I smiled and asked for his address. He said he forgot it. *Of course, he must be homeless.* A buddy behind him suggested his mama's address. I asked if he was married, and he said, "The woman run out on me." I asked about children, and he said he had "a couple . . . here and there." His buddies chuckled. Place of birth? He said, "Never been nowhere else but here." I thanked him and directed him to Doc. Fred asked, "What's he gonna do?"

Just check heart, ears, throat, I assured him. And look at his cut. Fred admitted it did hurt and moved to the table covered in sanitized white paper, where Doc sat him down and pulled the curtain closed. After several minutes, Fred came out smiling, sporting a fresh white bandage on his head. "Ready for my wine now!"

I said, "Okay. One last thing. Please sign your form."

Fred stopped dead in his tracks. He took the Bic pen into his fist and exhaled loudly as he deliberately marked a large "X."

Oh, my God. It was the first time in my life I'd ever met anyone who couldn't write his own name. Illiteracy shouldn't exist in America. Somehow, our education system had failed him. Fred hung his head and peeked at me with sad eyes, his jaw sliding back and forth across decaying teeth. I luckily remembered a fact of history. "That's okay, Fred. You know, the French king, Charlemagne, signed his name with an X, too."

Fred's face lit up and he stood. He said, "If an X was good enough for a king, it's good enough for me." He slugged some wine, then went forth to spread the word to his buddies.

I felt a deep satisfaction that I had not felt at college, of being part of something bigger than me, bigger than my own personal ambitions. At the end of the day, as Doc departed, he thanked us for the clinic's success. The gang celebrated, and I picked up a cup of wine, too. Stan looked at me askance. Not yet eighteen, I was not legally allowed to drink. I lowered the cup. But as soon as he turned, I lifted it again and toasted him behind his back, making Rudy and Soc crack up. Stan looked back at me, a grin spreading on his handsome face.

Over pizza, we all sat around shooting the breeze. Susan announced funds available for tutoring, and Rudy mentioned he had tutored with me. Stan asked to hear more, and we told the story.

———

One Saturday the previous spring, I'd invited Rudy to join my Unitarian youth group tutoring kids in Harlem. From the subway station at 125th Street, we found the place where Quakers organized opportunities for youth. The Quaker in charge, Woody, assigned Rudy and me to a group of lively Black and Latino pre-teens, who begged us to ditch tutoring and take them downtown instead. I proposed a trip to the Metropolitan Museum of Art, free to the public, and Woody agreed to pay bus fare down Fifth Avenue.

At the Museum, the kids zoomed from room to room, freaked out by real Egyptian mummies and nude Greek statues. Their eyes grew wide seeing war masks from Africa and patterned fabric from South America. We must have trekked miles before we sank, exhausted, on the grand steps outside. Rudy treated the kids to balloons, and I bought them fat pretzels with mustard. A girl got sick and threw up on the curb, right there on Fifth Avenue. Her composure impressed me—no whining, she just stood up and carried on. Back in Harlem, I told Woody how exposure to art is good for youth who are "culturally deprived."

Woody squinted. "Culturally deprived?"

In his gentle Quaker manner, he shared his view: These kids are steeped in culture—their own very rich community. Their extended families and neighbors watch out for them, share traditional foods, tell them stories, and expose them to many languages and dialects.

I felt hot with embarrassment. I didn't mean to put the kids down. Woody understood I was "well-intentioned," like the so-called experts who produce such terms as culturally deprived. He said they couldn't see how the term assumes the dominant culture is superior.

I had blindly absorbed the same false assumption.

On the way back to the subway with Rudy, I paid closer attention. I smelled fried sausages. I heard sounds of Spanish and Creole and slang, cooing of grandparents over toddlers, and music on radios while young people danced in the street. Rudy kidded me, "Ever since Chubby Checker taught the Twist, it's cool Black celebrities who set the trends for you White kids—how you dance, what you wear, and even the slang you speak."

Rudy and Woody got me thinking about my friends in Queens Village, the neighborhood I knew as a child. We spoke only one language; we got our stories from cartoons and commercials while we ate packaged TV dinners; we lived in single homes isolated from other relatives in small "nuclear" family units. Neighbors didn't sit on stoops, play music, dance in the streets, or watch out for each other's kids. It struck me that White middle-class culture could be another form of cultural deprivation.

———————

"You learned a lot that day." Stan said, as Rudy and I finished talking about Harlem. "We have to examine our false stereotypes," he said as he trashed the empty pizza box. "You know, not everybody is willing to learn." That sounded like a compliment. He licked the tomato sauce off his full soft lips and an uninvited thought flashed through my mind, *What would it feel like to kiss him?* I quickly banished the idea.

Stan mentioned our project for the next Friday, applying for grants for community businesses. He said he was studying a model program in one of the poorest Black neighborhoods in New York: Bedford Stuyvesant. "That's where Janet's father works," Rudy said.

Stan looked surprised. Rudy told Stan he learned that when he walked me home after our day in Harlem. "Janet's father invited me in."

"So," Stan said, "let me get this straight. After spending a whole day out with his daughter, a White man invited you into his home."

Rudy smiled. "Okay, at first, I freaked out. But he wanted to talk about civil rights. He's a reasonable guy. In favor of youth programs—good for the kids and good for the cops."

Stan stiffened. He turned to me and asked, "And just what does your father do in Bedford Stuyvesant?"

"He's a lieutenant for the New York Police Department."

Stan stiffened and numbly stated, "You're the daughter of an Irish cop."

Uneasy, I watched his face flood with clashing emotions: disbelief, anger, suspicion. He finally looked straight at me and, sounding almost hurt, asked, "Why didn't you tell me your father is a cop?"

Chapter 4
RIOTS AND SUSPICIONS

Why hadn't I told Stan that my father was a cop? Clarence had railed at what anyone could see on news footage on TV: Police often arresting and injuring Black men, even killing them without consequence. He'd called cops "racist pigs." I feared losing Stan and the gang as friends, and I was right. After learning my father's job, Stan had looked at me as if I were an alien, "the daughter of an Irish cop."

An *Irish* cop. I bristled, remembering our talks about canning stereotypes. As if to excuse his lumping all cops of a certain descent into one negative stereotype, he said, "In our community, the Irish are known to be . . . *unfriendly* to Black people. Understand?" I understood well.

———————

I recalled a childhood Christmas at my Irish grandparents' home. Under the tree, my sisters and I spotted the manger—new to us. Treating it like Grandma's own "dollhouse," we played with the wooden figures of sheep, shepherds, wise men, and angels. I especially loved the baby in the wooden crib because in Unitarian Sunday school we learned that Jesus loved everybody—neighbors, poor people, and even enemies.

Demonstrators in Harlem, 1964

My sisters and I therefore felt shocked when Grandpa, at the dinner table, used the word "nigger." We stared at him. Dad and Mom had previously warned us to never say that word, along with "hell," "damn," and "crap." Grandpa explained the word came from Negroes themselves because they were too ignorant to say the word "Negro" properly and demonstrated by slurring the word. I'd never seen Grandpa look so mean. Seeing my sisters and me staring at him, he gestured for us to follow him to the icebox and chuckled as he gave us each an extra Coke—our sweet Grandpa Duffy again. I felt confused observing his switch from unfriendly Irish to friendly Irish.

An Irish cop came to mind who, two years before, in 1964, shot and killed a fifteen-year-old Black boy. The boy's death set off a riot in Harlem. The NYPD called in from all precincts hundreds of special duty policemen, including my father. I sat with my mom and sisters in our Jamaica apartment, terrified by the scenes on TV—crowds surging, cops pushing, people crouching amid sounds of shouting, gunshots, sirens—yet scanning the screen for a glimpse of Dad.

The faces I saw among the people roaming the streets conveyed fear, anger, and hopelessness, like they didn't give a crap anymore what happened to them. Kids my age set garbage cans on fire and burned White-owned stores to the ground, while sirens of fire engines blared in the background. Mothers with infants ducked through shattered glass windows to steal stuff and slinked away looking afraid. I cringed as streams of people poured into the streets. Some pumped up their chests, I imagined, to stamp down their fear: Unarmed, they faced police with drawn pistols. I hoped my father was not among police who swung nightsticks and bloodied heads of men who wouldn't back down.

Dad finally arrived home. I jumped up from bed to hug him, but he seemed unapproachable, exhausted from trying to control the uncontrollable. Some cops had been attacked. I wanted to ask if he knew any of them, of if he himself had beaten anyone. I'd felt fear just watching. Had he been afraid? But I didn't dare ask anything. His eyes looked red and glazed like he'd seen things he didn't want to talk about.

From later news reports I pieced events together. On July 16, 1964, James Powell, a Black boy about my age, was hanging out with friends, when they got hosed and called "dirty niggers" by the white janitor, Patrick Lynch. The boys chased Lynch inside the building. An off-duty policeman, Lt. Thomas Gilligan, stumbled upon the scene. Afterwards accounts differed except for one indisputable fact: Gilligan shot Powell dead.

Word went out in Harlem about Powell: "Another Black teen killed by a cop." Outrage erupted. A civil rights group held a peaceful rally on 123rd Street, but later a preacher, Rev. Duke, led a march to the police station to demand the arrest of Gilligan for murder. His fiery words, which he later regretted, sparked a powder keg. A crowd tried to push into the station, but police dispersed them by firing shots into the air. On Lenox Avenue, people threw bottles from rooftops and one hit a cop; police seized a youth. The story spread that while the boy was shouting he didn't hit a cop, he got dragged to the station house and beat up.

Six days later the rioting left hundreds wounded, more than five hundred arrested, and one person dead. Dad and I finally spoke. I couldn't bend my mind around the cause of such mass madness. He said, "No one cause, many deep problems." He believed people exploded because of desperation—desperation over discrimination and families trapped in a downward spiral of poverty. Earlier Irish immigrants had faced hiring blocks, too, which led them to government jobs in fire and police departments. It was true the Irish filled the ranks of the NYPD. My father joined, not because policing was his dream job or because he wanted to act tough. He'd wanted to go to college but needed the steady pay and benefits for his wife and three girls.

Dad went on to reveal he did regularly hear other cops make jokes or say hateful things about Negroes. He figured they'd heard hate at home, as he had, which poisons generation after generation. He had determined to break free from the "cycle of hate," and deliberately taught my sisters and me that prejudice is not only wrong, it's stupid. "Prejudice means, *pre-judging*," he said. "You don't judge a book by its cover, and you don't judge people by their color." For that, I felt proud of Dad. But what about the other cops who regularly made racist cracks? Wouldn't they be more ready to use a night stick, or gun, against a Black person? Wouldn't their individual hate and prejudice rot the entire police department? While I grappled with these questions, I stayed clear of Freedom Place.

———————

I spent time painting with Bill. We expressed freedom his way— by making art. At Squires's Restaurant door, seeing his sleepy eyes and crooked beret, I figured he'd spent the night painting and taking periodic naps curled up in a booth. He slurped down the cup of coffee I brought him.

Bill handed me tubes of Winsor & Newton oil paints: Naples yellow, cobalt blue, alizarin crimson, and titanium white, which I squirted onto my wood palette in little spirals. He asked me to mix up some beiges for skin tones. Bill had always painted the faces. I looked at him quizzically, and he nodded. Feeling trusted, I enjoyed mixing a full range of skin tones: palest porcelain white and creamy beige with a blush of cherry; tan tinged with golden olive, light cinnamon brown, and milk chocolate; and a dark purplish brown the color of eggplant. All mixed from the same three primary colors and varying amounts of white.

Bill smiled but said we wouldn't need the dark tones for English squires. I got it. I could mix the rich eggplant color another time. I thought, *If I ever painted Stan's face.*

I worked up courage to return to Freedom Place the following Friday. Stan greeted me, making my name sound like "Stuffy." I felt like leaving. But Socrates brought me to the back room, where I found the gang celebrating Rudy, who was at Queens College for Orientation. He'd been accepted into the spring SEEK program. And even better news: Rudy got his 4F! He could stop infecting himself to keep out of that immoral war. A guy called Jamil sat stiffly on the couch and said, "You let White people in here?" I felt slapped.

Soc said, in his disarming way, "That's Duffy. She's cool."

Jamil wouldn't look at me, but I studied his thin light brown arms. I held up a black coffee mug and a white piece of paper. "Jamil, you call yourself Black and me White, right?" He looked at me sideways like I was crazy. "But look, your skin is not black like the mug, and my skin is not white like paper." I placed my arm next to his arm. "Looks to me like our colors are only slightly different shades of beige and tan." Jamil didn't answer.

"Right on, sister," Socrates said with gusto. "Duffy, you may be White, but you got a Black soul."

I took that as a great compliment, and the gang nodded and laughed. I noticed Stan observing us from the threshold of the door. He asked me to his office. I joked he sounded like a principal as I stepped inside, but he remained serious, saying, "Open your eyes. Miss Duffy. In fact, you are lily White, part of the privileged race, and Jamil, though on the fair side, is still Black, part of the oppressed race." He sat and said, "Take a seat, White folks."

Still standing, I said, "Why do you call me 'White folks,' using the plural?"

"Because when I see your White face, I see *all* White folks."

My heart pounded. I could hardly believe these insulting words were coming out of the mouth of a man I respected and believed worked against prejudice. If he was playing some kind of

game, I didn't play. I said, "I thought you didn't like stereotypes."
Stan didn't look at me. I said, "This is about my father being a
cop isn't it?" His silence confirmed it was. I sat down. "You know,
I never heard anyone here talk about their father's job. I didn't
think it mattered." I caught myself making dumb excuses and
stopped. I had once apologizing to Rudy for the same ignorance.
I said to Stan, "I'm sorry. I should have known that being a cop's
daughter does matter."

After a moment, he said, "It's Friday night."

"What about it?"

"Tell me something. Why aren't you out with your friends?
At a movie or something?" I told him I'd rather do something
useful and share my skills. "That's very 'White' of you," he said
and swiveled around to face me. "Why do you *really* come here?"

I wished he'd stop the suspicion. I told him I came for the
same reason as everyone else, to work for a good cause. "That's
what we are to you—a *good cause*? Look," Stan said, "we Black
people fight to change the system, you know that, right? Make
no mistake, Jamil is Black. If he gains freedom, aren't you afraid
you'll lose?"

If Stan's goal was to stoke my fire, he succeeded. Screw
him—pitching such a narrow vision of winners and losers. If
even one person is oppressed, nobody wins. I believed if Jamil
gains his rights, I gain a just society. Martin Luther King knew
that, and we both knew that, and I told him so. I declared, "It's
myself I fight for. I'm not free if I have to worry about those who
are not free." I said something about "enlightened self-interest."

Stan said, "Duffy, you're smart. You really should focus on
your degree."

Focus on my degree? I could have reminded Stan of his
previous advice: that I'd learn more about America on the streets
of the ghetto than in any college course. My mind crawled with
confusion. Maybe it *was* time for me to study more and spend
my free nights with people who appreciated me.

———

Several days later, I invited my friend Penny over for spaghetti. I knew Penny sometimes worked with Stan on community events, and I hoped she might help me figure him out. Freedom Place had given me some friends and a sense of purpose I didn't want to lose.

Her warm hug cheered me up. She leaned down to pet Felice, and I put on an album by Harry Belafonte, one of her favorite singers, to distract from the noisy traffic outside. She talked about her classes at Hunter College, the CUNY campus on the East Side of Manhattan, and about her part-time work at the Museum of Modern Art.

"You work at MOMA?" I said, envious.

But Penny didn't give a hoot about modern art. She said, "I zip right up the elevator to the penthouse restaurant to waitress." I didn't think I could ever waitress. "The tips are good," she said. "It's the class snobbery that's tough." Waitresses were not allowed to chat with diners or even make eye contact. No jewelry, makeup, accessories, or any personal expression. I told her I just couldn't picture her, my vocal friend, sticking her red hair in a net and keeping her mouth shut. She said she needed the money. She asked me about work.

I told her I kept my job painting with Bill. And that I also volunteered in Jamaica. I got to ask her what she thought of Stan.

She said, "He's good-looking. And he knows it."

"Do you think he has charisma?"

"Charisma?" Penny smiled and said, "Sweetie, do you have a crush on him?" My friend knew me well. I said that Stan was too old for me. "Look, Janet, do you think the older men you work for, Bill and Stan, kind of fill in for your father?"

I stood up abruptly, collected the dishes, and washed them in the sink. She pulled out a towel to dry. I thought, *The men I work for are so different from each other.* Bill, an artist, paints scenes of aristocrats; Stan, an activist, works with street people. Bill, so out of shape, and Stan, so muscular. Penny found it interesting that the two men I worked with were Black.

Penny said we shared an interest in issues of race since tenth grade, and recalled the survey I designed for our class, 99 percent White. I presented the results at an assembly: Out of the hundred kids I interviewed, I found almost all supported integration in education and jobs, but fewer in housing and social circles. Basically, the more intimate the relationship, the less support for integration. I said, "Hardly anyone liked the idea of interracial marriage."

She asked if that surprised me. I thought about the interracial couples at church, who—in the South—would be breaking the laws against miscegenation. "I did figure that kids in the North would be more open-minded."

"Back to Stan," Penny said. "Did he ever approach you?"

The jolt I felt at our first meeting popped into my head. Since his warm hand shook mine, a jiggling fantasy had taken up residence in a corner of my mind of Stan wrapping me in his heat and strength. "No," I said, "He never approached me."

"Is Stan married?"

"I don't know." If he did have a wife, that would end any sweet feeling I carried for him. I would never consider a relationship with any married man. Penny knew that. Sitting on the sofa bed, Felice curled up on Penny's lap, I told her that Stan acted suspicious toward me since he found out my father worked as a policeman.

"Oh, of course," Penny said. "But, sweetie, if he really didn't trust you, he wouldn't let you near his place." She stood to leave, hugged me and said, "He's just playing with you, to test you, to find out who you are."

Stan wants to find out who I am? I thought. *So do I. I've been asking myself that same question for years. Am I dutiful or rebellious? Scholarly bookworm, or creative artist type? A dependent daughter or independent woman? To which tribe do I belong? What does it mean to be a White person working for Black people?*

I'd told Stan, "I want to free myself," but I wasn't always sure who my *self* was.

———

On Sunday, I knocked on the Squires door and heard resounding classical music, unusually loud. Bill answered the door holding a paintbrush upright, his eyes wet.

"Anything wrong?"

He pointed to his radio—which for the first time I noticed was shaped like an arch of a cathedral—the source of loud mournful sounds. "Handel," Bill said, squeezing his eyes shut. He said, "My soul vibrates, as if I *am* the cello." His Buddha belly filled and emptied of breath. Choked up, he spoke. "Now *that* is soul music." I thought of soul music as mostly sung by Black singers. I asked if I, a White girl, could feel such depths of soul?

On the mural before me, newly painted figures appeared to come alive, strolling through Willoughby, our vision of kindness. It was so unlike New York City where workers in a rat race commuted underground. I pictured myself escaping to the sketched storybook mansion on the hill, sitting at dinner with the English family politely chatting. Voices of my own family intruded, shooting cutting words at each other. Once, Mom had crawled under our dining room table to pet our cat Beauty, but in minutes she crumpled to the floor, sobbing. My chest ached in sympathy.

Bill rescued me from the memory. He handed me a new sable hair paintbrush. Looking at my eyes now wet like his, he said, "Duffy, you got a lot of soul. Now mix up some greens for the grass." I smelled the oozing paint. I filled my cup with oil, gripped my palette, and climbed to my spot on the scaffolding. We painted way past dusk, listening to soul music from centuries before, the only other sound the brush of sable on whitewashed wall.

I'd worked in silence like this, doing homework side by side with Mom late into the night when she attended the Fashion Institute of Technology. One night, as she applied inks and watercolors to her design of a flowered gown, worthy of the elegant ladies in Willoughby, I watched in awe as a delicate woman emerged.

I missed those close times with Mom. I missed our family. Barbara, now married, rarely visited; our parents struggled with their reconciliation; Maureen sometimes visited them and hung around for a meal. But my mother and father hardly ever stopped off to see how I was doing in college. Maybe they felt I didn't care about them.

But I did care. In the past, to show love and support, I'd go with Mom to Al-Anon or with Dad to an AA meeting. But the divorce changed everything. The agreement, Mom had informed us, required that Dad pay child support, but only until age eighteen. Did that mean that then he'd abandon Maureen and me? He'd already more or less disappeared from our lives. Because he felt ashamed about getting drunk? So much hurt in so many hearts.

"Hey, Duffy, time to wrap up for the evening." As Bill and I put away our brushes, I let out a deep sigh. He asked, "You doing okay?" Bill's eyes looked tired but still shone with a peace I saw as soul. I confided that I wasn't sure I was on the right path. He told me to look inside myself. He said my parents couldn't give me answers.

Ain't that the the truth, I thought. *Not my sisters, teachers, rock stars, girlfriends, or boyfriends either.* His wise words reminded me of Emerson, a Unitarian minister, who preached about finding the truth within.

He said, "You won't ever get yourself together if you care what other people think. Define yourself, Duffy. Your soul will guide you."

At Freedom Place opportunities flooded in, and Rudy called to say Stan hoped I could lend a hand. I wondered, What's changed? I readily answered the call, and Vicky handed me a funding application for after-school programming. In the back room, I sketched ideas for art projects.

Stan stepped into the room, and I tensed, not knowing what to expect. Looking over my sketches he said, "You're good at art." I told him about Bill. Seeming impressed, he watched me draw.

He sat opposite me and said, "Last week I heard knocking and found a stocky White man at the door." He paused. "He introduced himself as your father."

"You're kidding." It wasn't like Dad to check up on me.

"He didn't tell you he visited me?" I shook my head. Stan said, "My first thought was, so this is *Lieutenant Duffy*. I have to admit, I stood on guard, expecting him to grill me, this man his daughter worked for on Friday nights. But he disarmed me."

"I know my father can be charming."

Stan said, "He seems smart." True. I told Stan that once Dad had turned me on to great authors at an early age. Stan said, "I agree with Rudy. He is a reasonable man. I liked him." My stomach relaxed. Stan told me my father thought I carried the world's burdens on my shoulders, and he supported my work for civil rights. "And we found something in common," Stan said. "We're both vets." Dad had served in World War II, and Stan, the Korean War. Stan said, "We both signed up for the army."

I told him my father always attributed the GI Bill for his head start in life. He took advantage of the college benefit to take a few courses, and the low mortgage rate really helped.

"The GI Bill did not help me." Perplexed, I asked why not? Stan told me the few colleges set up for Black folks were too far away. I hadn't realized that. "The rest didn't accept Black folks."

That, I knew. I'd watched a news story with Dad a few years before about James Meredith, an outstanding student who'd served nine years in the air force and had been accepted by the University of Mississippi. However, discovering he was Black, the university blocked his admission. Meredith took his case to the Supreme Court and won, but that didn't stop threats from White rioters. Kennedy had to send in the National Guard.

Stan told me the GI housing benefit was also useless. Banks drew red lines around Black neighborhoods and would not give mortgages there. "And White neighborhoods were not exactly opening up their arms." I knew that recently Dr. Martin Luther King Jr. had led hundreds to protest housing segregation in a working-class neighborhood of Chicago, where he braved jeers of thousands of White people. King had hoped the protest would bring "hate out into the open," and it did just that. White people threw rocks, injuring thirty—one stunned King himself.

Stan said, "I eventually got a mortgage because I owned a business." He told me something I'd never learned. That the army had been segregated when Dad served in World War II. Black soldiers had first fought in separate "colored" regiments in 1866 and every US war since. In the middle of the Korean War, segregation in the US Army officially ended.

Stan said, "In Korea, I fought side by side with Pete, a White guy. We got through the war together and, arriving back home in America, we set up this carting business together. But we had to live on opposite ends of town."

How awful, I thought. Yet I knew my grandparents on both sides still firmly supported segregation. I'd lived in a "de facto" all White neighborhood growing up and still did. That fact made me feel damn uncomfortable.

I zipped right up to my parents' apartment, relieved to find Mom already asleep and Dad alone and sober. Over Sanka decaf, I asked about his visiting Stan. Dad said, "I saw a fit man going for a piece of the pie—smart." Interesting, Stan had called Dad *smart*, too. I felt relieved they'd passed each other's tests.

I blurted out. "Dad, about your parents—why are they so bigoted?"

He grimaced. A history buff, he thought the root of our problems lay in the past. Long ago in Ireland, the Irish suffered at the hands of the English, who'd slaughtered and enslaved them. The Irish were called "the Blacks of Europe." The failure of the potato crop in the mid 1800s forced millions to flee famine. Our ancestors arrived in New York City and Boston, desperate for work, but they faced signs like: "No Blacks, no Irish, no dogs."

"The Duffys," he speculated, "were probably among the Irish who'd found some low-paying work in New York, just when Abraham Lincoln issued the Emancipation Proclamation." The Irish and other immigrants in the city depended on the cotton coming up from plantations for work, and they feared the emancipated Blacks coming north would take their jobs. It became a battle for survival. "Soon," Dad said, "a racial uprising erupted— the worst in American history."

"The worst?"

He pulled out a rare document, "Draft Riot of 1863," by J. T. Headley, which he'd bought at an estate sale hoping to better understand the riot he'd witnessed in Harlem in 1964. He said, "In New York, a century apart, two terrible riots exploded."

"Why?" I asked.

"Imagine people full of fear. Then the country gets hit by the draft—the first draft in history, way before Vietnam." During the Civil War. Black men were ineligible because they were not considered citizens; rich White men escaped by paying a substitute. "The fighting fell to working White men," Dad said. "In New York, that meant mainly Irish. They rebelled."

My fingers gripped my chair as Dad told how anger exploded into a five-day rampage. On the East Side, mid-town, a disgruntled crowd soon turned into a stone-throwing mob. At first, they focused on symbols of injustice—the draft office, the mayor's residence, the *New York Times* office, a couple police stations—and set them on fire. Then they destroyed homes of Black people and the first pharmacy owned by a Black man. Their threatening Black sympathizers scared me, because they would have called me a *sympathizer*. They attacked abolitionists and threatened two White women who'd married Black men. Violence escalated. They hurt a Black fruit vendor and a nine-year-old Black boy. They lynched eleven Black men. They threw a three-day-old Black baby out the window to its death.

I recoiled in horror.

Dad continued. Brandishing clubs, a mob of several thousand, including women and children, advanced on the asylum founded by White women that housed over two hundred "colored orphans." They stole food and clothing, then set the orphanage on fire.

"Sickening," I said. "Really, the cruelty is too much to grasp." Dad said the state militia finally quelled the riot. "What about the orphans?" I asked. He said the orphans had escaped. "But who—what kind of person—would try to kill children?"

I remembered Dad arriving home from duty in Harlem in 1964 and telling Mom that some cops, some Irish, had called the Black rioters "animals." They obviously knew nothing about their own beastly history. Dad believed that the underlying cause of both riots, and any riot, is oppressed people rebelling against discrimination. In the last century, White people exploded; in our century, Black people.

"However," he said, "there's a huge difference in the *scale* of the damage." In Harlem in 1964, the riots left one person dead and hundreds wounded, and the destruction was limited to one Black neighborhood. Terrible enough, but much worse in 1863: rioters killed hundreds, injured thousands, and destroyed fifty buildings in several neighborhoods around the city.

I again asked, "How is that possible?"

Dad said, "Mob mentality. I've witnessed it." Rationality goes out the window. Base instincts of fear and rage take over. Seemingly normal people become capable of horrendous acts. Noticing my distress, Dad turned to me and said, "I know sometimes the truth is shocking. But history teaches us. Education can save humanity. It can civilize us and help us tame irrational impulses. Oppression always backfires. We gotta wise up and stop making the same stupid mistakes."

———————

At Freedom Place the following Friday, I sketched more ideas for a youth art program. Stan asked where I got my art talent? I laughed. "Definitely not from my father. Art comes from my mother's side." Stan asked if my mother was also Irish. I said, "No, she's Austro-Hungarian." He smiled and said they didn't get too many Irish-Austro-Hungarians hanging around down here. He assured me I'd make a good art teacher.

Later, I settled on the couch in his office for our regular discussion. Half-joking, he said, "Tell me more about your father. I want to know how 'the White man' thinks."

"Oh, he's not the typical 'White man.' He's open-minded. He picked up those attitudes from our church."

"The Catholic Church?" Stan asked with surprise.

I smiled. "No. You know, it's a stereotype that all Irish are Catholics." I told Stan that all four of my grandparents were Catholic, but my parents rebelled against Catholicism. "They couldn't accept that innocent babies are born with 'original sin.' And they knew they couldn't handle more than three babies even though priests warned them if they used artificial birth control, they'd go to hell for that mortal sin." I said, "They chose a religion that taught that it's fine to plan for babies, and babies are born *good*, not sinners.'"

"There's a religion like that?" Stan had never heard of Unitarian Universalism. We called ourselves UUs. I told him that in

Sunday school we learned about the teachings of Jesus as well as Buddha and other wise thinkers, like Mahatma Gandhi, who won a war through nonviolence. He said I sounded proud of my church. I was. I loved our principles—love, peace, justice, democracy.

"We call ourselves 'seekers of the truth,'" I said. "We're free to question and think for ourselves."

"That explains a lot about you, Duffy," he said, as he sat back and smiled broadly. "Your father bucked tradition."

"Exactly," I said. "He also rebelled against his family's prejudice. He wouldn't teach his girls to hate." Stan asked what he did teach us. I remembered him taking the family to the movie, *South Pacific*. "Afterwards Dad played the soundtrack, and wanted us to learn the song, 'They Have to Be Carefully Taught.' Children will play with any kid who's fun. Fear of people of different colors has to be drummed into them."

He asked if fear was drummed into me at school.

I thought, *Stan wants to peel back the onion*. My mind reeled back to third grade. I told Stan about my teacher, Mrs. Rousson. "She was the first Black person I ever met. In fact, the *only* Black person in my elementary school. Our class was accelerated, but she made time to talk to us about Rosa Parks. The Montgomery boycott was all over the news. We kids knew it wasn't fair to force people to the back of the bus."

"Good to hear little White folks have some sense." This time, his tone in saying "White folks" sounded not like an insult, but a gentle tease.

"Yes, Stan, and she told us little White folks to dream, to believe 'anything is possible.'" I remembered that she'd told my parents I have many gifts, and it would be hard to choose the one to follow. "Since then," I told Stan, "I believe if I can dream it, I can do it. I loved Mrs. Rousson. I felt so proud when she, my teacher, rose up to sing at school assemblies, looking like a star, like Mahalia Jackson. I cried when she belted out 'America, The Beautiful.' 'God crowned thy good with brotherhood . . .'"

73

Exhausted from spilling my guts out, I thought we'd pack it in. But Stan probed. "Duffy, those liberal White folks at church, do they practice what they preach?" I thought they did. Together we recalled how Dr. Martin Luther King Jr., a year and a half before, stood ready for a second attempt to march over the Pettus Bridge in Selma, Alabama. He put out a nationwide call to clergy. More Unitarian Universalist ministers showed up than from any other denomination. King hoped the presence of clergy would fend off violence, but the mounted police charged anyway. Stan remembered two of the Black victims: Cindy Amelia Boynton, hospitalized, and Jimmie Lee Jackson, killed.

"The night before the march," I said solemnly, "thugs attacked a Unitarian minister, Reverend James Reeb. Beat him unconscious. He died in the hospital." Stan and I sat for a moment in silence. The minister's killing had made national news, and Stan knew Martin delivered the eulogy for a White minister. King said that Rev. Reeb, who lived in an integrated neighborhood, showed that "men of different races and classes might live, eat, and work together as brothers."

"Another Unitarian traveled to Alabama, Viola Liuzzo," I said. "A lay woman like me." I told Stan she'd grown up poor in the South under the Jim Crow laws, and as a little girl, she noticed that her White family received small privileges unfairly denied to Black families. In 1965, she left her five children with her husband and drove from Detroit to Montgomery, where she met the marchers arriving from Selma. Twenty-five thousand people made it and celebrated while Dr. Martin Luther King Jr. praised the courage of the marchers and allies of every occupation and religion from all corners of America.

Viola offered a ride in her Oldsmobile back to Selma to a nineteen-year-old Black man. A car full of Klansman pulled up beside them and shot into the car. The young man survived. My voice cracking, I said, "Viola died instantly."

After a respectful pause, Stan said, "Your church folks were safe in their White churches and houses up north. They chose to risk their lives. Why?"

I answered with a quote from John Donne's poem, "No Man is an Island": "'. . . every man's death diminishes me.' We believe, along with King and his followers, that our fates are interwoven and that a life spent working for justice is a life well-lived."

"And you, Duffy, that's why you take risks coming here?"

Into my mind popped epithets, "White nigger" and "nigger-lover," both hurled at Viola by the lawyers defending her accused murderers. A cold fear arose along my spine.

Stan noticed my shivering, stopped probing. I took a deep breath. I couldn't say why I wanted to volunteer in neighborhoods deemed dangerous or why I grew angry when excellent students were blocked from school because of color. I supposed a passion for fairness had become part of me without my giving it much thought.

My mind floated to my childhood when I watched the movie, *Giant*, which Stan had also seen. I said that during the scene when a White owner of a diner bullies an elderly Mexican man with his family, I broke down crying. "Why? All I know is that whenever I see someone hurt and abused like that, it feels like it's me being hurt. And I have to do something."

Grandma Duffy, 1960

Chapter 5
DEATH

Our parents came down to pick up Maureen and me. Dad looked pre-occupied, but sober and wearing a neat suit, his wavy hair combed back. I felt hurt that he criticized my mini-dress—it was the only dress I had. He said, "And look at your shoes. Don't you have a better pair?" No, I didn't.

Our family entered the funeral parlor filled with scents of perfumes, chemicals, wax, and wicks burning. We found, already settled in the room, Dad's well-fed family from Boston, Aunt Florence, her daughter Marion, and their husbands.

"Hello, Edmund," said Florence. "I only see you at funerals."

I wanted to say, "Because you cut off contact." When Dad left the Catholic Church, Florence had scolded him, "You rejected God. You will never inherit a *penny* of my wealth." I looked down at her shoes—so tiny—and wondered how she kept her balance. She looked like a top-heavy opera singer ready to belt out an aria. I imagined her singing, "A Penny from Heaven—But Not for You." *She's unfair*, I thought. Rebelling against a church, a man-made institution, is not rejecting *God*.

Florence, wearing a pearl necklace and matching earrings, allowed Dad to kiss her cheek. Dad said, "Florence, you remember Janet? She's in college now." He stood proud, though his relatives treated him like "the black sheep." Dad's brother

George, his thin hair in a crew cut, waved to us. He was the favorite nephew because he'd graduated college, landed a prestigious job at IBM, and, most importantly, every week he attended Catholic Mass.

Florence studied me head to toe. My scuffed shoes, I regretted, gave evidence of my turning out poorly, as godless and hopeless as her nephew. Dad's relatives knew our family's "skeleton in the closet," and seemed to feast on it bone by bone. Most families keep a skeleton in a closet, but ours had been on full display for years, practically dancing in the window under neon lights.

Dad's cousin Marion caught my attention. Her apricot lipstick made me think of Mom's story of Marion on a train filled with soldiers. She was accompanying Mom on her way to an Alabama army base to marry Dad during World War II, and Marion reportedly had quite a ball weaving through the cars, her blouse loose around her shoulders, her lipstick smeared on her chin.

Hard to imagine youthful impulse in Marion, who now stood in the parlor beside her mother and banker husband, the epitome of propriety. They stared with disdain at Mom and Dad, forgetting that Jesus taught forgiveness, looking ready to throw the first stone at these lost lovers for their trespasses: a scandalous divorce, now "living in sin."

Their narrow eyes turned to my older sister Barbara as she arrived sporting white go-go boots and a stylish Vidal Sassoon haircut. I caught a few mean words that buzzed through the room. "Such heavy eye-makeup, like that Jew, Barbara Streisand." Maurice, Barbara's dapper husband, appeared in a smooth jacket. Hands covering mouths, eyes darting, Florence and Marion bent their heads to speak to little ladies with bluish hair permanents, and I imagined them saying, "A French foreigner, a common nightclub singer, and—imagine—as old as Barbara's father!"

I turned to approach Grandma Duffy, Dad's mother. At a wake a year before, she'd enjoyed the family gathering so much that she'd told everyone she looked forward to the next wake. Now here she was, with piles of powder and rouge on her pale face, wearing her best brocade, white lace, and pearls. Her waxy hands held a crucifix and rosary beads, but her mouth would never pray again.

Mourners took turns praying at her coffin. I too went to kneel, feeling Marion's narrow eyes watching to see if I crossed myself. I didn't. I thought death a mystery. I thought of Grandma's name, Lily, my middle name. Later, I told my sisters what I'd whispered: "Grandma, I'm sorry for the big fight you had with Mom and Dad over trying to teach us prayers."

Maureen asked if we remembered Grandma sprinkling holy water the night we slept over on her big white bed. "And the statue hanging over us of the bleeding man with nails in his hands and feet. How scared we felt."

A priest appeared on the threshold of the wide doors, his black robes flapping, as if emerging through a time tunnel from the Dark Ages. He spoke about celebrating the devout Lillian Duffy, but his tone turned grave: "God's only son died for us, lowly sinners . . ." Dad rocked back and forth on his feet. I knew he didn't believe any of this literally.

After, women prayed with rosary beads; men played cards and told jokes. Johnny Walker appeared—two bottles plopped down on the table. Relatives watched Dad to see if he'd take a shot. Luckily, he did not. But Grandpa Duffy took a full whisky bottle to an empty card table.

I couldn't stand the stink of whisky. I asked Mom, "Can we go now? The wake's over."

Mom said, "Over? No, it's an Irish wake—the party's just begun!"

She asked my sisters and me what we liked about being Irish. Maureen loved John Kennedy, the first Irish Catholic president; Barbara enjoyed fun at the St. Patrick's Day parades in New York City, proudly wearing "Kiss Me I'm Irish" buttons. Into my mind intruded the Irish draft riots, but I spoke of how Dad teared up when hearing a wistful tenor sing "Danny Boy."

Maureen mentioned the painted smile on Grandma in the coffin and said, "I hardly remember her smiling. She always seemed so *businesslike*." Mom reminded us that Grandma *did* work in business. Every day she dressed in a grey fitted suit, the hem down to her calves. (She thought knees were ugly and not to be seen.)

Barbara recalled the day Grandma took us to Manhattan, our first time on the subway. The dark tunnel, studded with yellow lights blinking like bats' eyes, terrified and thrilled me. A train going in the opposite direction whizzed by so close, we feared we would collide. Barbara said that none of her friends had grandmothers who worked outside the home.

Mom revealed that Grandma had never wanted a career, but Grandpa's illness forced her to work. "His nerves were shot," she said. "I give Lil credit—she just picked up, got a job, and kept that family going."

That news startled me. I hadn't seen Grandma as a pioneer, or Grandpa as broken down. I looked over at him, tightly holding onto the deck of cards while Dad told him he'd just dealt a hand to an empty chair. "It's for Lil," Grandpa said, sobbing, toasting her with a swig of whisky. Dad and George led their father out as he cried, "What will I do without my girl?"

———

Days after, our family of five visited Grandpa Duffy at his house in Queens Village. He looked thinner and whiter, his grief thickening the air. Feeling sorry about his loneliness, I thought of his jolly chuckle and how he'd passed on that good trait to Dad.

"Where is Lil?" Grandpa muttered to himself. I, too, missed her presence; it felt odd being in this house without Grandma standing on her short legs, bobby pins in her wavy white hair. Grandpa didn't seem to see me, Maureen, Barbara or Mom—not even Dad, his son.

But I looked at them. Feeling light-headed, tears blurring my eyes, I noticed their lips moving but words sounded muffled.

I felt a flood of love for my family. I blinked hard, like a camera shutter, to take a mental snapshot, to capture them in the flesh in that moment, knowing that, someday, we were all destined to fade away, like Grandma, into skeletons.

Grandpa's skin seemed as thin as a veil. "Lil, Lil," he cried, yearning to be with his wife. His spotted hands gripped a bottle of scotch. Dad grabbed it as if to pull Grandpa out of quicksand, but I feared Dad would sink in with him. Dad had not carried on his father's religion nor his father's racism, and I hoped Dad would stop carrying on his father's alcoholism.

"Pop . . ." Dad said. "You have to stop drinking or you'll kill yourself."

———

"You still want to learn about *real life* in America?" Stan said when I returned to Freedom Place after a lapse.

I said yes. Sitting in his office, I noticed on his desk a framed photograph of himself with two young boys. No woman or wife in the photo, but I thought, *They must be his sons.*

Stan closed his fingers together like a steeple. "Well, here's a real-life assignment: There's a man, Mr. Griffith, owner of a company in town. He's 'the Establishment.' Rich and White." Stan told me one of Griffith's sons was trained and bred at West Point to be an army officer. "He's part of the White elite in Vietnam who directs Black grunts to the front lines to die." Stan paused. "I just heard the boy got killed." We took in that grave fact. Stan continued, "The better angels of my nature mourn for the boy. But, I'll be honest, I also thought, *One less racist in the world.* I'm not proud of that, Lord knows, but it's the devil in me."

I shifted in my seat. He asked if this was too much *real life* for me. I told him to go on.

"I feel for the father. For all our differences, I found that Griffith did deal straight with his company's union about hiring more Black workers. But politics, status, color—none of that matters now. What matters is that his son died. How could I not feel sympathy, man to man? He's lost . . ." Words caught in his throat. He continued, "I want to send him a letter. That's where you come in. I want you to write it."

"But Stan, you know what to say."

"I've tried to write but can't get a damn word down. Duffy, here's your assignment: write a letter for me to that rich White man whose young son died in this devilish war."

Working alone in the back room, I picked up the challenge. I turned in the finished letter to Stan before going home, exhausted.

———————

The phone's ring woke me, and the voice at the other end of the line sounded throaty and tentative. "White folks?"

"Stan?"

"I read the letter."

"I figured—it's almost midnight." He apologized. I said, "Well, I'm awake now, what's up?"

"Your letter. I went over and over it, each and every word, looking for just one that I could change. But there's nothing, not even a punctuation mark, that I'd alter. Sitting here reading it, I feel . . . shaken." Surprised, shaking a little myself, I asked why. He said, "Because you got into my head."

I explained that I simply wrote what he'd asked me to write. "I understood . . ."

"You understood too well, Duffy. You wrote with *my* voice in the letter." He paused and then read, "'I feel sad that your son, any son, should die in a war, in a world where there is still war. . . . The feelings you had for him while he was alive still exist in you. You are deeper for having conceived a son, for loving him, and for dying a bit with him. . . . I, too, have sons.'

"How is it, Duffy, that you came to write about *my* sons? I never told you about them."

I said I'd seen their photograph in his office.

He read another line: "'As soon as they are pushed out from the warm womb, we tell them where and how to live, we try to give them as much of the good and beautiful, so when they encounter the ugly, they can stand up and carry on.'" He sounded puzzled. "How could you know my hopes, the way I *feel* about my children?"

I said, "Stan, knowing you, I imagined the way you would feel."

"*Knowing* me. That's what I'm saying—you're in my head. It makes me edgy. To have someone that close to *imagine* what I'm feeling. Especially White folks."

"Oh. Sorry to creep you out," I said. "You know, it's funny that even when you're complimenting me—I think that's what you're trying to do—you still have to badger me."

"Listen." Stan read a sentence, "'True life is elusive, forever escaping man's clutching hands. Like love and freedom, life cannot be sheltered or possessed. It can only be challenged, played with and fought for. And in daring sometimes we lose.'"

Stan's voice choked up, then he went on, "Tell me, how can these words, about life and death, come from someone so young?" Before I could answer, he said, "If I don't tell you tonight, Duffy, I'd never tell you . . . I want you to know what I really think of you."

I held my breath.

"You are a beautiful person."

Heart pounding, I felt overwhelmed.

"Good night, White folks."

———

I felt buoyed after Stan's midnight call but didn't hear anything from him all week. My next time at Freedom Place, he mentioned nothing to me about his call or the letter, let alone his feelings. I focused on my art program project.

Stan called me to the back room for something different: Chinese take-out instead of pizza. The gang and I chowed down on fried rice and spring rolls. When everyone else went back to their assignments, Stan asked me to his office. I settled on the plaid couch, and he swiveled in his chair to face me. He said, "You know, I sent Mr. Griffith the letter. I rewrote it in my own handwriting and sent it off as if it were mine. I stole it."

"Stan, no, I wrote it for you."

"Griffith called me after he read the letter," Stan said. "Right there on the phone, he cried. This big and powerful man, he broke down and cried." I listened, feeling sympathy. Stan said, "I still want to know how you, so young, could write with such depth about death?" I told Stan about Grandma and Grandpa Duffy dying. Stan paused to honor them. "Still," he said, "how could you understand how it would feel to lose a *child*?"

I sighed. I told Stan my mother's sister Pauline died at seven years old. Mom's mother (Nanny) totally withdrew into grief. My mom felt so miserable at home that, as soon as she turned eighteen, she eloped with my dad. Stan remained quiet. *Maybe*, I thought, *he didn't often hear White folks from the other side of town talk about their personal struggles*. I faced the photograph of his sons and said, "They're cute. You miss them when you work late?"

Stan sat back in his chair. "Now that's a personal question. But I'll answer. On the few nights I do work late, they get good care from their mother." I thought, *Their mother—his* wife? I asked the boys' names. "The four-year-old is John," he said, "and the six-year-old is Emmett."

"I never heard the name, 'Emmett.'"

"You never learned about Emmett Till? I guess in August, 1955, you weren't even in school yet."

"Let me think. I was about to start second grade."

"I see," he said. "Well, that summer, Emmett Till left Chicago to visit his uncle Mose in Mississippi. A pretty young woman, running a grocery store, accused Emmett of flirting with her. The boy died for that crime."

"For *flirting*, the *death* penalty?"

"Not from any judge. Two men broke into Mose's home to take the boy. Three days later, kids fishing in the Tallahatchie River found the naked body of a boy . . ." He stopped. "Duffy, are you sure you want to know?" My heart felt like lead, but I nodded. Stan described the barbed wire around his neck, his face completely disfigured, one eye dislodged and a gunshot wound in his head. I scrunched my eyes shut. "His mama insisted on an open casket—she didn't want to hide the brutality. In Chicago tens of thousands walked by him to pay respects."

"Did they find the killers?"

"They tried the suspects: the pretty woman's husband, Bryant, and his brother, Milam. The trial made national news." Stan retrieved a newspaper clipping he'd saved. Reporters described the Tallahatchie courtroom: Black people sat on one side of the room, White men with guns on their belts on the other. Jurors slugged beer. Witnesses were called. Local boys, cotton pickers, testified they'd gone with Emmett to Bryant's store to buy candy. One boy said Emmett showed Bryant's wife a picture of his school up north, Black and White teenagers sitting together in class a year after the Supreme Court Ruling, Brown vs. Board of Education.

I'd sat next to Rudy in homeroom in New York. *No big deal.* But Mississippi was another world. Stan said that Emmett's mama tried to warn her boy, but Emmett didn't mind, according to Bryant's pretty wife, who testified that he dared to put his arm around her waist. A commotion rose in the courtroom at the idea of people of different races *touching.*

Stan said, "The trial was a drama. I'll never forget the moment when Emmet's uncle Mose, a sharecropper and preacher, stood up and pointed right at Milam, looked him in the eye, and said 'Thar he. Thar he.'" Goosebumps broke out on my arm. Stan said, "Think of it! A sharecropper accusing a White man in court. Nothing like that had ever occurred in Mississippi, understand?" Stan closed his eyes and threw his head back. "At that moment I heard the chains break. Everything was going to change. I knew it, Black folks knew it, and White folks all across the country knew it."

"So, the case was over—"

"Not so fast, Duffy." The defense lawyers claimed the body, disfigured and decomposed, could not be identified.

"So much for law and order."

Stan described the God-given order in Mississippi: White men on top, followed by White women; and down at the bottom, Black people, hardly human. Stan said, "A Black boy flirting with a White woman—the end of the world as they knew it!" When the jury acquitted Bryant and Milam, rage exploded around the world. I felt that rage, too.

"The kicker is," Stan said, "the following year Milam admitted in a *Look* magazine interview that he did shoot Emmett, 'thought nothing of it.' That's Mississippi."

In Mississippi, three young Freedom Riders tried to register voters and the Ku Klux Klan shot them dead. I told Stan I'd met the brother of one of them, Andrew Goodman. He regretted how young lives were wasted.

Stan shook his head. "Take the Mississippi Delta where Emmett was killed," he said. "In the 1950s, *zero* Negroes registered to vote. A decade later in the Delta, *sixty-three thousand* Black people registered." He believed that those Freedom Riders exposed the evils of White supremacy and, like Emmett Till, they became martyrs. Martyrs spur progress, Stan contended. Emmett was on the mind of Rosa Parks when she refused to go to the back of the bus, which sparked the Montgomery Bus Boycott, inspiring Martin Luther King Jr. to march from Selma to Montgomery, which spurred Congress to pass the Voting Rights Act of 1965.

"So those victories keep you going?"

He said, "I keep going for Emmett . . . and Rosa."

I smiled. "I thought you'd say Emmett and *John*, your sons. If you had a daughter, would you name her Rosa?"

Stan smiled and cocked his head. "If I had a daughter, I don't know what I'd name her. But I'd want her to be like you."

———————

A few Fridays later, a young man wandered into Freedom Place, looking dazed. His eyes scanned Rudy, Arthur, and Soc. Seeing me, he recoiled like he'd seen a ghost and blurted, "A blue-eyed White devil."

Stunned, nobody moved. Then Soc jumped in and said, "We don't believe that shit around here, man." He ushered the guy out the door. Stan asked what was going on. Soc told him, then turned to me. "Duffy, you got blue eyes, but you ain't no blue-eyed White devil. You more like an angel."

Later, when all had gone, I sat across from the photo of his little sons, and Stan asked if I felt afraid. I shrugged it off. I said it seemed the boy was just trying out words drummed into him. I'd heard the term "blue-eyed White devil" before, when used by Elijah Muhammad. Stan said Malcolm X had used the term, too, before he broke with Elijah Muhammad and made a pilgrimage to Mecca, where he met devout Muslims from all nations, including some White pilgrims. "Malcolm had a revelation—that beautiful people come in all colors."

I laughed. "How about Soc, standing up for me, calling me an angel?"

A strange look crossed Stan's face. He stood to peer at the dark street through blinds of yellow wood. He said, "I once thought I met an angel." I leaned back on the plaid couch to hear his story. "She was lily White, with the bluest eyes I'd ever seen. I thought I must've died and gone to heaven. I'd been injured and was just gaining consciousness in the army hospital in Korea, and this White nurse was treating me so sweetly, I didn't want to be discharged. I'd never been that close to a White woman. Her skin looked like cream—I wondered if it felt different than mine. I felt the urge to touch her hand. But at once I retracted the idea—knowing I could never, ever, touch her. That's when the full meaning of being Black hit me."

His story brought my mind back to the evening I first met Stan, when he hesitated to shake my hand.

Stan talked more about Korea. "My war buddy, Pete, told it straight: 'In war, race don't mean a goddamn thing. Just watch my back.' We made it home alive to America. But we hit the same old walls. I swore I'd tear down those walls for my sons—"

"You had sons—back *then?*"

Stan smiled. "No, they were not yet born. But in my gut, I always knew I'd have sons. Two. I wanted the best mother for them. I found Constance." I noted he didn't say he married his wife for love. "She makes sure the boys are *ready* for school. I ensure their *right* to a good school." I asked if he worried his boys would lose that right. "Look, Duffy, some politicians even fight Head Start—to help poor three-year-old children. The top dogs know education is power and want to keep it all to themselves, like in the good old days."

"Good days for them anyway," I said.

Stan again looked out the window. "In our times—when *history* is turning around—we must take risks. But Constance wants me around at home, safe and sound." Stan said she doubted real change from his community activism was possible. He said, "Truly, what excites me is aiming to achieve the *impossible*. If I told her that, she'd think I was a fool. You see?"

What I saw was a man confiding in me dissatisfaction with his wife. He said, "Don't get me wrong, I honor Connie." He straightened his back. "Never mind. What's important is that I fight for my sons. So their passions won't get suppressed." He pressed his lips, but words spilled out. "So when they become men and ever love a woman, Black or White, they'll be free to—"

"Touch her."

Stan stopped cold, eyes wide, staring at me.

"Yes, Stan. Like the White nurse."

I'd said too much. Stan drove me home.

From his silence I sensed he believed he'd also said too much. Penny once noted, "When a man tells you he's not happy with his wife, he usually wants a romance." A romance was not possible for Stan and me. We both knew that. We cared deeply for each other despite our difference in age and race. But the main barrier: his marriage. Without saying a word, we each realized we'd come too close to a dangerous edge that neither would dare cross. We said goodbye, formally, knowing that we wouldn't be seeing each other any time soon. I wobbled up the stairs to my apartment and cried for hours.

———————

The next day, while Bill and I finished details on our mural, "Willoughby," I felt immersed in a watery realm as Bill and I listened to *La Mer*, Debussy's dreamy symphony evoking the sea. I said, "I feel like *myself* when I'm painting. It calms me."

"You know, Duffy, you are calm and balanced. Placid as a lake. And that makes you easy to be with. I'm balanced too." To demonstrate, he rolled his heavy body from side to side. I laughed. A British friend of his once told him that he was "unflappable." That was true of *Bill*, but not me. Just then I felt like flapping doors inside my chest were swinging open, then slamming shut. It may have seemed to others that I was placid, but that was just the surface. Below the water swam a fire-breathing creature, full of passions, desires, impulses.

Bill asked me to paint faces of a young couple, and I fleshed them out, my mind still stuck on Stan. I wondered why he told me about his infatuation with the White nurse; and what ever made me blab about touching White skin? We almost crossed a line. He would say I got "too much in his head." Well, Stan got too much in my head, too. My mind knew I'd be wrong to hang out with him any longer. But my heart felt squashed.

Bill noticed how in "Willoughby" I'd rendered the couple holding hands. He said I painted with feeling. "Duffy, you have a real gift for art."

His words cheered me. Art had been a source of solace, ever since I could remember. I said, "Bill, you once told me, 'You have to find out who you are.'" He nodded. "Well, I think, I know who I really am. I'm an artist. You think I could be an artist, like you?"

He looked pleased. He said, "You already *are* an artist. But stick with college—you'll need a good day job." I said I would live simply—all I needed was a room and food. Bill got real, saying, "I often sleep in this loft. Some nights no heat. Some days nothing to eat."

Climbing down from the ladder, I knocked a can of brushes and it clattered to the floor. The thought of Bill going hungry troubled me. Too often the word "artist" was coupled with "starving." Since I felt determined to be an artist, I'd have to develop serious survival skills.

Chapter 6
VERA AT VASSAR

I longed to talk to Vera. She loved the arts and could advise me on how to meet challenges of the artist's life. She had a genius for making meaning out of our messy lives. Her parents had lived through the Holocaust and crossed the Atlantic to create a new life. Best friends in senior year of Jamaica High School, after our graduation ceremony the previous June, we clustered with our friend Annie. Their parents snapped photos of them in their caps and gowns. But Mom sat in the back with Doug, a stranger she'd soon marry, taking me from New York and my friends. Vera and I made a vow to "forever share our journeys." In the summer we exchanged letters, but I could never reach her on the one public phone in her college dorm.

One Sunday night in October, she called, and I was thrilled to hear her say, "Hello darling." She invited me to visit her at Vassar and had even arranged a ride with a dorm mate's boyfriend. The following Saturday, I traveled up with a boy named Robert in an orange Volkswagen Beetle. He turned the radio loud and sang along to Simon and Garfunkel lyrics, making it clear he didn't care to talk. Fine. I preferred to look out the window and enjoy memories of Vera.

Vera and Janet

I'd first met Vera when, as juniors, we auditioned for the fall play but didn't make it. I asked her about the author of the essay she'd read, and she said, "He's Romanian, from my home country. I was born in Transylvania."

"You're kidding!" She thought I was reacting to the common association with Count Dracula. I told her that my grandmother was also born in Transylvania but called herself Hungarian. Vera told me Transylvania had been ruled back and forth by many ethnic groups. The year she was born, Romania ruled. I encountered Vera again a few months later when I joined her in advanced honors classes. After school she asked why I transferred mid-year. I said, "An administrator's mistake."

I told her that in September, 1964, when my family moved to Jamaica, Dad brought me to school to register. A tall, gaunt man, Dr. Horowitz, seated us in his small, dark office. I held out my tenth-grade report card to show the row of A's. He waved me away. He handed me my schedule, saying, "Here, Miss Duffy." He'd placed me in *regular* classes. I pointed out that I was an honors student.

Huffy, he said, "You're new at our school, Miss Duffy. We'll review it next term." I turned to Dad, who backed my request for more challenging classes. Dr. Horowitz said, "We don't want to overload your daughter, Mr. Duffy."

Dad's face reddened. Did he catch Horowitz's condescending tone every time he said, "Duffy?" Did Horowitz believe, despite my records, that an Irish girl had little aptitude for scholarship? He stood, towering over us, but Dad and I didn't budge. I said, "At least Honors English." Horowitz closed the folder.

Dad raised his voice. "My daughter skipped eighth grade. She was reading *The History of Mankind* by Hendrik van Loon in *fourth* grade, for Christ sake!" True, I had read the first parts of that book, fascinated by evolution. I just wished Dad hadn't said, "Christ." With pursed lips, Horowitz scratched out a schedule that included Honors English. In December, my guidance counselor reviewed my records and, without question, assigned me to advanced honors.

Vera suggested we walk to the pond down the hill from school. She felt dismayed by the Jewish administrator's prejudice. "I'm Jewish myself. Which I never knew—until I arrived in America a few years ago." Sitting on a bench by the pond, she told me in Communist Romania, her parents hid their Jewish heritage because of anti-Semitic attacks throughout much of Europe. "Before I was born, the Nazis sent my grandparents to Auschwitz to be exterminated like rats. A brave Hungarian hid my mother." After the war, the Communist youth group recruited Vera, a schoolgirl with academic brilliance.

During our senior year, Vera and I were inseparable. Jamaica High, bursting with Baby Boomers, dismissed seniors at noon. On most days, we walked to her family's apartment in Jamaica where she nourished me with pea soup before we did our homework. Afterwards we read poetry and shared confidences, attempting to figure out ourselves, our boyfriends, our families, and the world. Vera had to learn the rules of a new culture in a time when so many—students, women, and Black people—rebelled against old rules. We were developing our personal identities as the American identity itself was being newly forged.

We often fantasized about an ideal place where we'd have unfettered freedom to study on a beautiful campus far away. She said she had an immigrant's ambition of fulfilling the American Dream and applied to the Ivy League.

My dream centered on a small liberal college in Ohio, Antioch, founded by Unitarians in their spirit of open-mindedness. What attracted me most was their special program of work-study—I felt hungry to learn from real life. I applied only to Antioch. When I was notified I'd been "waitlisted," I felt devastated. Admissions never received the recommendation from Bill, and I blamed myself for not checking on him. But, by that time, really, I understood that my dream of going away had always been nothing but a childish fantasy.

————————

Robert's Beetle crossed the Whitestone Bridge toward Poughkeepsie, and we moseyed along the Taconic parkway lined with trees turning colors.

My mind flashed back to summer green leaves—Dad at the wheel, me about eight, asleep on Nanny's bosom in the backseat, heading for her lake house in Rhinebeck, near Poughkeepsie, in the Catskills. My sisters and I had taken vacations there for granted, but now I dreaded its loss.

————————

One year before, Nanny put the lake house on the market. We'd never vacationed there outside of summer, but then I asked to go as often as possible. She agreed and took me there last fall, winter, and spring.

For the long Columbus Day weekend, 1965, I planned a solo "retreat" inspired by Henry David Thoreau's book, *Walden*, which Vera and I had studied. Thoreau wrote that most people endure lives of "quiet desperation," and he deliberately chose to live simply, close to nature. I wanted to follow his desire to "drive life into a corner" and "know it by experience" to be either "mean" or "sublime."

When Nanny's driver pulled up to her country house, I felt elated seeing for the first time Long Lake framed by the magical colors of autumn woods. That weekend I did many things I'd never done before. I took a rowboat out on the lake by myself and beached it on a small island, watching a scared deer splash into the lake and swim away. I drew the old barn, wrote in my diary, and played with words for poems. I slept outside under the night sky, filled with dazzling stars, invisible from the city.

Back home, I invited Vera over to talk about my adventure, and Nanny arrived to cook us Hungarian goulash. Vera spoke to Nanny in Hungarian, their mother tongue. I'd rarely seen Nanny's face beam with such delight as when she conversed with Vera, seeming to forget her Jewish heritage. Nanny gladly offered to open up the lake house again during our winter vacation for Vera and me. I thought of two more Jewish classmates, Annie and her friend Alma; they'd invited me to a wild Chuck Berry concert where we'd bopped in our seats.

My three girlfriends joined Nanny and me at the country house in February, all of us delighted at our first sight of the frozen lake. I'd never seen it glistening with ice. We girls clomped on snow-filled roads winding along Nanny's property and screamed with laughter sledding down the steep hill toward the lake. After dinner, we retreated to a large bare bedroom. Annie, bright as a star, adopting a slight British accent, entertained us with stories of her recent trip to England, home of our adored Beatles, where Brits gladly adopted American blue jeans and rock and roll.

I related another time when Annie had stood before us talking excitedly—in our English class when Dr. Silver, with affectionate admiration, asked her to conform for once in her life and read her composition out loud. The topic: "What I Hope to Be." Her brown eyes sparkled as she spoke about her ambition to be a writer.

Annie laughed at my recollection and said writing was still her ambition. Vera shared she wanted to be a linguist. Alma, a lawyer. I'd struggled to choose one role—writer, artist, psychiatrist, anthropologist, marine biologist. I said, "So for my composition, I came up with, 'My biggest hope is to be a Person, A Whole Person.'" My friends got a kick out of that. We shared other dreams and confidences. Alma blurted out, "Why don't we take off our sweaters and bare our breasts?" Surprisingly it was Vera, the only one with developed breasts, who quickly squashed the idea.

Nanny cooked as usual: beef browned in gobs of butter, served with milk. Later, hearing Annie and Alma chanting, "Milk and meat, milk and meat," I remembered kosher rules and asked Nanny not to mix meat and dairy.

In the evening we gathered around a fire Nanny built in the room overlooking the lake. Vera looked at me and said, "How remarkable that my first American friend has a grandmother born in my hometown of Cluj!" She said that Hungarians and Romanians had been terrible enemies, and that disturbed me. I said, "In America we fight over race, while in Transylvania, they killed each other over ethnicity."

Annie said, "Then throw religion into the mix!" Vera said that during the Holocaust in Hungary two thirds of the Jewish population were killed. Nanny said nothing. She offered us popcorn to pop over the fire. I had feared she might spout off anti-Semitic remarks, but she seemed to genuinely like my Jewish friends once she'd met them. She asked Vera about her family in Transylvania.

Vera shared the story of her family before she was born. Her father suffered in a concentration camp and friends offered to hide Vera's mother along with her daughter Marion and baby Agnes. But the baby cried too much. If the Nazis found the friends harboring Jews, they would *all* be killed. Her mother was forced to put Agnes into an orphanage. Nanny asked if they all survived. Vera said, "My father, mother, Marion survived. Not Agnes. The orphanage was bombed." I saw Nanny, who'd never recovered from losing her child, Pauline, mop her eyes.

Robert turned from Poughkeepsie's main street onto the Vassar campus and steered toward the dormitory, where Vera promised she'd be waiting for me. I shifted, searching for her among the students buzzing around—all female and White, some wearing jeans and peace buttons. By a stone building, I spotted Vera's Old

European look—fabric wrapping her bosom, a long skirt over sturdy boots, standing as tall and still as an ancient Greek caryatid.

Vera rushed to embrace me. Seeing my usual dress—short skirt, black tights, dangling earrings, and beat Greenwich Village loafers—she said, "Oh my beatnik friend, I missed you so much." Robert informed me where to meet for the ride back and scampered off to find his girlfriend. Vera called a warning, "Dorm Angels are on guard!"

I asked, "Dorm Angels?"

She smiled. "Seniors watch us like hawks and enforce the rules: *Gentlemen* are confined to the parlor area. *Ladies* must keep a proper distance." I said the rules were from the 1950s. She whispered, "But of course I find a way to break the rules." We laughed.

She put her arm around my shoulders and led me inside. In the sitting room where girls studied, their long hair hanging over heavy books, I breathed in the thick smell of abundant antique carpets on polished wood floors. Vera led me to her favorite spot, an isolated window seat beside stained glass. She sat on a pillow and puffed up another for me, tapping it as if summoning a cat. Settled in the corner, I asked, "Are you still so much in love with Ken?"

"Deeply," she said. Her eyes got dreamy as she recalled her first night with him.

Vera's parents had taken a winter cruise the previous December. Vera threw a party. Annie brought Alma and a couple British guys to drink and dance, and Vera's 1965 New Year's Eve celebration was one we'd never forget. Party over, Ken joined Vera in her bed. I slept in a spare room.

As we sat in the window seat, I said, "You woke me up in the middle of the night!" I laughed. "All wrapped in a sheet, you looked like the goddess Venus."

She clapped her hands at my description. "I was bursting with joy. I just had to wake you up to tell you that Ken and I had consummated our love. Imagine. At the most intimate of all moments of my life—surrendering virginity and becoming a woman—you, my friend, were *present!*"

Vera and I also recalled the second trip we'd taken together that year to Nanny's Rhinebeck lake house. In spring, this time accompanied by our boyfriends, which Nanny surprisingly allowed. We were once again present for each other, making love in separate rooms in one of Nanny's unfinished houses we'd discovered unlocked on the other side of the lake.

Vera smiled and noted how close my grandmother's property was to Vassar. I told her that Nanny would soon sell it all. The loss felt like a signal of the end of childhood.

Upstairs, Vera opened her door with flourish, saying how grateful she felt getting the single room, because she was "a bookworm who required privacy." It contained only a narrow bed, a small desk, and her books. It looked similar to how I imagined Thoreau's simple cabin on Walden Pond. I told Vera, "You're certainly living your life far from 'the mass of men' and their 'lives of quiet desperation.'" I thought about my daily trek in a packed subway car deep underground, desperately enmeshed in the *mass of men.*

We sat on the two wooden chairs that faced shelves of her beloved books, some in the foreign languages she spoke. I noticed a book of French poetry, which her professor had lent her after a one-on-one conversation. Thinking of my condescending French professor, who barely deigned to look at his students, it was hard to not feel envious. Here at Vassar, Vera was clearly living the dream we'd once dreamed together.

I pulled down a book by Pascal that we'd studied in our French class the previous year, and she recalled how passionately our teacher, Mr. Herald, had read aloud to us. She recited the lines we'd memorized: *"Le coeur a ses raisons que la raison ne connait point."* My translation: The heart understands things the mind knows nothing about. I said I loved that Pascal, a mathematician, elevated emotions above calculations but added, "Sometimes my jumbled emotions do need a shot of reason." Vera asked to hear more. I spilled it all out: disappointment with college, the commute, my parents, Dad's drinking, the death of Grandma and Grandpa Duffy.

She softly asked if other parts of my life brought happiness. I said I felt grateful for my sisters; my own apartment; painting with Bill; and seeing friends, Penny and Rudy. Vera asked about Rudy. I told her he'd got me volunteering in the Black community every week. She lifted her brows and asked, "What drives you?

I said that my Unitarian Universalist faith taught me to work for justice. I told her it was actually a Unitarian minister and abolitionist in the 1800s, Theodore Parker, who penned the phrase, "the moral arc of the universe," made famous by Martin Luther King Jr. I hoped my work might help bend *the moral arc* just a little higher. Vera understood. I described Stan's cause, and she said, "When you talk about him, your eyes light up." Before I answered, she picked up a flowered Romanian shawl and said, "Darling, you must be hungry. Let's go for a picnic."

———

The day had warmed up. In the cafeteria we picked up grapes, bread, and cheese, which she spread out on her shawl on the lawn. I blurted out my new dream of becoming an artist. Smiling, she said, "You are gifted with an artist's eye. Is art in your heart?" I told her, yes. "Then you must follow your heart." Her faith in me buoyed my spirit. We set out to the edge of the campus to explore the woods.

Vera and I locked arms as orange and plum leaves formed a mosaic to walk upon—everything quiet, save the crunching underfoot. Yellow leaves jumped in our eyes like popcorn against the blue of a perfect sky. I said in a low tone, "How can decaying leaves be so beautiful?"

Vera quoted the first lines from "Spring & Fall: to a young child," by Gerard Manley Hopkins, a poem we'd studied together: "'Margaret are you grieving over Goldengrove unleaving?'"

I picked up the last line. "'It is Margaret you mourn for.'" My voice cracked.

Vera asked, "Darling, what is it?"

The musty air of decay stuck in my throat. When I could speak, I brought up the fear I wanted to ask her about. "I feel like Margaret, shaky about the familiar falling away. My new path in art, what will it take? I'm all right with living simply, but—being poor?"

She inhaled and asked, "So you believe that poverty for an artist is a requirement, like a rite of passage?" I nodded and fell back on the leaves to look up at the sky while drinking in her words: "The journey of the artist is sacred, worth the risks. Don't be afraid. Do what you love, or you quickly forget who you are."

Being with Vera made me feel like my true self. Enlivened, I stood and shook off the leaves, ready to explore the woods. As we strode down the path, she said it was fun being with me. We sat on a fallen log to catch our breath, and her expression turned sad and serious. I asked what weighed on her mind, and she took her turn confiding in me.

"I carry a heavy load," Vera said. "I plan to double up on courses in order to graduate in three years, not four." I asked her why. She said, "To make up for the year I was put back." When she arrived in New York from Romania, she had to take a year immersed in English. "I don't want people to think I'm dumb."

"Vera," I said, "you speak four languages. No one in the world thinks you're dumb!"

She insisted she would graduate at twenty-two, the same age as the rest of her class. Then she revealed the real reason: "Ken thinks I'm a sophomore, like he is." I asked why he'd think that? She said that when she met Ken, she was just entering her senior year in high school. "Ken mentioned he was eighteen, and I said, me too. Then he said he was in college and again I said, me too."

"Vera! You just made that up?"

She adjusted herself on the log, her long skirt stretching across her knees. "It just popped out. At eighteen, smart kids go to college. I wanted him to like me." She took a deep breath and said, "You know, darling, you said you feel shaky. Me too. Sometimes I feel on such shaky ground." My mouth dropped, realizing how much I counted on her being a steady pillar. She said when she and Ken became lovers, she vowed to tell him the truth. "But the confession stuck in my throat," she said, looking pained. "I couldn't bear it if he stopped loving me."

How awful, I thought. One misstep can take a good person down a bad path. How hard to find a way back. "Vera, just talk to Ken. He loves you. He'll forgive you. Anyone can make a mistake."

She thanked me, stood up, and tapped me. "Look up. Over by the pond." Peepers and crickets were chirping and above the trees the sun broke through a cloud, shooting down an oblique ray of intense light. It looked like a searchlight.

I moved towards it, waving. "Over here, shine your light on us!" We stood mesmerized by the particles dancing before us in the sunlight. As we circled back, I noted the woods' resemblance to a Dutch masterpiece. I said, "Oh, if only I could paint such beauty." Vera said she believed I had the talent to master such skills, and I encouraged her to speak the truth to Ken.

At the edge of the woods, Robert waited by his orange Bug. Vera scribbled down Ken's phone number and address in New York City near Columbia where I could leave messages. We hugged and again vowed to always share our journeys.

Chapter 7
NO SATISFACTION

"**D**o *what you love, or you quickly forget who you are,*" Vera had told me. On Friday morning heading to college, I added to my book bag a camera and a new letter from Vera.

I descended underground, where stale air hit and bodies crowded me against an iron pillar. I pulled out a book by Saint-Exupéry and opened it to the scene where the Little Prince from another planet observed Earthlings piling into trains, dashing in one direction and only hours later dashing back in the opposite direction. He considered such behavior utterly irrational. The F train thundered into the station. If the Prince observed me now, pushing through the doors, snatching a seat while grim workers hung over me on straps, I thought, *I bet he'd consider me a full participant in the madness.* I figured that about this time, Vera was making her way to class across a wide green lawn. I re-read the line in her letter, *Do what only you can do.*

———

After classes, I chose to do something different. Instead of routinely following the crowd of students to the subway, I turned the other way to walk a few blocks St. Nichols Park. I inhaled the fresh November air.

I climbed a rock to get a marvelous view of the park's wide extension north and south. The ledge I stood on formed a natural granite barrier to the college campus above me, and far below me I saw the green roof of a subway station on a gray street at the edge of Harlem.

From my bag, I dug out my little camera, hung it around my neck. I jumped down to walk the dirt path. A gnarled and twisted tree hanging over a rock caught my eye. Battered by seasons of hurricanes and ripped of leaves and branches, only the skeleton remained. I kneeled on the damp earth and snapped. I smelled decay and turned to photograph the snarled roots. I'd loaded black and white film—perfect for the stark beauty before me.

Further down the hill, I sat on a mossy boulder and reached into my bag for paper to answer Vera's letter. I wrote: *Shorn trees bare their essence. Branches fork endlessly, like veins and capillaries in my body. Beauty "only I can see."* I planned to send some of my photos. I leaned back, closed my eyes, and allowed the sun to warm my face. The squeaky sounds of squirrels and birds made me glad to be alone.

The snap of a twig. I sat up, alert.

Behind me, up high, I saw two Black kids in baggy pants— one tall, the other baby-faced—heading toward me. The way they bopped down the hill reminded me of Rudy and me walking home from school. I shot them a bright smile and called out, "Hi!" They nudged elbows and shot straight up to me. I said with forced cheer, "Beautiful day, isn't it?" Neither answered. Their eyes landed on my camera, dangling, its black strap cutting my neck.

I said, "I'm at the college." I pointed up but kept my eyes on them. "You know, City College? Do you go to school? Or did you take off early like me?" They said nothing, I kept chatting. "Every day I walk near this park, but never stopped. Today, I thought I'd take some pictures, you know?" No reaction. Nervous, I stuffed my papers in my pocket, stood up, and tried to engage them, saying, "Look at the trees now—like skeletons, right?" They stared like I was crazy.

I took a quick glance down the hill. Not another soul around. Way down, the green roof at the subway station. A dirt path—I moved toward it. "Well, I gotta go. On Fridays I work with kids your age in a neighborhood near where I live in Queens. South Jamaica. We work for civil rights—do you? You know, the Great Society?"

I walked faster, my camera bouncing against my chest, shoulder bag tucked under my right arm. They scurried right alongside me; I kept talking like a Pollyanna. "I have a job, making art. Do you like art? I work with an artist. A Black artist."

The tall boy pivoted to face me. I could see the tiny hairs above his lips. His jacket hung back from his shoulders. I felt his hands on my waist, down on my hips, on my thighs, then fingers crawling up to lift the edge of my skirt. I knocked his hand away. With both hands he pulled me closer and pressed his body against mine. He made groaning noises, saying, "Oooh, pretty White girl, let me feel your creamy *ofay* thighs,"

"You're not acting nice," I said as I pushed him.

He looked confused. *Nice?* He stopped pressing, but still held onto me. The baby-faced one pushed up behind me. The tall one humped his body harder against mine. I looked him in the eyes and mustered a sharp teacher's voice, "Now stop that! I'm on your side." He stopped moving. I said, "You know where I'm heading tonight? To Queens, to work with kids like you. They want a better chance. This is just the kind of thing that gets you guys in trouble. Don't make things worse for yourselves."

Pressure from behind stopped. Babyface appeared on my side and said to the tall boy, "Ah, let her go." And he did. I thought, *I'm free!* I flew down the hill, terrified, but unharmed—the boys didn't even take my camera or my wallet. I nervously laughed, thinking, *How did I ever come up with* Be nice?

———

All the way home, I couldn't stop shaking. I needed Mom. When she opened her door, I smelled alcohol, and noticed her smeared mascara. *Had she been crying?*

She moved to her closet to change out of fashionable work clothes, and I followed, bursting to confide my narrow escape. She pulled a sheet off the sofa—a sign she'd slept there, not with Dad. I sat near her, dying to speak, but she spoke first, telling me that my father had been on a binge the entire week. She said, "Disgusted, I told him last night to get out and sober up, but he was so plastered he fell on the bed, unconscious."

Now, obviously, was not my time to talk. I listened to Mom describe the stench, Dad lying on his back, vomit dribbling down his chin onto the sheets.

———

The next time I saw Dad, he was holding a sharp knife, intending to carve the turkey but reluctant to put down a can of beer in his other hand. Nanny snapped at Mom for overcooking the mushrooms. Maureen lay on the sofa, curled up in a fetal position. *Ah*, I thought, *our traditional family Thanksgiving.* Done carving, Dad turned on the game on TV, plopped in his recliner with another beer, and opened the *New York Times.* I looked over his shoulder and read the headline: "Racism and the Elections: American Dilemma, 1966."

I said, "I read that, about Negro clergymen." I paused. Dad could get riled up when drinking. But he answered calmly, "Yeah, at the Statue of Liberty. Remember the poem?"

On cue, Maureen and I recited, "'Give me your tired, your poor, your huddled masses, yearning to breathe free.'" Dad smiled, looking glad we remembered those lines.

Dad said he agreed with the ministers that African Americans are treated like "crap." So were Irish Americans. I swung to sit on the hassock facing him and said the Irish weren't dragged here in chains. "True," Dad admitted. But pointing to the game on TV, he went on about how Negroes had gained the right to play sports, go to White schools, live where they want, work where they want. Legally, it was possible for a Negro to be elected *president* of the United States. His wry smile revealed he thought it unlikely. Legality is not reality.

"Jesus, Mary, and Joseph!" Nanny called out from the kitchen, where she was tapping powdered sugar on her apple pie like a Norman Rockwell granny. She sputtered, "Why so much talk about *Schwarzes?*" Her tongue rolled out a nasty trail of German words that I was glad I didn't understand. She sounded like a mad woman, reminding me that the Black clergy had prayed at the Statue for more "sanity" among White Americans.

One of the ministers said that racism makes us all sick. I said in a low voice to Dad, "This Thanksgiving, I'm deeply grateful my parents decided not to pass down the sickness."

Mom called us to the table in French, "*Mangeons!*" She snapped off the TV. Maureen and I sat side by side, Dad took his place at the head of the table, and Nanny sat as far away from him as possible. She'd celebrated when Mom had divorced him, and now that "godless Irishman" had popped back up. Mom said a word of remembrance for Grandma and Grandpa Duffy. Dad wiped away a tear, got up, and returned with another beer. Mom shot him a dirty look before leading a toast, "*Bon appetit.* Here's to Barbara in Paris, enjoying Maurice's family."

Maureen said, "Barbara's so lucky!"

"Paris," I repeated with dreamy longing, my eyes on the reproductions of Renoir and Monet paintings that Mom had hung on the walls. I pictured the Impressionists setting up their easels in Paris parks and imagined myself bursting up from this table and rocketing to a cafe along the Seine River. I plopped a scoop of mashed potatoes on my plate and drowned it in gravy.

Mom asked Maureen about her French class. "*Tres bien*," she answered. She'd earned high grades without laboring. Mom asked me about my French class. I shrugged.

Mom looked blankly at me. I knew she wanted everything to be perfect for me. A year before she'd told me, "I'm not worried about you. Water seeks its own level." It seemed that she—like other family, friends, and teachers—assumed that, all on my own, I'd magically breeze through college and make a splash in whatever field I chose. I did not feel afloat on that dream boat.

———

Rudy called, alarmed that Doc faced eviction from Interfaith hospital. Just weeks before Christmas, Stan was rallying a crowd to show support and hold off the bank. I'd miss classes, but remembering Doc's clinic, I wanted to help.

I walked the twenty minutes to the hospital and found the entrance blocked by chicken-wire barricades. I stopped, astounded at seeing personnel in white coats throwing baby cribs on top of old desks. It looked like a scene from a revolution. A scowling nurse barked, "No one is allowed inside!" Rudy appeared and assured the nurse I stood on Doc's side. She said she'd been instructed by Dr. Matthew to "keep the marshals out." *Marshals. What the hell is going on?*

Stan rounded the corner, and we made eye contact. My heart raced, and I realized I'd hoped to see him. Right behind him marched Sue and Vicky, Pete, union buddies, civil rights activists, and a flock of elderly people from the local Baptist churches. Socrates came marching around the corner. "Hey, Duffy," he called, chest puffed out. "Everybody and their mama here today." He led men with weathered faces. I recognized Fred and other men from Doc's clinic at Freedom Place draped with placards with slogans like, "We Love Doc!" and "Save our Hospital!" Wearing no coats, hats, or gloves, they showed no sign of shrinking from the cold as they joined the protesters and mumbled along with the song, "We Shall Not Be Moved."

I asked Stan, "Did you promise them some wine afterwards?" He winked.

Reporters arrived from local church papers and *Newsday*, and the reporter from the *New York Times* brought a cameraman. Stan said Doc's story worked for the White media. When I questioned his meaning, he asked, "How many Black faces do you see on TV? Any Black experts, anchors? Any stories about successful Black folks?"

Stan was called to introduce Doc. He leapt up the steps and briefly gave Dr. Matthew's background: a neurosurgeon and director of Interfaith Hospital, the only hospital in New York State where Negroes shape policy; "Please welcome, Dr. Matthew."

Doc spoke with charm. The City of New York had entrusted the hospital with welfare patients. He only asked that the city pay the funds they promised, to avoid eviction of the eighty frail patients, most of them White. He ended by saying that a minority group runs Interfaith, but want to make a contribution, not to the Negro people alone, but to *all* Americans." Enthusiastic applause followed.

Stan returned to my side. I thought Doc's message patriotic. Stan believed he knew how to play on Americans' beliefs. He refuses handouts. He projects the image of a moderate Black man acceptable to the mainstream; he does not threaten American capitalism or way of life. "That's why the White media is all over Doc."

Shortly afterwards, Doc broke in on a loudspeaker. "Mayor Lindsey's office just called in." We waited, hushed and hopeful. "Promises will be kept—the city will pay!" The crowd whistled and hollered. "Victory!"

Stan's face lit up. Two little boys ran up to him and jumped into his arms. Following right behind in high heels, an attractive curly-haired Black woman kissed him on the mouth. Stan introduced his wife, Constance, and two sons, Emmett and John.

"Nice to meet you," Constance said, smiling. She told Stan, "We won't stay, it's too cold. I just wanted the boys to see their father in action."

Rudy was speaking—something about a rare and swift victory—but I heard hardly a word. I studied Stan interacting with his sons. Adorable—no surprise. But I hadn't pictured his wife so vibrant. I found myself upset. Did I harbor a dream that maybe someday Stan and I would . . . would what? How stupid of me. And wrong.

I heard Rudy say, "Things turned around! Right in front of my eyes."

I thought, *True, right in front of my eyes.*

<hr />

At Bill's studio a few days later, he perked me up by paying me my share for "Willoughby," and saying the owner of the Squires chain raved about it. However, plans for more murals were stalled. My chest constricted. I asked Bill how he could stand not knowing where his money would come from. He said that was the price of independence. He once had a steady paycheck from the post office, but because he wanted to paint during the day, Bill chose to work the night shift.

"But when did you sleep?"

"At work." He'd read a scientific study on sleep and the data showed that if people broke up their sleep, they needed less. Bill took three short naps each night. I asked about his boss. Bill said one night his supervisor did show up and caught him sleeping. "At first he was all over me about it," Bill said, "but I showed him the packed mail bags, sorted, ready to go. He never bugged me again."

Bill left that job to be a full-time artist. I'd had fun being his apprentice. But now we had no more murals to paint. Bill said we could earn some change through the holidays by painting Christmas decorations on shop windows in Jamaica. He had a few beauty salon customers.

I needed more than change. And tracing snowflakes, Santas, and candy canes on cold windows just didn't turn me on.

PART III:
WINTER, 1967

Chapter 8
LIBERATION

braced myself to face the flood of college students expected by the seasoned clerks beside me. We waited behind the textbook counter in the Barnes and Noble bookstore where I'd been hired as a temp to help handle the crowd from all over Manhattan, which would soon be coming straight at us. The winter term had just begun, and they'd be in a hurry.

On alert in the back room, I focused on the entrance to our counter. A young man entered. With long black hair and dressed in a black turtleneck, he seemed like a student but did not hurry and did not come forward.

Just then the surge began, obscuring the man. I jumped to serve the mob of students shouting out titles they needed. I liked the rush, the cacophony, the energy of running back and forth from the stacks to students who came from NYU, Cooper Union, and CUNY campuses—Brooklyn, Hunter, and City College. Last September I'd been studying just like them; now in January I stood on the other side of the counter serving them. That suited me—I liked earning a steady paycheck.

The rush over, I looked up, startled to see the man in black still standing by the door, his head down. In contrast to the frenzy, he stood perfectly still. He wore no coat. I wondered, *Who is he?* He lifted his head and caught me looking at him. He approached the counter with a shy smile that made me smile, too. I asked what title he wanted. He hesitated. I asked the author. He didn't know. We laughed. He admitted he didn't need a book. "I wanted to talk to you," he said. "Your eyes are so blue, like your jacket." I wore a soft blue corduroy suit, my one outfit for work. I pulled back, surprised by this personal attention. "Are you free?" he asked. "I mean, for coffee? I'm Don."

I agreed to meet him outside at the back door of B&N at five o'clock. Venturing into the icy cold, I pulled my jacket around me and saw Don scurrying toward me—in shirt sleeves. Noticing my concern, he said, "I don't have a coat." I looked at him, speechless. He said, "It was stolen. Don't worry, I'm not cold."

This guy's a little crazy, I thought, laughing, as we dashed to the coffee shop right across the street on the corner of 18th Street and Fifth Avenue. The revolving door spun and spit us out near the counter, welcomed by the aroma of fresh brewed coffee. The chatter of working people filled the shop as we took our coffee to a back booth where he crammed his husky body between the wall and tiny table. With soft brown eyes, he slowly scanned my face from my chin up.

He said, "Looking into your eyes, I feel like I'm swimming in blue."

"You sound like a writer."

"I am," he said.

I took my turn studying him. I figured he might be Italian from his olive skin and black hair so thick I felt tempted to touch it. I sensed that beneath his shyness lived wildness. His hands covered the entire tabletop. I said, "You remind me of Michelangelo's statue, "David," with his oversized . . ."

"Oversized?"

". . . hands," I finished. We smiled. He said I sounded like an artist. "I am," I said. "In fact, I have to go to class. I study at the Art Students League." He said he also had a class, in literature, that started in fifteen minutes, but he'd rather be with me. I got up. "Gotta make it to 57th Street. Where are you heading?" He said City College. "Wow, funny coincidence." I told him I'd started there the previous fall.

He followed me to the door and over heads of people between us, he called, "Friday, I'm going to a film. Want to come?"

"Okay!" I yelled and watched him heave his large body through the revolving doors and, coatless, throw himself into the cold night.

———————

Ready to date a man I knew only two things about, his name (Don) and his major (English), I punched out on the clock by the back door of the bookstore, and there he was. Don took my book bag, noting how heavy. I'd bought books as soon as I got paid. I couldn't resist the discount. He liked my choices: poetry by e. e. cummings, *The Way of Life* by Lao Tzu, Conrad's *Heart of Darkness*, and an art book on Cezanne. He said, "If you read all these, you'll be so smart you won't need college!"

I smiled. "Like Mark Twain said, never let school get in the way of your education."

He agreed completely. We walked to the theatre a few blocks down Fifth Avenue to see the film, *The Lower Depths*—a classic adapted from Gorky's Russian, acted by Japanese actors, subtitled in English. How I loved the mix of cultures in Manhattan!

Don commented afterwards, "It's a dark story, but you got the humor—I like your laugh." He knew a warm bar where we could talk.

"I don't drink. I'm seventeen."

He looked confused. "But you already started college—"

"I skipped a grade," I said.

On 18th Street, we crossed over to the same coffee shop, same booth. Through my tights, the leather felt cool on my thighs. He dipped French fries into ketchup, and I savored a gooey grilled cheese. He told me he worked at a publishing house, reviewing new books and writing blurbs for the jackets.

I figured he had to be intelligent, and he must be stable—he'd worked full time at the same job for six whole years, while going to college at night. He told me that in May he would finally graduate.

"Congratulations. I figure the two extra years makes you twenty-four?"

"Yes. And here I am falling for a seventeen year old."

Falling for me? Wow. That's fast.

He said, "So, you took a break from college?"

Funny, "break" was exactly how I had described it to my parents. We were sitting under a small artificial Christmas tree in their apartment. Mom turned white and said, "You mean, *drop out? You*, Janet?" She sounded like I'd killed someone. Maybe I had killed a bright spot in her mind, her pride in me. It did hurt me to make the decision. But Dad liked my idea; maybe my working lessened his burden.

Don searched my face. I told him, "College had been my dream. Now my dream is to be an artist." I thought of Bill. "Sometimes you have to give things up to be your true self."

Don reached over and grabbed my upper arms. I felt his breath on my neck. "I understand," he said. His sudden contact startled me, but his hands felt wonderfully warm. The waitress came to clear our plates, Don let go of me and I stood and picked up my book bag. "Stay, please," he said. "You know, you come and go, like Ruby Tuesday," referring to the hit by the Rolling Stones. "I don't know where you come from." I told him I lived an hour away by subway. He said, "The subway? Why descend into the cold *lower depths*," he asked, "when I have a place nearby?"

He moves too fast, I thought. "You hardly know me."

He said, "I want to know everything about you." The puppy dog look in his brown eyes made me sit back down. He pumped me with questions about my family, my life. I told him about

Freedom Place, what it had meant, and how I missed it. Don saw my excitement, and said he'd like to go there with me. I felt curious to see how Don and Stan would get on.

———————

The next Friday, at Freedom Place, Socrates peered out through a crack in the door. "Who is it?"

"Quit playing around, Soc, it's Duffy." He asked who the guy was, and I said, "My friend. It's freezing. Just let us in."

Socrates opened the door, eyes twinkling behind his rosy shades. He said, "You losing track of us." He told me that Rudy went to college now, and Clarence, the guy who loved to fight, joined the Green Berets. Don recoiled at the mention of Vietnam. Soc said, "I'll tell Stan 'Duffy's here,' watch his face get, like, all lit up." Soc looked at Don. "Don't know, though, what he'll think 'bout this cat. We ain't never had no long-haired hippie here before."

Don laughed. "I'm not a hippie."

"Stan!" Soc called. "Duffy here."

Stan opened his door, and as Soc anticipated, his face did "get all lit up." Then he saw Don. He gripped Don's hand, hard, it seemed, while he looked him straight in the eyes and asked, "Did you come to visit or to work?" Don said he'd like to contribute. Stan flashed white teeth. "Tell me, young man, what is it you think you have to *contribute*?"

Don said. "I'm a writer."

Stan's brows lifted. "A writer? What kind?" Don said a copy writer. Stan said then he must be concise and persuasive. "Exactly what we need tonight."

I asked, "What's up?" Stan poured coffee, and we all sat on the sofa in the front room, where Stan gave an update about Dr. Matthew. Since his victory over the eviction, he'd received more contributions for the self-help group he'd started called NEGRO.

Don asked what the acronym stood for. Stan said, "You sound like Duffy, with her *college* words." I told Stan I'd taken a break from college, and he frowned.

Don said, "You were telling us what NEGRO stands for."

"National Economic Growth and Reconstruction Organization," Stan said. "Its mission is to build hospitals, rehabilitate slums, and generate Negro-owned businesses. I agreed to help raise money. Doc thinks big. His goal: Almost three million."

"Wow!" I said, "You're right. Doc thinks big." I had some ideas for eye-catching images. Don said he could draft letters, ads, press releases.

Stan set me up to sketch in a cubicle, then turned to Don and said, "Ready to work? Come into my office."

About an hour later I heard grunting and opened the door to Stan's office. I stopped in disbelief at what I saw: Stan and Don in an arm wrestle! Both men seriously staring down the other, faces tight, biceps popping. In the struggle, locked arms fell one way, then the other. Finally, Stan lowered Don's arm down to the desk. I felt like laughing, but I just handed Stan my sketches. He offered a lift home, and while Stan got his keys, Don whispered, "I want you to know that it was *Stan* who challenged *me*. I'm ten years younger, stronger—I could have easily taken him down. But when you appeared, I sensed he needed to *prove* something. Weird. So I *let* him beat me."

———

Stan didn't seem happy about dropping Don off with me but accepted my invitation to my apartment—the first time either man would see it. In the elevator I heard the Blues Project, Maureen's favorite band, signaling she was still awake. We found her on the couch, petting our kitten, looking beautiful with her fine hair falling across her soft sweater. She smiled and said, "Janet's told me a bunch about both of you."

Don moved straight to Maureen, but Stan stayed at the door

by an easel, looking uncomfortable. He said, "You girls live here by yourselves?"

"Yep," Maureen said. I showed Stan and Don my painting of a whisky bottle between two floppy dolls.

"Do you mind if I ask," Stan said, "where are your parents?"

I laughed at his confusion and quickly explained the divorce, remarriage, another divorce. "Now they live together, when my father's sober."

"I see," Stan said.

"See what? That it's screwed up?"

Stan nodded with a wry smile. He said he had to go and told Don he'd drop him back at the subway. Don said he wasn't leaving and followed Maureen into the kitchen to get a drink. Stan paused again at the door to look at the painting on the easel, a portrait of a Black man in a blue denim shirt, his face painted in tones of rich sienna browns. He asked, "Who is this?"

"Just a model," I said. I told Stan how I'd carried the wet painting home on the subway and a White businessman kept peering up from his newspaper, his eyes darting from me to the painting. "When the man stood up to exit, briefcase in hand, he said, 'Nice painting.' But then sneered, 'Is he your *father*?' His hatefulness shook me up."

Stan's face crunched like he felt the sting himself. He asked why I painted the man from the back. I laughed and said, "No artistic reason. I was late and got the easel behind the model! Only part of the man's face was visible, and he was looking forward into the distance—I thought the angle added mystery. It makes you wonder what the future may hold."

"Duffy, you're an artist. I mean it, a *real* artist. You know, I'd love for my sons to spend time with you." I thought, *His precious sons?* He said, "To draw and talk with you, pick up your perspective, see with your eyes. To just be in your *presence*."

Overwhelmed by his sudden admiration, I kept my eyes on the painting. Stan frustrated me. I never knew if he was going to confide in me, challenge me, ignore me, or tease me. Now he praised me, affirming my call to art.

———————

The next week, I asked Don to supper before classes at Squires Restaurant on Lexington Avenue to see the "Willoughby" mural. I told him how Bill mentored me, and he said, "Another father figure." I asked his meaning. "Like, the other night, when Stan learned you'd left college, he acted like a disappointed father. I felt like I needed to prove myself by performing the Tasks of Hercules."

I found that hysterical. Don asked, "So now, is it okay for me to be your guy?" I laughed and nodded. He asked to see the parts I'd painted on the mural. I pointed to a girl's face. He said, "Sweet face, like yours." I looked at his face and told him he had dreamy eyelashes. He said not to arouse him before his class.

Don asked why I respected Bill. I said, "He earns just enough to do what he loves. He doesn't care about other people's opinions. That makes him free. And that's how I want to be."

Don leaned in. "That's how you are now! You can't be chained," he said, referencing the song, "Ruby Tuesday." We moved in line to pay. Don tilted my face closer to his. He said, "You know what you want and how you feel." He raised his voice. "You want to be *free*. I love you!" People standing by the cash register stared. He pulled me to him and kissed me. His lips, so large and soft, swallowed me up.

We laughed as we dashed down to the subway. I noticed he hadn't yet bought a coat. He said, "The truth is I don't like wearing coats. I want to be free to sense life fully, as it is. If it's cold I want to *feel* cold."

An unusual man, I thought.

He said he'd join me waiting for my train, wanting every minute to be with me. He inserted tokens, and we pushed through the turnstile and skipped down the metal stairs. He said, "When you finish painting, come meet me. Take the IRT train down to Sheridan Square Station, Greenwich Village. I'll wait for you there."

My legs wobbled. I asked myself, *Am I ready for a romance? Will Don pull me off track?*

He held me steady. "Come spend the night with me." In the dank station, a sweet scent on him stirred me. "Come," he said. "Just to sleep. I'll sleep on the floor. Or we can sleep together side by side if you like, just sleep. I promise I won't do anything you don't want me to do." *I am being seduced*, I thought, queasy, feeling both aroused *and* cautious. I told myself, *Pull yourself together*. I picked up my paint box. My train to school rumbled in, the doors opened, and as I slid in, I turned to look at Don.

"Ten thirty," he said. "Sheridan Square. I'll be there. Just come."

———————

I didn't know what to do with the nude body standing in front of me. I began with what I could handle—the face, the eyes, the lips. I approached the neck and shoulders tentatively. I followed the body's sweep, traced a line from collar to hip, marveling at the anatomy, everything hanging naturally. A touch here, a touch there, now coming together. I finished my drawing and set up my oils for painting.

I first looked for the deepest darks, as Bill had taught me, located usually next to the brightest lights. But boundaries between dark and light got lost, muddying my colors. Edwin Dickinson, a kind teacher, a respected artist, took my brush from my hand and loaded it with pale golden yellow. He swished the sable all over the areas of light—the breasts, abdomen, thighs. Under his experienced strokes, the colors remained distinct and the figure took form on the canvas.

I couldn't concentrate. My stomach flipped each time I thought about Don, who'd extended more than an invitation. He'd issued a gentle command: "Come spend the night with me."

Class over, carrying my wet canvas and paint box, I hurried to the cold subway station. An inner voice said: *You have goals, don't get side-tracked*. A counter voice said: *If you take the uptown train to Queens you'll sleep alone in your bunk; if you go downtown to the Village, you'll be held in Don's warm arms*. My knees trembled—from desire or indecision?

I chose a train and peered out the smeared window. On the platform at Sheridan Square, there stood Don, just as he promised. Catching sight of me, he beamed, ran up, and hugged me. "I'm so glad you came!"

I had to inform Maureen and called her from a payphone since Don said he had no phone. He guided me past quaint buildings in the West Village to Christopher Street, lined by young, bare trees. I asked, "Is this where the beatniks lived?" He laughed and said lots of artists and writers lived here.

We stopped outside a bar/cafe, in the basement of his rooming house, and he unlocked a private door. "No visitors allowed," he whispered. "But my landlady is mostly deaf." We tiptoed up two flights of stairs to his room at the top, with just enough space to stand between the bed and the dresser. I hardly pictured a man as expansive as Don living in such a neat, Spartan room.

"Don," I said, "I'm here to sleep, right? You promised, just sleep."

"Just sleep." He took off my coat and hung it in the tiny closet. In the cool room, he hugged me and rubbed the ribs of my burnt-orange sweater. He spread his hands on my back, and surely noticed, no bra. I supported women's liberation, and I simply didn't need one. He tripped on my paint box. He moved the wet canvas, looking at the nude I'd painted. "I can model for you," he said, pulling off his shirt to reveal impressive muscles. He struck a pose similar to the statue of David.

I laughed. "To paint you, I'd use ochre colors. But there's no room to paint here!"

He stepped into the hall shower—I heard him humming "Ruby Tuesday"—and returned in only a towel. He reluctantly agreed to pick out a shirt for me and watched me undress and slip it on. I got under the covers of the narrow bed, and he joined me naked, radiating welcome heat. Soon I felt his penis hard against my thigh. He kissed me and moved his hand along my body.

"Don," I said, pulling away. "I'm not ready."

His hand had already slid between my thighs and touched the moistness there. He said with a husky voice, "You feel ready to me." I felt the desire to let go. But I didn't want to lose control. I pushed his hand away and reminded him he'd promised we could just sleep side by side. That was enough for tonight. He asked, "Why wait?"

"I have no protection."

He said not to worry—he promised he wouldn't ejaculate inside me. *Ejaculate.* The word excited me. But a question spilled out. "We could make life. Are you ready for that?" I added, "It's a serious thing, having intercourse—"

"Intercourse," he repeated and rolled on his back laughing. I asked him what was so funny? He said, "So stiff and formal, the way you said, *in-ter-course*."

I realized my stupidity. How could I sleep so close to a man and expect him to "just sleep?" I sighed. "I probably sound like a little kid to you."

He said, no, he saw me as a lovely emerging woman. He yawned, and said we had to sneak out early before his landlady woke up, so we'd better get to sleep. Relieved, I inched closer to the wall and decided never to stay over with him again. Before he fell asleep, he asked, "Hey, on Friday I'm going dancing. Do you like dancing?"

We met to go dancing at the Dom. Beforehand, Don bought Chinese dinner in Greenwich Village. Sitting close, I again noticed that sweet scent on him. I asked about his family. As I'd figured, they were Italian. The Gallos lived in Brooklyn. He said he loved his mother's sausages and pasta, but he rarely went home for dinner because, afterwards, "everybody went for each other's throats." He said he never knew his father, and as for his step-father, he'd kill him if he ever saw him again. He'd abused Don when he was a little boy—I'd never heard of such an awful thing.

But Don said he was over it and had his own life now. I asked how he broke free. His trick: to see everybody as characters in a play—insane, tragic, or hilarious. "Great material for writing," Don said. "Seeing the shit on the page, outside of me, I could see the way out." I found that profound. He suddenly stood up, attracting attention. "You gotta shake that shit." He shook his hair, shoulders and arms. "Time to go dancing!"

We reached St. Mark's Place on 2nd Avenue and approached the Dom, the hip hot dance spot. A big man Don called a "bouncer" nodded for us to go in. I followed down stone steps to a landing where another big guy blocked the stairs. He recognized Don and waved us in, saying, "Just getting started, man."

We descended more steps to a new universe—a dimly lit dance floor where colored lights twinkled in the high ceiling; piped-in music bounced off glossy black walls in a large industrial space transformed by artists. Tangled with wires and pipes, the room looked like a big riverboat, powered by heat from bodies in motion and ready to sail on the rhythms of favorite soul and rock artists: The Four Tops, Stevie Wonder, Chuck Berry, Aretha Franklin, Otis Redding. Two of the few White faces in the crowd, Don and I moved among faces hard-set on having a good time. As the crowd got bigger, the music got louder—so loud we couldn't hear each other talk. Words had no place here. Neither did our minds. Only our bodies belonged, all of us planted on the same thundering dance floor booming to the beat, rocking our bones.

Vibrations pulsed up from the floor through the soles of my feet to my legs and energized my hips.

Sweat and body odors, lotions and perfumes blended in with earthy smoke that Don recognized as pot. I admired dancers' clothes: dark, tight and sleeveless, or light, loose and low-cut. Hair ranged from straightened to braided to natural. The picked out hair of Afros created crowns around their heads, the first time I'd seen that. Don's long black hair flew wild. I let my wavy hair loose, too. Lights flashed. A girl with silky hair like Maureen rolled her head, and under the startling strobes the flickering light made it look like she had three heads.

As one disk ran into the other, our Whiteness seemed to be forgotten, or coolly accepted, and I relaxed into a feeling of immense freedom. All of us—freely moving individuals forming one throbbing crowd—moved to the same beat, nothing separating us from the music, its overriding rhythm binding us all.

Then I lost sight of Don. In the darkness I felt anxious on my own, a blue-eyed girl searching for my partner among the brown-eyed dancers around me, fully awed by their rippling movements, the way they bounced their backs, their spines undulating in waves from hip to neck. I mirrored the movements using muscles I didn't know I had. I moved my pelvis, finding a rhythm satisfying to myself. There were no clear partners on this floor—two or three dancers might face each other for a song, or part of a song. A Black guy faced me, and we moved in the same rhythm until he floated on.

I spotted Don dancing alone with self-absorption and undisciplined movements. When "Ruby Tuesday" was played, he circled back to me. He drew me excitingly close, for a slow number, and on my thigh, I felt that he was hard. Over the music, he yelled in my ear, "Dancing is liberating. Once, right here on this floor, just moving to the beat, I had an orgasm!" Someone started a quick clapping to the beat of the Stones' song, "Let's Spend the Night Together," and everybody joined in, all of us clapping louder and louder until we reached an exhilarating group climax.

When the time came for us to pull ourselves up the steps, piercing streetlights forced us to come down from hot ecstasy to face a cold, drizzling night. A church clock showed the time: two in the morning. Exhausted, I dreaded the subway and walk home in the rain. Don put his arm around me and hailed a cab, and I thought, *Looks like tonight will be the night.*

———

In his room, nervous, I watched Don remove his shirt, and while he showered, I heard my inner voice say, *Take the bull by the horns.* On impulse I tore off my sweater and when he returned naked, I pressed my torso against his. His hands on my narrow back, he pulled my small smooth breasts further into his chest. I felt my nipples harden. We stood meshed for a long moment, and then he did an odd thing. He sprawled on his bed, pulled out a shaker of powder, and asked me to rub it on him.

"*Baby* powder? I started laughing. "That's what I *thought* I've been smelling on you, but didn't think a man—" He shut his eyes and surrendered like a smiling dog ready for a belly rub. "Okay, *baby*," I said, and applied the powder over the black hair on his chest, abdomen and thighs. Caressing him excited me. I slipped away to shower, returned to lay close to him. But he was knocked out, totally unconscious.

———

In the morning, I sat on the edge of Don's bed and scratched soft black charcoal on newsprint, aiming to express the raw instincts and urges in him that excited me. He woke up and asked, "Hey, what are you doing?"

I said, "Trying to capture you."

"I don't wanna be *captured*." He shielded his eyes from the sun to look at the portrait: his arms encircling the pillow, his large hands gripping it like a prized possession. "I love your lines. They look driven." I gifted him the drawing.

The aroma of roasting coffee rose up from the basement cafe. We quickly got ourselves downstairs, ordered coffee and buttered croissants, and sat at a round table. Don brought a book to show me, required for his psychology class: a new collection of writings by Wilhelm Reich, an author new to me. Don said Reich built on Freud's theories on sex and libido. I knew about Freud from my mother and father, who'd spent time in psychoanalysis. "Society views sex as a force to be strictly *repressed*," Don said. "Like when teachers line children up in a row and tell them not to talk or move." *Exactly how my kindergarten teacher had scared my class*, I thought.

Don said Reich believed the opposite, that sex *affirmed* life. He lived in Germany when Hitler came to power, and after he published *The Sexual Struggle of Youth*, the Nazis went after him. He escaped to the United States, but some conservatives in America, who feared sexual liberation led to anarchy, burned Reich's books. I thought, *Banned in the "land of the free"?* "Reich died in prison," Don said, closing the book, "but his ideas live on."

Back in his room, Don told me that Reich had invented a box called an Orgon Box. Sitting in it stimulated orgasms. This box was another strange thing I'd never heard of. Don said even Jack Kerouac wrote about it, in *On the Road*. "I just think it's great to get juiced up." I agreed orgasms were healthy. He flopped on his bed and extended his arms—his fingers almost touched the walls. I said he must feel boxed up. He said, "No, I'm juiced up." Reaching out to me, he noticed his watch and said, "Fuck! Gotta go!" Friends were waiting for him in Brooklyn.

———

We knocked on the door of a beautiful brownstone an hour later. I'd never been inside a home in Brooklyn. Don's friends let us in, and the smell of oil paint and the canvases tilted against the walls signaled they were artists. They studied at Pratt, one of the best art schools, and Peter had used his creativity to artfully wrap a gift for Emily, now perched on an easel in their living room.

Emily peeled off the hand-painted paper and held up the cover of the Stones' latest album *Between the Buttons*. Peter played the album, blasting, "I Can't Get No Satisfaction." We listened to song after song. I wasn't used to spending an entire afternoon doing nothing but sitting on soft cushions listening to music, eating, and hanging out. Instead of relaxing, I felt edgy. Peter took out a skinny crooked cigarette and passed it around our circle. It smelled like the smoke in the Dom that Don had identified as pot. *Shit*, I thought, *I've kept away from pot all this time, and I'm not interested now.* Don passed the thing to me and urged me to try it. I took a little puff and coughed. After a few rounds of little puffs, the music became so intense to my ears, I had to lay my head back against the couch as lines from "Ruby Tuesday" blended right in with "Let's Spend the Night Together." Torpor overwhelmed me, and, closing my eyes, I fell into a daydream of languishing on a riverside, sun sparkling on rushing water.

It's dark. I'm in the kitchen. Don discovers peanut butter. We spread it on crackers and the crunchy chewing sound—so funny. Don knocks over a bottle of milk and some spills on the floor. A wild angora cat comes from nowhere and happily licks it up, and Don says, are you *laughing* over spilt milk? The cat smiles—no kidding—like the Cheshire cat in *Alice in Wonderland*, and I almost pee. I rush to the bathroom. Pizza shows up. Don spreads peanut butter on his pizza, making me weak with laughter. Don lays his finger to his lips and points to Emily and Peter cuddling up on the couch.

My arm tingles as Don touches it, saying, "Let's go into the other room." I see a big bed there and from nowhere I hear my inner voice say, *better not stay*, but my weak legs do not obey and down I lay. Don kneels at the bottom of the bed, says with urgency, "We must have each other tonight." I go on alert. I try to sit up, but my belly lacks strength. I must rally, I think. I don't want to think but I should think, I think. But . . . what is Don doing? He tugs at my feet, my body is sliding down, then quick fingers at my waist, a button snapped open, jeans jerked down. Cool air on my bare legs perks me up. I hear, *We must have each other tonight.*

Undies off, legs pushed apart.

I hear myself whisper, "Oh, wait. Do you have . . .? I have no . . . protection—"

"I'll withdraw."

"What?" I snapped out of my stupor. His breath pounded in my ear like wind through a window of a speeding car. I felt pressure between my legs, a pain, then less pain, more pleasure. My body, filled up, rocked up and down as he moved deliberately to the rhythms of his own pleasure in building intensity until the last moment when, with amazing self-control, he pulled out. Then nothing. Emptiness. He wiped my sticky thigh with a hand-kerchief, then collapsed next to me, his weight making the bed bounce. I wanted to roll towards him but with my lips tingling, heart pumping and my whole body vibrating I couldn't move.

I heard Don mumble, "How are you doing?"

"Doing?" I whispered, "It's done. What have I done?" My mind, now awake, bombarded me with questions: *Does this mean Don loves me? Do I love him? Are we in love?* I stared at the peeling paint on the ceiling and words meant for him arose out of my mouth: "You may have planted a seed of new life in me—are we ready for that?" No response. I turned and saw Don asleep. I wriggled away, got up, and washed my face.

———

Probing fingers awoke me. Light streamed over us as we lay sandwiched between blankets on the living room floor—I hardly remembered moving there from the bed. I felt Don kneading my inner thighs with insistent strokes, my whole body alive with excitement. But something felt incomplete from the night before and left me wanting more. His lips fell on mine and I released all resistance, let my mouth fall open. Don seemed to sense my abandon and kissed me again and again on my mouth, my neck, my breasts until I felt like singing. I rolled over him, and felt him under me, our hearts beating in rhythm. Our breath rushed in and out like waves at the shore, receding and pounding, until I exploded. Then once again, stillness. I imagined our entwined bodies a sand sculpture with the ocean splashing over us and felt broken shells within me dissolve and wash away. I felt part of him. *Yes, this must be love.* He tumbled down next to me and while he slept, I picked up a scrap of paper and wrote to him.

> *Under her*
> *under her under*
> *and after your fingers*
> *opened her*
> *and you said*
> *"we must have each other tonight"*
> *you were into her*
> *you were under her*
> *she was singing with open mouths*
> *you were deep down under her*
> *under her, under.*

I read my poem to Don the next day, Monday, at the coffee shop during our lunch break. He noticed the influence of the poet, e. e. cummings, who broke a lot of rules. He said, "This is not your first poem." True, I said. "And I'm not your first lover." True again. "And . . . not your first orgasm?" No first there either.

The waitress arrived with our eggs, for him, sunny side up, and for me, over easy. He said he could hardly focus at work, his mind kept replaying our lovemaking. I said, "Me too. I missed you. And today, back in the grind."

"Hey, we can break out of the grind," Don said. "We can choose liberated lives." He threw up his arms. "When I graduate, let's get away." I asked where we would go. He said, "Pick a place."

"Like what?"

He said, "How about Tangier?"

"Where is Tangier, exactly?"

He said Morocco. Oh. I'd wanted to go to Africa since I was fourteen, when Kennedy started the Peace Corps. Don said in Tangier the beaches were gorgeous and hot. That sounded great. "A whole new world," he said. I regretted I had no money to get there, but he said that we could "work our way over on a freighter." In a hundred years, I never would have thought of travel by freighter. He said we'd take a job on the ship and "get paid to travel." He leaned back, his hair sliding from his face, and he began describing life in Tangier. "I'd bake in the sun. Men there are free to take off their shirts."

"They're taking off their shirts—boys and girls—in San Francisco." In Golden Gate Park, hippies had started off the New Year with a "human be-in." Nothing like it ever before. Timothy Leary egged kids on, chanting the mantra, "Turn on, tune in, drop out."

"Cool," Don said. "Let's save up and go cross country."

San Francisco sounded more possible than Tangiers, but I didn't have the money to go anywhere. That morning I'd found out that my temporary job at the bookstore was ending. Don knew his company was looking for office help. Offices didn't interest me, but Don asked me to work and save for three months. "Then we'll take off and be free."

Later at a Chinese Restaurant in the Village, we planned our trip. Don had arranged my interview that Friday. "You're sure to get the job," he said. The waiter brought fried noodles and dip.

I said, "We'd save more money if we didn't eat out so much." Don's room had no fridge or hot plate, he told me, and his landlady's rule was no food in the room. "Since when do you care about rules?" I asked.

He dipped a noodle into the orange sauce and looked me in the eye as he sucked off the spicy goo. "Tell me about your earlier lovers."

I laughed and shook my head. The waiter brought bowls of wonton soup, and, hungry, we spooned it into our mouths. I said, "Only a boyfriend in high school." I saw a chance to make a point. "We used birth control, and we should —"

Don cut me off. He said, "I got this. Don't worry." He continued to pepper me. "That kid brought you to climax?"

"Let's say he assisted. I brought myself to climax." Don leaned in, looking turned on. I told him that I'd discovered orgasm myself. He asked when. I said, in kindergarten.

Don held his noodle mid-air. "You had an orgasm in *kindergarten*? Now you're pulling my leg."

I trembled, not sure about sharing with a man such secret, intimate parts of my life. I told him about my scary kindergarten teacher, how she once grabbed me when I arrived late, and threatened to drag me to the office of the principal. The teacher saw my terror and relented. After school I needed comfort, but found Dad out working, Mom busy, and my sisters arguing. I hid in the bathroom where Dad had left open his Playboy magazine. I escaped to my bedroom and rubbed myself against a corner of my bed. I sank into a kind of trance—I didn't know what was happening, but I felt a stiff tension followed by a sudden a burst of good feeling.

"This is so fucking far out," Don said and put his spoon down. He said, "I never imagined—" The waiter took our soup bowls and laid down a platter of shrimp with lobster sauce. Don dove into his meal but I felt too worked up to eat. When the waiter brought our check, he offered a container for leftovers. Don reminded me of the no food rule. Then he said, "Fuck it!" and swept the shrimp and lobster sauce into the box. "Tonight, we're breaking the rules."

———————

Don put the forbidden Chinese box on his bureau and took me in his arms. He said, "I love that you reach climax. Because lots of girls can't. It's frustrating for the guy."

"What about the *girl?*"

He corrected himself. "Yes, especially frustrating for the girl."

I sat on the bed and kicked off my shoes. I said, "Right after the first time we made love, you fell asleep on me." He apologized. I laughed and said, "After orgasm, your blood pressure drops so fast, you can't help it. Orgasms are like natural tranquilizers."

"Mmm," Don hummed. "Orgasm is the topic of my paper for psychology. I want a favor." He pushed my torso down on the bed and raised his body over mine. "You could help with my research. Describe your experience."

"All I did was hump."

"Did you use toys?"

I answered, "No toys, no nothing." He asked me if my parents knew, and I said, "Eventually, but they didn't stop me. Their parenting style was laissez-faire." I told him they'd rejected guilt about sex when they left the Catholic Church, and besides that, they believed in Freud's idea that sex was natural.

Don rolled to my side, lifted up my sweater and, with his finger, traced a line from my bare breasts to my waist. "You explored your own body and liberated yourself; you discovered what gives you pleasure." He inserted his hands under my waistband. "I want to satisfy you. Tell me what you like."

"I'd like at this moment for you to put on your condom."

His face fell, but he kept his hands on me. He told me he didn't have a condom.

I said, "Wait, didn't you just tell me, 'you got this, don't worry?'"

"Right, because I *do* practice birth control—withdrawal. It works. Trust me." I felt his fingers stroking me. "I have to get inside you," he said, and pushed a pillow under my hips and entered me. I felt exquisite pleasure. I tensed, about to—Abruptly he stopped, leaving me lost in a void. He boasted about his control, saying it took every ounce of will power for him *not* to ejaculate inside me. "See, I promised to withdraw, and I kept my promise."

I desired a different promise from him. And I decided I wanted some rules—new rules I didn't want us to break.

Chapter 9
MY EIGHTEENTH BIRTHDAY

The Stones' hit, "I Can't Get No Satisfaction," played incessantly, in the Café-Bar below Don's rooming house, but at that moment I felt content. I said, "Tomorrow I can order a beer, too—I'll turn eighteen."

"Wow, the end of childhood." Don delighted me by gifting me a pair of sexy dancing shoes, sparking memories of the Dom. He asked my special plans to celebrate my "new womanhood." I'd go to the Museum of Modern Art, since my days were free while between jobs. Don said he would skip work to spend the day and the night with me. His lips to my ear, he said, "Making love to you is a dream."

"I love feeling you inside me," I said, "But I'm not sure about, uh, the unfinished end."

"The *end*?" He pulled back.

I whispered, "I want you to *finish* inside me."

His brows gathered. He said, "I don't want to get you pregnant."

"Exactly. So why are we taking risks?" Gulping down a swig of beer he told me he knew his body, he always pulled out on time. I said, "All it takes is one Olympian sperm to swim up to the mother egg and, bingo!"

He shook his head. "You kill me with all the little sex facts you know." He chugged his beer and ordered another. He lowered his eyes to my breasts. He said, "When I fondle you with bare hands, they tingle. Plastic gloves block sensation, right? Same blocking effect with a condom." I said I wasn't talking about condoms. "What else then," he asked with a grimace, "foam?" I said foam didn't work well either—only seventy-five per cent effective—but withdrawal didn't even *count* as a valid method of birth control. He disagreed and informed me of the medical term for withdrawal: *coitus interruptus.*

"Funny," I said. "*Interruptus* is just what it feels like when you pull out. Interruption is not satisfying." Don brooded, saying it seemed to him that he'd brought me satisfaction. I said, "Yes. But worry diminishes it."

Don asked, "Who gave you these ideas?" I told him, Dr. Schwartz, my gynecologist, who'd prescribed the Pill. He brightened and said, "The Pill? Far out! It's total protection." I agreed it was ninety-nine percent safe. But the prescription expired six months ago. "So," he said, "fill the prescription!"

I couldn't. My doctor had taken me off the Pill. She had concerns that the drug was too new, untested, with unknown consequences. "I'm too young to risk harming my reproductive system." Don looked frustrated. I pulled his face to me and kissed him. I said, "Let's go upstairs. I have a surprise for you."

In Don's room, I pulled out from my bag a bright blue circular case. He smiled and asked, "You brought a toy?" I said, sort of. He opened it, gaped at the round beige object within and said, "A tiny Frisbee?" I laughed and said it's a diaphragm, just as safe as the Pill. A tube of jelly came with the case and, reading the label, he hissed, "*Spermicide*! And the diaphragm is *rubber*. I hate rubber," he said, throwing "the thing" at me.

I snatched it. "Let's try it," I said, pulling down my jeans. "First we take off all our clothes." He followed my lead, and we both sat naked on the bed. "Now we lubricate with jelly," I squeezed the tube, making squishy sounds. He said he liked jelly and licked my ear.

A buzz made him jump to his feet. "It's midnight!" He smacked the off button on his alarm clock. "You are now eighteen years old!" I laughed, still holding high in my hand the jelly-filled diaphragm. He laid it on his bureau and pulled out from his closet a bottle of champagne and two glasses. "A toast! To our laws in the State of New York. At seventeen, a girl can legally consent to sex, and, at eighteen you have an important *new* right." He popped the cork, and champagne burst out. "You can now legally drink a glass of fucking alcohol."

I laughed and added, "Also, I no longer need my parents' legal consent to marry."

Don didn't follow up on the *marry* thought. He gave me the champagne and said, "It won't last." I took just a sip. Don took gulps from the bottle, discarded it, and surrendered. "Go ahead if you want, put in your . . . *thing.*"

I inserted it and lay back, feeling grown up, not a kid anymore who just let things happen to her, but a woman, taking responsibility. Don lay on top of me, nuzzling my hair, and asked how he could make my birthday night special. I said, "Stay inside me." He nodded and I wrapped my legs around his waist. "Slow, steady . . . *stay.*" I felt hot sparks inside me, my belly contracted, my heart expanded into outer space, my sense of time suspended. No hurry, no fear, only allowing pleasure to burst into bloom. He kept his promise to stay through the end, and a still joy spread through my body.

Tired, hanging over a table in the downstairs Café the following morning, I said to Don, "You fell right asleep last night before

I could ask you—" Our coffee and plates of fried eggs arrived, and as he bit into a slice of crusty toast, I said, "About last night."

He dropped his toast and declared, "Planned sex is the death of spontaneity." Stunned, I thought, *How unfair!* I questioned him about our lovemaking—didn't it make him happy? He swallowed and said, "I'm happy when I feel all of you, your soft flesh, every fold."

"I get that," I said, "and with the diaphragm you could still feel all of me, couldn't you?"

"No," he said flatly, stunning me again. "To me sex is liberation, the pleasure of an open road. The *thing* was like a stop sign." He held up a knife to represent a stop sign. "It blocked my sense of liberation and my pleasure."

His resistance confused and hurt me. I picked up my fork to pierce my egg and squeezed my eyes to stop tears. I stood up, told him to forget the museum, and left the yolk oozing on the plate.

I cried on the subway, I cried at the grocery store, I cried walking home to my lonely cat. I smelled the turds in her box, emptied the dusty gravel, and refilled the litter. A pile of Maureen's clothes hung on a kitchen chair, papers cluttered her desk, and unwashed dishes filled the sink. In the last week, I'd hardly been home except to pick up clothes and paints for my class.

Don called from work to apologize. "I'm a prick, to treat you like that, especially on your birthday." He didn't know what got into him; I thought of that bottle of champagne he downed. He said how stupid to gripe. "I love how we make love." I could picture his big brown eyes drooping. He said, "I feel more for you than I've ever felt for anyone. I love you."

His words softened the pain, but I turned down his invitation to return to the city. My family was giving me a party. "Tomorrow then," he said. "Friday, when you come for your interview. I told Human Resources how smart you are. I'm sure you'll get the job. Then you can stay with me. We'll go dancing to celebrate. I have your dancing shoes." I considered but declined. I needed time with my sister. In his silence I heard disappointment, but he pressed me. "How about Saturday night?" I said, maybe. He said, "You're not blowing me off, are you?"

I told him that maybe I'd see him the next afternoon, when I went for my interview at his company. Maureen arrived home from school just as I was hanging up. She smiled when she saw me, we hugged, and I told her I'd missed her. She asked how it was going with Don, like she sensed something. I shared that he'd been "a little stubborn" but had apologized. Looking at her, so lovely and caring, I felt I needed to apologize to *her*. I said, "I'm sorry I've left you on your own so much."

She looked down. "I'm okay," she said, then shrugged. "Hey, happy birthday!" She handed me a macramé necklace made of beads in my favorite colors—greens and aqua blues, with a peace sign dangling on the end. In her card she'd circled the words, "I love you." I told her I loved her, too, and admired her beautiful necklace, which looked like she'd made it. She said, "Yes, art runs in the family, except for Daddy—" Maureen's face dropped. She said, "Daddy's gone away again."

I felt sorry I wouldn't see Dad on my birthday. I asked how long he'd been gone. She said, "A bunch of days. Mom's so fed up this might finally be the end."

I told her, "You know our parents. For them, not even divorce was the end." She slumped to the couch and curled up. Her childhood plumpness had bloomed into teenage voluptuousness. I wondered if she took care of herself. For a junior in high school, she was sharp and independent minded. But with more chores to do, she had less time to study. I asked, "Before we go up, do you need to do your homework?"

"All done."

———

On the elevator I told Maureen that I actually looked forward to Mom making a fuss. And she did. She gushed when she swung open the door of her apartment, wearing a fashionable white cape. She handed me a cardboard box, with apologies for not wrapping it.

She'd bought me a brown mini-dress with white dots and said that with my figure—"skinny like Twiggy"—I'd wear it well. I kissed her cheek, and in the kitchen alcove I spotted a Sarah Lee box of chocolate cake. The doorbell rang. I thought it might be Barbara and Maurice.

I opened the door, surprised to see a man. I took him for a salesman. A black toupee nested atop his oblong face. Black framed glasses matched his hair and turtleneck; his round belly popped out of a striped jacket.

"Happy Birthday, Janet!" I wondered how this salesman knew my name. He said, "I'm Saul, Maureen's boss." She worked at the pharmacy near the subway station. He scooted over to Mom, said, "Hello, Beautiful!" and gave her a sloppy kiss. He made sure we knew the lovely cape she wore was a gift from him. "She's such a beauty," he said and turned to a framed photograph on the wall, a shot of Mom at twenty when she worked as a Powers model—her wavy hair falling to her shoulders, Judy Garland style. "She still has the same delicate neck, one that deserves diamonds," he said as he wrapped his stubby hands around her throat.

I shot Maureen a look as if to ask, "What the hell is going on?" Maureen whispered that he's "courting her." I could hardly imagine it. Saul handed Mom a bottle, Johnny Walker, a label that triggered bad memories. At dinner they knocked off a few glasses of wine while Mom soaked up his flattery. I ate quickly, itchy to get out of there.

"Birthday girl, this is for you." Saul handed me a box wrapped in a loud orange; inside, a polyester blouse with hideous green stripes. "It's mod," he said. I barely mumbled a thank you.

Mom said, "Saul, how thoughtful." She kissed his cheek, and he pulled her wiggling and giggling onto his lap.

"Gotta go!" I said and stood up.

"But your birthday cake," Mom said, rising to get it. She stuck in candles, lit them, and turned out the lights. She told me to make a wish. I said to myself, *I wish . . . this man would go away.* I made a second silent wish for happiness—for me, my sisters and Mom, and for Dad, wherever he may be. I blew out the candle, and it went completely dark. I groped to find the switch, and when I flipped it, I saw Saul's hand stuck up my mother's skirt. I almost puked.

Mom jumped up, face red, hands fluttering. Saul rose with a heaving noise and dropped on the turntable a schmaltzy Perry Como album. He grabbed Mom to dance with him to "Sweet Adorable You."

"Thanks for dinner, Mom. Bye!"

Maureen followed me to the door, where she yelled, "I got a lot of homework to do."

Outside in the hall, I said, "Homework? You told me you'd finished it." She laughed as we ran away down the cement stairs.

———

After my interview at Don's company on Friday, I cautiously passed by his desk to tell him I'd start my job on Monday. He looked so glad, I softened and thanked him for recommending me. He ventured to say, "So, if we're going to work together, can we be friends again?" I felt anger in my heart trickle away, and I smiled. He said he'd still love to take me dancing, and I asked him to call me the next day, Saturday. That afternoon I had an idea to pick something up for him.

Saturday morning, Maureen and I caught up. We played with our cat Felice between chores. I sorted laundry, separating socks from bras, darks from lights, while anticipating a call from Don.

Maureen noticed a red envelope stuck under our door, opened the door, and saw the Sarah Lee box with the remains of my birthday cake. I ripped open the envelope and read Mom's note: "Darlings: I've gone to Saul's to advise on décor. Be back Sunday evening. Adore you."

Maureen said, "Oh, my God. What if she *marries* that jerk?"

"Let's forget about him," I said. "Today, let's have fun." I played my Spencer Davis Trio album loud and wiped the kitchen counter while bouncing to the beat: *ba-ba-ba-ba ba-BOOM, ba-ba-ba-ba ba-BOOM.* Turning around, I jumped, startled to find Maureen's friend, Aviva, watching me.

"Surprise! Happy Birthday!" Her furry coat hanging off her shoulders, her sky-blue dress bringing out the gold in her hair, she asked in her raspy voice where I'd picked up "those cool dance moves." I told her at the Dom, she said, "Oh, my God— *the Dom?*" Her dancing instructor had described the club, and she longed to go there. I told her Don and I danced there to the Spencer Davis Group song now playing: "Gimme Some Lovin'." She said she could use some loving. I told her Don had asked me out dancing that night, but I'd said no. Maureen suggested that I invite Don to party with us at home. Aviva said, "Groovy! Hope he likes teeny-boppers." Maureen asked her to help prepare meat-balls and together they pulled apart the ground round and rolled chunks of beef into little pink balls. Aviva dropped them in the oiled pan, then blurted out, "Janet, are you and Don having sex?"

I laughed at her bold question and said, "Yes. Just yesterday, I picked up a prescription from my gynecologist." Her hazel eyes wide with curiosity, she asked if I used birth control. "Yes, she gave me the Pill." I asked her if she had a boyfriend, and she said she would if she weren't afraid. I told her which methods were safe, and not so safe, like withdrawal. She didn't know about it. I explained, "He pulls out before he ejaculates."

"Ooh!" Aviva said so loud that Maureen and I cracked up. I said that withdrawal is as useless as rhythm, the method Catholic priests told our parents to use, which resulted in three girls in four years. Aviva joked, "It turned out your parents had a lot of rhythm!"

The doorbell rang. Two more of Maureen's girlfriends arrived, and all five of us stood chattering and hugging each other. Ruthie tossed back her red hair. She wore a petite black mini under a camelhair coat. Stocky Natasha, wearing hair pulled back in a matronly bun and a heavy coat and boots, stood in sharp contrast. Her Russian Orthodox parents insisted she dress in long skirts, turtlenecks, and jumpers that flattened her breasts.

Maureen brought out potato chips, and we sat in a circle snacking. She said, "We're celebrating Janet's birthday, and a new job, too."

Aviva clapped. "Our pioneer!"

I said I was only a year older than them.

Ruth said, "Maybe, but you're miles ahead. We only dream about college, and you've already started."

"And already dropped out," I said with a bit of regret. Ruth said she admired me exploring real life. I didn't simply read about civil rights, but actually volunteered. Natasha wished she could take art classes.

Aviva said, "I'm only fifteen. You're eighteen, a woman! With a job in New York, a lover . . . and your own gynecologist." We laughed. Feeling lost in some ways, it warmed me that they thought of me as a trailblazer.

Don called from the Cafe/Bar. After we spoke, I announced, "He's coming to our party!" Everyone cheered except Natasha, who had a curfew. Looking at my paintings, she said her parents forbade her to study art because art jobs are hard to find. "But, Janet, you found a job with an artist." She sighed and pulled on her boots to go home. I remembered that Natasha lived near Bill's studio, and I offered to introduce them. She agreed eagerly. As we walked, I told her that Bill might need a new assistant. She asked if I trusted him. I said absolutely. Her handsome face flickered with excitement for a moment, but with her soulful dark eyes downcast, she said her parents would never allow her to work for Bill.

I thought, *Poor Natasha. I wonder if she'll ever dare break the rules.*

I introduced Natasha and offered Bill a piece of cake. "Someone's birthday?" I told him I turned eighteen. He said, "A big one!" When I wrapped my arms around his huge waist, Natasha's eyes opened as wide as the moon. She turned to the canvas on the easel and marveled at the eight-foot-long panorama in pinks and oranges of a sunset on the beach. He had been working on this Fire Island painting forever. Bill said, "The patron wants it, but I ain't ready to let it go."

He talked about how he worked back and forth between details and the big picture. He wanted a viewer's gaze to move in a circle around the scene and sense the harmony. "I got that," Natasha confirmed. "And all in dots—*pointillism*." She told Bill she wanted to study art, and he said they should talk. I noticed how similar their stocky bodies were, and how comfortable they seemed together.

I told Bill I worked a job, took an art class, and left college. Bill looked surprised and asked, "Can't you study art at college?"

"Let's eat cake," I said, and found plastic forks amid the garbage next to towers of old coffee cups. We ate sitting on rickety chairs around his radio, switched it on to a popular station. Up came the hit by the Byrds, "Turn, Turn, Turn," with words from the Bible that I hummed, "A time to love, and a time to hate; a time of war, and a time of peace." I thought, *So true, the whole wide world is turning around us.*

I stood to go, and Bill made me promise to finish my degree. "It will help you get a better day job," he said. I left him and Natasha getting to know each other.

I saw Don galloping up Hillside Avenue as we both headed to my apartment building. He said he'd missed me, and he kissed me. He handed me his gift of dancing shoes I'd left behind.

In our apartment, he beamed at being greeted by three high school girls in mini-dresses and beads. He wore his usual jeans, black turtleneck, and black leather jacket, which Aviva dressed up by pulling off a strand of beads from her neck and laying it around his. Maureen put out bowls of spaghetti and meatballs, and Don called it the perfect meal—"hot, tasty, and cheap."

I laid Detroit Wheels on the turntable, ducked into a corner to put on my polka-dot mini, and emerged in my new dancing shoes. The girls adored them. Maureen turned down the light and lit candles, giving our room the feel of a club. "So let's dance," Aviva said.

Don started bopping to "Devil with the Blue Dress." His black hair flying, he shouted, "Move your *arms!*" We all raised our elbows and punched our fists into the air.

Maureen grabbed a tambourine and dropped on a single by Little Richard, "Good Golly Miss Molly." Ruthie grooved to her own rhythms, her red hair like fire around her. I felt my mini rise as I thrust my torso back and forth. I hoped to catch Don's eye, but his eyes focused on the tambourine Maureen was passing to Aviva. "This is fun," Aviva said, bouncing, and banging the tambourine with abandon. Her blonde hair tumbled over her face, and her legs revealed a dance student's strong thighs.

Maureen and I considered sleeping arrangements for Ruthie and Aviva. I kissed Don goodbye at the door, and he said, "Sorry to miss your pajama party."

"Aww," we all moaned.

Then Maureen had an idea: Why didn't Don and I sleep in Mom's apartment, vacated for the weekend? He and I unlocked Mom's door and, turned on after all the dancing, we stripped off our clothes and spread out on the spacious double bed. Holding on to Don's thick hair, I whispered, "I have a surprise for you. I'm on the Pill now—"

In the bright of day, I felt odd in my mother's bed. I slipped on her raspberry silk robe and turned on the radio, surprised to hear "our song." The last chorus of "Ruby Tuesday" played out, beginning with "Goodbye," and ending with "Gonna miss you." I switched it off, put on Mom's album, "The Girl from Ipanema," and, hungry, whipped up egg batter. Don, naked, stumbled to the kitchen.

I asked, "How about French toast?" I spooned butter into the pan, dipped slices of bread into the batter, and when the butter bubbled, laid the bread into the sizzling pan. As I swayed to the music, Don came up behind me saying he loved the way my hips swelled. We ate quickly and sloppily. He licked maple syrup off my mouth.

Noise at the door startled me. I gasped. I pushed Don's head away, thinking Mom had returned! But it was Maureen. She yelled, "Janet let me in!" Don stumbled for his shirt, and hopping on one foot, pulled on his jeans. Maureen sounded agitated. "Mom stopped in our apartment. She'll be up any minute!" I ripped off Mom's robe, searched for my clothes. Maureen had told Mom I'd slept up here. Mom was okay with that, and when she offered food for the girls' breakfast, Maureen dashed up to get eggs and bread, a chance to warn me. She said, "Quick!"

"Quick what?"

"Get Don out! Mom will be up the elevator any second!"

Don was already out the door. "Take the stairs!" I shouted down the hall after him.

Maureen, at the lyrics, "She just doesn't see," shut down "Ipanema" so fast I hoped she didn't scratch the record. I fell to the floor, groping under the bed for my panties.

The metal sound of a key in the door. Maureen and I froze.

Mom sang out, "Hello, darlings," as she floated into her apartment, and saw me dressing. She asked why I wore dancing shoes. I explained that Maureen threw a birthday dance party for me downstairs, and we dressed up like we were in a club. "What fun." While her back was turned Maureen stripped the bed and I picked up plates from the table. Mom noticed bowls with traces of egg batter. "Oh, you ate already?"

"So hungry," I said, "And I bet Maureen and her friends are really hungry." Mom gave Maureen a box of eggs, a stick of butter, and a bag of bread. "If you want French toast, take the maple syrup," she said, puzzled where it could be. I grabbed it, added it to Maureen's pile, gathered the bedding in my arms, and promised Mom I'd wash the sheets.

She shrugged and said, "No need for just one night. You're not dirty, are you?"

"Ha. No," I said. "We gotta go."

Maureen and I heard the Rascals blaring in the hall. We entered our apartment to see Don dancing in the middle of the room, boogying to "Good Lovin'" with Ruthie and Aviva around him clapping and laughing. When Maureen passed with the food, he got distracted by the maple syrup. Aviva snatched the bottle. I yelled over the music, "Don, you should go!"

A knock on the door. I sighed. "Too late." Mom entered and halted at the scene before her. Maureen turned off the music, and Don sat down on the sofa. My arms wrapped around the laundry, I pointed with my head. "This is my boyfriend, Don."

He said, "Nice meeting you."

Mom stared at him. I shielded myself behind the sheets. No one spoke a word. Don, for some reason, put his feet on the coffee table. Mom scanned him: long hair, leather jacket, sunglasses, and a strand of beads. She judged people by their looks, and I knew Don had lost his case.

Mom said to Don, "You forgot something." Between two fingers, she dangled a pair of men's Fruit of the Loom underpants, flicked it into the pile of laundry I held, and coolly turned out the door.

Later—Don gone, girls gone, Maureen out working at Saul's pharmacy—I sat on the couch, mind vacant. A knock on the door. I let Mom in, but not in the mood to talk, I slumped back down. She pulled up one of the kitchen chairs to sit opposite me, crossed her legs, and said, "Really, don't you think that man's hair is outrageous?" I agreed with her by saying Saul's fake hair was outrageous. She told me don't be smart. "I'm talking about that man you're fooling around with." I told her his name. She asked, "Why did you choose a bum?"

"Mother, you are so wrong." She asked his background. In a wooden tone, I shared what I knew: Italian, from Brooklyn, supports himself, works a good full-time job, and will soon graduate college. I knew that nothing I could say would dissuade her from disliking him.

"Does he smoke pot?"

"Sometimes."

"Do you?"

"I tried it."

Long silence. She asked when I started having sex, and I said when she got me birth control pills. She looked confused, and I reminded her that when I turned seventeen, she took me to our family doctor because she thought my breasts were not big enough to attract a man. "Remember?" She nodded and explained that the doctor thought the hormones in the Pill might help me develop. "Janet, I never knew you were angry about that."

I told Mom I wasn't angry. "It made me feel sad, like I wasn't good enough."

Mom stood up, lit a cigarette by the window, and said in a low voice, "All this behind my back." I thought, *I might have told her about my life if she ever bothered to check in with me.* After a silence, she turned to me, blowing out smoke. I opened the window for air. She said, "You're making impulsive decisions."

Now I did feel angry. I reminded Mom of her impulsive relationships: Dad, Doug, Dad again, now this Saul.

She said, "He asked me to marry him."

"Which one?"

Mom looked annoyed and took a drag. "Your father doesn't want to marry again." No surprise there. The image of Saul as my stepfather made me shiver. I said softly she didn't need to marry. Certainly not the first jerk who came around. She shook her head, crushed out her cigarette, and joined me on the couch. "Janet, I came down to talk about *you*."

I thought, *That would be a first.*

She said, "You're taking pot and sleeping with a man."

"So?" I said, "Do you think you're the only woman who wants a man in her life? Didn't you start dating Dad when you were, like, fourteen? I'm eighteen—remember? The same age you were when you ran away with Dad." Mom looked horrified that I might be planning to run away with "that man." I admitted Don and I had talked about a trip. Silence. She asked if my motive was to get away from her. I said, "Mom, it's not because of *you*. It's *me*. What *I* want. I want to learn about life. To travel to cool places, meet other artists." I told her I'd probably come home to the city, maybe go back to college, get a day job and a room of my own. "I don't care about marrying. I don't want to lean on a man, like . . ."

"Like me?" She rubbed her forehead like she had a migraine coming on. "Janet, I know I've made mistakes. You're young and can find the right man. Without men, women are nothing."

Nothing? I resolved that I would never use men to define myself.

———～———

On Tuesday evening, in his rooming house after my art class, I gave Don back his Fruit of the Loom. I said, "You didn't *know* you were dancing with a bare butt?" He laughed and said it had felt good letting it all hang out. I snuggled up closer to him on his bed.

He asked how I liked my first two days at his office. I said, "It's okay. But my supervisor is so prissy. Priscilla is the perfect name for her. She walks like a bird, wearing those stupid cat eyeglasses. I think she set up the guy—the one who wears the 'Bomb Hanoi' button—to check up on me. I'm good at typing, I'm fast, I don't mind it. But my first daily task at nine: bring mail to the director, Fred. Then file all day, which is incredibly boring. By the afternoon I can't keep my eyes open—thank God you order ice-cream sodas."

He called it the "three o'clock sugar charge!"

I said, "I feel like I'm at a dead end without a degree. I've been thinking maybe I should go back to college." Don looked flabbergasted. He reminded me I'd just freed myself from school, so now I could experience real life. "The life experience I yearn for is not *filing*," I said. "Hey, I'm no good at it. I *am* good at academic things. I know that game."

Don agreed that school is a *game*, one that requires sitting in classrooms for four years. He said, "Think about how much more you'd learn if you spent those four years living in four different countries, one country a year. Learning the language, the culture." Wow, I thought, that would be a spectacular adventure. But I challenged him, saying it was easy for him to say, now that he'd earned his degree. He said college got him out of the Vietnam draft. "When I graduate, I'm getting outta here. I thought you wanted to go with me."

"I do," I said, "but I can't imagine how." He asked if I liked the beach. "I love the beach, and I want to see San Francisco and the Pacific."

"Yeah, then let's head west," he said. "We could start in Provincetown."

"Isn't that north?"

"Yeah, in Massachusetts, off Cape Cod. It's the best place to begin, to make some money for our trip," he said. He would earn buckets waiting tables, like he did in past summers, and I'd make money drawing. "P-town is famous for its portrait artists, and you sure can draw. We'll jump start every day at the beach." I told him it sounded like a dream. He looked gleeful. "In the fall when it's cooler, we'll buy a second-hand car and hit the road."

He had a license. It seemed so adult, driving a car.

"We'll toss your paint box in the trunk and head out cross-country. If we need money we can stop in towns along the way, I could waiter, you can sell some paintings. Then move on again." It sounded great. He reached out to me and said, "Can you hold on until May, just two months away?"

———————

After my art class, I stayed at Don's as usual. Wednesday morning, we arrived late to work. Don flew to his desk, but I had to punch the clock before I dashed to collect Fred's mail. I found the bin already empty, and Priscilla there to remind me, with a dirty look, that Fred needs his mail first thing. I apologized.

But the following morning, Don woke yelling, "Oh shit! I didn't set the alarm!" I leapt out of bed in a panic. I thought, *Only my first week on the job, I can't be late twice!* No time to apply makeup. I pulled on the same dusty blue corduroy suit, and we raced down the stairs to the subway. Near 19th Street, we bought one bagel and gobbled it down as we pushed through the glass doors to the office. I punched in, again too late to get the mail, and slinked into my seat. Priscilla stood up and all typewriters in the room stopped clacking. All I heard were her heels clicking over to my desk and her cold voice. "Your pay will be docked for lateness."

At lunch, Don looked disturbed and told me that the boss, Fred, had confronted him at the water cooler. Don said, "The guy's my mentor for three years, I never saw him pissed off. Not about my job performance. It's about you."

I felt sick with embarrassment. I promised I'd do better. Don shook his head and said, "Fred is not blaming *you*. He reprimanded *me*. For hanging around your desk, displaying romantic interest, blatantly arriving late with you in the morning."

Yeah, I thought, *virtually announcing we'd slept together*. Office gossip distracted staff, his boss had said, then asked Don point blank, "What the fuck are you doing to this girl?"

———————

I couldn't wait to get home, to see Maureen and change my clothes. I stewed about the shit at work. Then more shit happened at home. I couldn't wait to tell Don about it at work. The next day, we separately left the office and met up at a luncheonette decorated in green for upcoming St. Patrick's Day. I felt ashamed that my reputation at work had sunk so low. Don squeezed my leg and promised he'd take me to his favorite Irish pub, but my mood did not lift. He held my hand and asked what troubled me. I said, "My mother stopped by to see me, and brought a guy with her."

"Who?"

"Her boyfriend, Saul. My mother had complained to him I was seeing a tough guy, but I defended you. I said, 'Don is *not* tough.'"

Don's head jerked back in surprise. "You don't think I'm tough?"

"Come on, Don, it's not funny. Saul is a jerk," I said. "Big guy, but weak. Saul pummeled me with questions. I told him, I don't answer to you, you're not my dad. Saul said, 'Your mother is worried sick, she doesn't need you to give her more grief by picking a guy who's no good.'"

Don's face hardened. I shared more. "I told Saul my life was none of his business, but he jumped all over me, saying, 'The guy is corrupting you with pot. I'm warning you, you better stay away from that bum, and keep him and his drugs away from your little sister. If he comes around here again, I tell you what I'll do—I'll break his legs, I'll break both his legs!'"

I exhaled in outrage and frustration. "So that's the totally ridiculous craziness I deal with," I said, and looked to Don for sympathy.

Don withdrew his hand. I asked him what was wrong. "What's wrong? The man *threatened* me!"

Stunned that Don took Saul's bluster to heart, I said "Don, it's absurd. He's a fool, just showing off for my mother. Don't worry, he's just a pot-bellied coward. He'd never actually *do* anything."

"The man said he'd break my legs. I mean, fuck, break both my legs?!"

Chapter 10
DOG AND STAN

Don did not, as promised, take me for a beer at his favorite pub on St. Patrick's Day. I met that Friday with Doc. I received his invitation via Rudy to assist at another clinic. Still hanging onto my job at the publishing house, I left work to head to Interfaith Hospital. Doc's appreciative greeting lifted me, and together we waited in the lobby for poor folks to show up.

"The desperate destroy their lives," Doc said. "Turning to alcohol and drugs, they lose everything." He recalled how I'd put the men at ease at the clinic at Stan's place. I said they avoided intake questions, seeming ashamed. Doc said the poor are secretive by habit and they fear formal institutions. His staff had blanketed South Jamaica with flyers, and we hoped a few brave souls would show up for a check-up.

Doc posted me at the entrance, and after a while, I opened the glass door for a skinny Black woman who dragged herself toward me. From what appeared to be a bulge in the thin fabric of her skirt, a child emerged, who'd been tightly clinging to her mother's knees as if to life itself. The smell of urine made me flinch. The girl, about five, held herself. I said, "Hello. Would you like me to take you to the bathroom?" Her dazed mother shook her hand loose and the girl stared at me out of deep sockets, her pupils like black holes. "What's your name?" I asked. The child did not speak. Her mother pushed her to me, and I took her hand and brought her to the bathroom in the lobby. Inside the little space, the odor intensified. She still held herself, wiggling, looking around, but did not move to the toilet.

"You can sit on the toilet now." My words didn't seem to register. I lifted up my own skirt and squatted over the bowl and, trying to make her laugh, made a pissing noise. No response. Standing, I asked her name again. She mumbled something, but now I couldn't understand *her*. How could she not know how to say her own name? Or how to use a toilet? She looked at me with wild eyes. *Maybe she thinks* I'm *weird*. I sat down on the toilet lid, and she let me bring her body closer. She was sweet yet I had to pull my nose away from her unwashed hair. I started unbuttoning her pants, and she caught on and pulled them down herself. Too late. She'd already defecated. I felt frustrated, like we lived on opposite sides of a chasm too wide for any bridge to cross. Not able to share even common words, I stopped trying to speak.

I pulled off her panties and dumped the feces in the toilet bowl. I flushed, rinsed the panties, and wrung them out. I helped her pull up her pants and I tucked the damp panties in her pocket. I lifted her to the sink and studied her in the mirror: her unfocused eyes, her matted hair sticking up every which way. She glued her eyes to the faucet. When the water got warm, I squirted liquid soap on both her little pink palms, and, just like Nanny used to do, I held her hands in mine, rubbed them together and wiped them dry. I flung the door open and deeply inhaled the sanitized hospital air.

I noticed the woman had made it to the desk. The nameless little girl dropped my hand to rush to her mother, who didn't seem to notice her daughter had returned. Maybe she hadn't even noticed her girl had been gone. Could she be high, on drugs or alcohol? My heart sank. I thought, *if her mother can't take care of this lost child, who will?*

Doc asked if I was all right. I said I felt dizzy and helpless. I told him the little girl had defecated in her pants. Doc said, "Consider, if you were homeless with no access to a bathroom, and you had to relieve yourself, wouldn't you do the same?"

———————

That very night, Doc offered me a full-time job. On Monday I gave notice at the publishing house, and a week later reported for my first day at Interfaith Hospital. My blue corduroy suit needed washing, so I had to wear my one dress, my polka-dot mini, and dressed it down with flat shoes. At the front desk, a Black receptionist called for Doreen, a large White woman who showed me up a flight to our workspace in the foyer. Dr. Matthew arrived with a light-skinned Black woman, pretty and proper, whom he introduced as his wife. They invited me to their office.

My eyes landed on a photograph of them with lots of kids. Doc said he met his wife when she was studying social work. Mrs. Matthew said with a slight smile, "We wanted a large family, so now I practice my skills on our children."

Doc said he had seven brothers and sisters. A family twice as big as mine, I thought. Behind him hung a framed degree from Meharry Medical College, Nashville, and I asked what inspired him to go into medicine. His mother, he said. "The day of my birth, when labor started, she rushed to the hospital right next door, Knickerbocker Hospital. They refused to admit Black people in the 1920s. The moment I heard her story, I knew I had to be a doctor."

"I can see why," I said, disgusted by the cruel discrimination.

"So I was born in a basement," Doc continued. His father was a janitor—the family lived in an apartment building beneath higher floors where middle-class white people lived. "I accompanied my father at times to fix things and observed White people's apartments. They had lots of books, so I checked out piles of books from the library and studied them until late at night."

Mrs. Matthews said that her husband was the first Negro to graduate from both the Bronx High School of Science and Manhattan College four years later.

Doc talked about his private practice in neurosurgery, which he relinquished to work on a grander vision. "Since childhood," he said, "I dreamed of directing a hospital where Black people were feely admitted."

I said, "And you've done that."

Mrs. Matthew said, "The hospital is one of our enterprises, all part of a larger plan to earn civil and economic rights for our people."

I leaned forward, excited by this lofty goal.

Doc said, "I imagine the Negro community as a sick patient with many ills, physical illness is only one. The others are poor education, unaffordable housing, unemployment—all symptoms of poverty. Today, the patient is getting only Band-Aids—a stitch here, a pill there—which doesn't cure the root causes. My vision is to treat the *whole* patient."

"Oh, yes," I said. I interlaced my fingers. "The whole picture. Everything is interconnected."

Doc said, "Let's take, for example, the mother and daughter who showed up at the clinic a week ago." Those two hadn't left my mind. He asked, "What's the first thing that woman needed?" I said to get off drugs. Doc nodded, saying he'd enrolled her in a drug treatment program at Interfaith. "And after the treatment is done," Doc asked, "What's the next step?" I said to be released. Doc said, "Yes, but released into what? Home? She has no home."

Feeling sadness, I asked Doc, "Then how can she stay well?"

Doc said, "Exactly. Housing is a necessary continuation of her treatment, along with food. How will she pay for rent and food?"

"She needs a job," I said.

"Right. But who will hire a Black woman, a drop out, a former drug addict?"

I shook my head, feeling dizzy and helpless again.

Doc said, "The way things are now, she probably will turn to welfare. Which is pitiful and humiliating. Being dependent, in despair, she's likely to escape by shooting up again. Then, to acquire money to buy the drugs, she'll sell herself or sell drugs." I said that was depressing—she'd be right back where she started. Doc called it "a vicious circle." He wanted to create a different kind of circle, a circle of success. He asked, "What if, after detox, she had an apartment and a job waiting for her?"

"She might have a chance."

Doc smiled with pride. "Giving chances like that is the work we do in my organization, NEGRO." I reminded Doc that the month before, helping Stan with Doc's NEGRO Fund drive, I'd drawn cartoons.

Mrs. Matthew's face lit up. She and Doc loved those cartoons, she said. And she'd been impressed on my job application with my academic credentials and experience in the Black community. "So you'll help with our grand vision?" I felt so inspired I had goose bumps.

After work, thrilled to be free of commuting, I skipped over to the grand Jamaica Public Library. From the periodicals rack I pulled an issue of the *Atlantic*, sat on a mahogany chair and settled into the luxury of reading. When I looked up, I caught sight of Stan studying at a table. My heart skipped. I hadn't seen him since his ridiculous arm wrestle with Don and couldn't resist saying hello.

Stan looked startled to see me. His face melted into a smile that rounded his cheeks. "Duffy, what are you doing here?" I had the same question for him. He said he was doing research. He'd spread out many photo stats, and I saw a newspaper clip with a photo of Doc.

"You're researching . . . Doc?"

He nodded and said librarians had dug up articles from the

New York Times going back years. "The man's easy to research—such a publicity hound." I asked what he meant. Stan said Doc loved calling press conferences. "Remember his eviction? How he threw up a barricade using baby cribs? The press took the bait and developed a melodrama: 'Dashing Mayor, Knight in Shining Armor, Saves Poor Hospital from Big, Bad Bank.'"

"In that melodrama," I said, "does that make Doc *the Fair Damsel*?" The image of bald-headed Doc in long golden hair made us both laugh, disturbing readers. Curious, I whispered, "Stan, what are you looking for?" He said he was doing simple "due diligence." I understood Stan had agreed to urge folks to invest in Doc's NEGRO. I said, "So you want facts to assure people about Doc's sterling character?"

He said, "Well, I began like that. But then I turned up . . . contradictions."

"You sound *suspicious* of Doc," I said, laughing at that absurdity.

Stan said, "Listen, I've known him since he hit town four years ago—a hero, setting up the first Negro-run hospital. Since then, I'm learning he's got his fingers in lots of other pies."

"Doc reaches out because he's got *vision*, you've said so yourself."

Stan said, "Lately I see less vision and more *ideology*." He said Doc believed in self-help: the best way for Negroes to lift themselves up is to own their own businesses. I mentioned Stan had his own business, too. "I do. And I pay my bills, while Doc almost got evicted."

I grew weary of the skepticism, and Stan must have sensed it. He asked me to sit, and I reluctantly slumped into a hard chair. He told me that though the city paid Interfaith, Doc still owes rent. Yet he purchased another hospital and took on more debt. "It puzzles me," he said, pointing to news articles. The black ink on the shiny white photostats dulled into blurry grey under my tired eyes.

I felt upset by Stan's nasty suspicions of Doc, who'd set up NEGRO to benefit poor people. I said, "I believe in Doc. Just today he and his wife laid out their vision, and I'm honored to work for them."

Stan's mouth hung open. "Say again? You *work* for Doc?" I told him I'd just started that day. He said, "And when were you going to tell me?"

I said, "I don't recall having to answer to you," and I spun around to catch my bus.

Stan followed me out of the library into the black night where wet snowflakes hit my face. *Can't be*, I thought. *It's the first day of spring!* Stan stood by his white Impala and invited me in. Damp cold creeping up my stockings under my thin mini dress convinced me to accept a ride. He turned the ignition, set the heat to high, and I warmed my hands in the hot blasts.

"Look," I said. "I really like my new job with Doc. I thought that you two were working together." Stan assured me they both did share the goal of improving the Black community. But he sensed something odd about Doc. He implored me to help him figure out why he'd *accept* the city's money to take in welfare patients, when he claims he's *against* welfare. That did seem contradictory, but I related that Doc fears that welfare leads to dependency.

"Nobody thinks long-term dependency is good," Stan said. "Independence is the goal." I got that. The education and training that Dr. King and President Johnson promoted in the Great Society programs were meant to lead to jobs and independence. "Exactly," he said. "And what if I told you Doc is *against* the Great Society?"

"I'd say you were mistaken. Can you please start the car?"

"Check this out first." Stan reached in the backseat for a folder of recent articles and flipped through them. He said, "Doc doesn't believe in 'welfare type relief,' and calls the anti-poverty program 'an extended form of home relief.'"

I felt stunned. But on my first day working for Doc, I refused to think about Doc's flaws. With struggle and conflict all around me, Doc's vision of prosperity and order gave me hope. I grabbed the door handle. "I'll catch the bus."

Stan turned the key all the way, the engine revved up, and the windshield wipers pushed slush from side to side. We crept slowly on clogged streets behind cars with brake lights as red as devil's eyes. Stan told me I was idealistic, so idealistic I could be gullible. He said to keep my eyes open at Doc's hospital.

"You mean, like, be a spy?"

"No, Duffy, just watch out he doesn't use you. For things you might not believe in."

"Like what?"

Stan said Doc met the previous summer with Richard Nixon. Doc, a charming gentleman in bow tie and spectacles, Stan speculated, could win the party Black votes, enough to elect Nixon President. "Impossible," I said.

We edged forward, stop and go. I ran one of Doc's ideas by Stan. "Doc says a handout humiliates people, jobs award dignity."

"A handout, if you were hungry, would help, wouldn't it?" Stan said that King made the march on D.C. all about jobs. The problem: a Black man was less likely to get a job than a prison sentence or a draft notice. I knew that was true. I floated another of Doc's beliefs: less government and more charity and self-help.

"Charity and self-help," Stan repeated. I knew I'd pressed a button. Stan believed people needed, not charity, but *laws and rights*. He said, "Without Lincoln's Emancipation Proclamation, we'd still be enslaved! Self-help. Huh! Black folks—aunts, big brothers, grandmothers, neighbors—we been holding our sorry selves up for centuries."

He turned to me. "Not like you White folks." He shook his head. "The way your parents cut you two girls loose to scramble for yourselves—shame on them." His words stung me, and I recoiled. He'd implied sympathy for my sister and me, but who was he to stereotype my parents, and all "White folks," as shamefully uncaring?

"I'm sorry," Stan said immediately.

My stomach churned. My hand gripped the door, I considered bailing out. I felt his eyes on me. He said he didn't mean to hurt me. I asked, "Then why did you say such a thing?"

He paused. "Duffy, I don't want to lose you. To Doc's camp."

"*Camp?*" I said, "I'm not in anybody's *camp*." Anger grabbed hold of me. "You know what I think? You're jealous Doc's got so much attention for his projects. After all your gang's work— attending meetings and writing grants for funds—what's changed? Nothing."

A pained look crossed Stan's face, and he stared blankly out the smeared windshield.

———

I broke free of Stan's Impala when he pulled up to my apartment building. Agitated, I ran up the stairs to my studio. Seven o'clock, Maureen out. I thought, *Good, I need to paint.* I ditched my mini for a sweater and jeans, pulled open my paint box, and slapped a blank canvas board on the easel. I squeezed oil paint on my palette and spilled harsh smelling turpentine into a metal cup. With a palette knife, I broke the white of the canvas by scraping on thick red and black paint. I layered in vertical slabs of white, and mixed red and black to create browns. Out of the painterly chaos a figure emerged.

The intercom buzzed. The clock read ten o'clock. My stomach growled. I dropped my brushes and pressed the intercom.

"Duffy, it's Stan." I froze at his voice. "I've been driving around, feeling lousy. I need to apologize."

"You were mean."

"You're right. Can we talk for a minute?"

———

I agreed to meet Stan in the parking lot of the Galaxy, the diner next door. I found his car running, heat on, and jumped in. "You have a minute," I said, and stared straight ahead. Working White men, heading to the diner, peered in at us and scowled.

Stan said, "I'm sorry for stereotyping White folks. It's not true what I said." I watched our breath vaporize on the windshield and thought, *It is true that Maureen and I are neglected.* I'd spoken harshly, myself, but at this moment I found apologizing the hardest thing on Earth. I finally said, "Me, too. What you've accomplished—it's not 'nothing.'" I thanked him for coming back and made a move to go.

Stan reached for, but didn't touch, my arm. He asked, "Do you still feel sore?"

I turned to face him. "Look, I don't understand these rivalries. All I know is my work for Doc, and for you, gives some purpose to my messed-up life." I said, "I have to clean up my paints."

Stan asked, "You were painting? What did you paint?" I said I painted my feelings. He asked, "How do you paint feelings? Is it abstract?" I described it as expressionist, emotional. Mere scribbles, but sort of a figure. Sort of him, actually. He asked to see it. I refused and said I was going to throw it out. He said, "Please, I must see it."

———————

I regretted giving in. In the elevator, Stan's eyes focused on the controls while I admired his handsome face and strong build. *All this tension between us,* I thought. *Why do we argue? I know he likes me, and I like him.*

I opened my apartment door. "Maureen?" I peeped in. "She's not home yet."

Stan stood back and asked me to bring the painting into the hall. I shook my head, still reluctant to show it. I said, "No, it's terrible."

"All the more reason I want to see it."

I told him I did it to let off steam. He got that but still wanted a look. My brain concocted excuses. But he moved closer, opened the door wider. There on the easel, lit by the harsh green light from the hall, stood the ghoulish painting. For several moments Stan studied it, his eyes narrow, his mouth twitching as though trying to hide hurt feelings. He took a big step back.

I broke. "Stan, I told you before that the figure was like you, but it's not. It is *not* you. It's *me*. The subject is my own anger." He remained silent and transfixed. "You were *on* me, you know," I said.

Stan said in a low voice, "Tell me what you were thinking when you painted the vertical white lines." I said classic columns, a symbol of order and harmony. He saw on the columns zigzags, like cracks. "They're crumbling," he said. "The *breakdown* of order and harmony. Is that what you're saying?"

"I'm not saying anything. Except that I felt pissed."

"Classical. A myth, then? Those squiggles merge to form a figure, arms pushing out against the columns. Samson?"

"I did have Samson in mind."

"He brought the whole temple down. Here, this wide Black face, I recognize my features." Yes, though distorted, Stan's features were unmistakable—broad brown cheeks, walnut eyes, full mouth, and glinting white teeth. "I'm grinning like a devil," he said. "Is that how you see me? I have to admit I did think of myself as more good-looking . . ."

"This is not a portrait of you!" I shouted. But Stan did not lift his eyes from the canvas. I said, "It's not realistic. I feel mean for even showing it to you." I snatched the canvas and ducked out the door into the hall, dashing for the incinerator.

Stan followed and blocked the hatch. "Please, if you don't want it, I'd like to have it."

"No, it's hideous." I hugged the wet painting to my torso, realizing too late I'd ruined one of my only sweaters. I said, "Stan, the wreckage I painted here is the wreckage around *me.* Me, trying to hold up good things in my life—my art, my sister, love, meaningful work. Everything else is falling apart." Exhausted, I tipped against the wall.

Stan moved in to protect me. "Duffy, what's falling apart?"

"Everything." I told him that my mother's boyfriend had threatened to break Don's legs, which turned him off, and he'd stopped calling. My job at Don's office grew impossibly awkward. "So I jumped at Doc's job offer."

A blonde woman in a pink robe and matching bunny slippers stepped out of her apartment holding a garbage bag. She stopped when she saw Stan and me. With a suspicious sideways glance at us, she dumped her trash down the hatch and ducked back into her apartment.

Stan said, "I better go. She might call the cops."

"Why?"

"I'm a Black man."

We stood in the hall staring at each other. He apologized again, and I did, too. "I'm sorry for ever painting this ugly thing." He said he'd accept my apology if I gave the painting to him. I begged off, promising to do a better one.

"This is the one I need to have."

"Why, for God's sake?"

"To remind me to be vigilant."

"Of what?"

"The destructive forces within me. In all of us."

PART IV: SPRING, 1967

Rev. Dr. Martin Luther King Jr. on anti-war march
with Dr. Spock in NYC, 1967

Chapter 11
REV. DR. MARTIN LUTHER KING JR.

Doc made an announcement to the Interfaith Hospital staff that thrilled me. Dr. Martin Luther King Jr. would be speaking at the Riverside Church in New York City on Friday, April 4th, and Doc had organized a van for all his staff to go. I felt as excited as I had at age fourteen when I wished I could fly to D.C., like a moth to sunlight, to hear Dr. King deliver his speech, "I Have a Dream." Because of Doc, I'd now hear Martin Luther King Jr. speak in *person*! Clearly, Stan had been mistaken about Doc opposing Dr. King's policies.

Doc asked me to do a special drawing. *Wow*, I thought, *I even get to draw on this job*. Doc asked if I knew that Dr. King opposed the US war against the Communist North Vietnamese. I sure did know. He said, "Martin is not wise to link the anti-war forces with the Negro cause." Doc reasoned that the public would think Negroes unpatriotic, which would hurt progress in civil rights. He looked at me and pointedly said, "Your job is to draw a cartoon that makes it clear Negroes must focus on economic improvement and denounce Dr. King's radical view."

Did I hear correctly? My boss just gave me a direct order to *denounce* my hero? I recalled Stan's advice to not act against my beliefs. I believed the war was wrong, as Dr. King did, so I couldn't possibly oppose him. But I had to start drawing *some-thing*. I found photos of King in magazines in the waiting room. *His face*, I thought, *projects courage and morality*; I refused to turn King into a cartoon. I portrayed only Doc—easy to caricature with his bald head, sideburns, bow tie, and white coat—and a speech balloon with him making a neutral statement: "Negroes Need Jobs and Housing."

———————

The day of Dr. King's speech, "Beyond Vietnam," Rudy invited me to join the gang on the bus Stan had arranged to go hear Dr. King in Manhattan. I yearned to join them, but too late: Doc and his wife ushered me along with staff into their van. We rolled past the streaming waters of the Hudson River, and the sight of the gloriously lit Riverside Church rising above us took my breath away.

Doc opened the van's rear doors and called to us, "There's a picket sign for each of you." Horrified, I saw he'd not only reproduced my drawing on signs but had added anti-King messages. I did not take one. I stood fixed on the sidewalk as Doc lined up his staff along the walls of the church. Across the street, handfuls of other fringe groups were protesting King, each periodically chanting the slogans printed on their signs. They took turns yelling out, "Bomb Hanoi," and "Segregation Forever!" A group of Black nationalists chanted, "A Free Black Nation, No Integration."

In contrast to the angry chants, shouts of laughter arose from the corner near the front of Riverside Church. Large Black women in choir robes burst into song: "Down by the riverside, gonna lay down my sword and shields, down by the riverside . . ." Hundreds of people, White and Black, young and old, streamed into the church. Then I spotted Rudy, Soc, and the gang. And Stan, who caught my eye. We walked closer to each other. Stan said, smiling, "Are you coming in?"

"I want to," I said.

He assessed the scene unfolding behind me: a reporter interviewed Doc, while picketing nurses walked in a dumb circle. Stan's face showed disbelief, "Doc is here to *protest*? He's *picketing* against Martin Luther King?" He turned to me. "What are *you* going to do, Miss Duffy?"

My face flushed with embarrassment. I'd been pushed into acting against my beliefs, exactly what Stan had warned me against. I said, "I want to listen to King."

"Well, let's go then."

Soc and Rudy beckoned us from the corner, and Stan waved and started walking to them. I lagged behind. He turned back to me with a questioning look. When I said nothing, disappointment crossed his eyes, and he continued walking. My eyes, glued to the back of his long grey coat, watched him recede. I yearned to follow but couldn't move. I saw Stan meet up with the others, send me a quick backward glance, then merge into the spirited crowd entering the church. My heart felt hollow.

Suddenly, Rudy popped up to peek around the corner. He came running for me. "Hurry, Duffy, this is history, you can't miss this."

If I leave Doc's group, I thought, *I'll lose my job. If I don't join Dr. King, I'll lose my soul.*

Feeling grateful Rudy hadn't given up on me, I raced with him up the steps of Riverside Church. But by the time we entered, the pews inside were so packed, not even standing room remained. We squeezed into a spot on a stone bench in the foyer where we heard Dr. King's voice piped in. His words resonated in my soul as he spoke from his heart, and his themes provoked associations with my own experience.

Dr. King stood firm in his belief that the issues of peace and civil rights are connected, a belief I shared, having been taught by my Unitarian Universalist faith to respect the inter-relatedness of all things. He spoke of how the poverty programs had aroused hope, which I myself felt while working for the South Jamaica community at Freedom Place.

Social progress stalled when the Vietnam War sucked up the nation's resources. Black and White soldiers fighting together in Nam reminded me of Stan and his White war buddy, Pete, who'd watched each other's backs in Korea yet, back home in America, faced strict segregation. *Why is integration so hard for some to accept?* I wondered, as Rudy and I sat side by side in the church just as we had as classmates.

King talked about angry young men, who doubted his path of non-violent protest, and I thought of Clarence, who'd frightened me at Freedom Place, seeming to advocate riots. I better understood that Clarence himself felt frightened by the violence all about—unchecked police abuse and the threat of the draft closing in—and wanted to fight back. Clarence chose to join the war as a Green Beret. I worried that under cover of the American flag, he'd release his anger by inflicting undue harm on innocents.

And the violence mounted daily. King reported a million Vietnamese killed, mostly children. A disgrace so appalling that Rudy had poured dirty dish water on a self-inflicted wound to avoid recruitment into an army where he could be ordered to kill peasant families. While destruction of villages ripped apart families in Vietnam, the conflicts over the war divided families in every state of America.

King's shocking perspective of America as the most violent nation vibrated in booming speakers. *What's happening to my country?* I wondered. *Are we losing our soul?* His words of spiritual truth filled me with life. I felt alive, here with my hero, in the same church, breathing the very same air.

Dr. King called for the world to move beyond the tribes of race and class. He called for nothing less than unconditional love, a force of unity. *Unitarians stand for unity*, I thought. *We follow Rev. Martin Luther King Jr. because he embraces our deepest values of justice and love.*

We believed his words that we could move from discord to a "symphony of brotherhood." My brotherhood poster, I remembered, won an award the year my beloved teacher, Mrs. Rousson, inspired me with her passionate rendition of "God Bless America."

Americans had to choose change and look toward the day "when justice will roll down like waters, and righteousness like a mighty stream." Those closing words King chose from the Bible washed over us in waves, and Rudy and I, arms inter-locked, found our cheeks wet.

On my desk the day after the speech, I found a clipping from the *New York Times*: "Dr. King Proposes Boycott of War." The writer appeared to believe that Negroes opposing the war would appear less patriotic and that Dr. King was speaking for himself. *Really?* Inside the church, three thousand devoted followers; outside, only handfuls of Black nationalists, White war hawks and racist segregationists, and Doc's peculiar picketers.

Another clipping appeared from the *Times*, titled, "Dr. King's Error." The editorial took a view similar to Doc's position that it was better to stay focused on the civil rights movement. They fervently objected that King compared American military methods to that of the Nazis. I wondered what would *they* call mass bombings, burning crops, spraying napalm on villagers?

Confusion rose in me about many things, but on this issue I stood fast. I thought, *Dr. King sees the whole picture. He's taking the high ground, and I will walk the path with him.*

I couldn't wait to march with Martin Luther King Jr! The following Saturday, April 15, he would lead us from Central Park to the United Nations, where he'd speak against the war in Vietnam.

Penny, also excited, met me on Eighth Avenue, where we streamed along with a river of people of all ages and colors. All of us in a high mood, we paraded in the sunshine up to Sheep Meadow in Central Park, where we headed for a San Francisco style "be-in." Penny asked random people where they arrived from. They answered: New Paltz, Rockaway, Stowe, Philadelphia, Cleveland, Cincinnati—as far away as Michigan and Wisconsin.

A White woman from Chicago told us that she and her party had slept overnight on their busses. "Eight hundred teachers like me," she said. "And housewives, grocers, students. We woke up at the bus station, clothes wrinkled, but rarin' to go." I wished that those who suspected that organized rabble-rousers instigated these protests could meet these plain folks.

Another teacher admired my Equal button, the one I'd worn since high school. Penny noticed a SNCC button on a young Black man, and said, "I know it stands for Student *Nonviolent* Coordinating Committee, but your new leader challenges King's non-violence."

He answered in good cheer. "You know, my man Stokely and King don't always see eye to eye about *how* to get our freedom, but I can tell you today they're gonna be up there on the UN stage standing together on opposing this hellish war."

When we got to Sheep Meadow, we were confronted with white wooden police barricades. Penny said, "Look at all the cops! They're expecting hundreds of thousands, Janet. Wouldn't that be amazing?"

I looked among the blue uniforms for Dad, maybe called in for special duty. I hadn't seen him in a month, and thought, *How odd if we find ourselves facing off on opposite sides of the barricade.* I heard a protester call a cop a "pig," a de-humanizing term that made me shudder.

Kids tuned up guitars while we waited for speeches by celebrities, like Tony Randall and Harold Pinter. Someone announced that Peter, Paul and Mary would perform. I loved that group. I'd watched them on TV recently. Mary sang with Harry Belafonte and at the end of the song she kissed him on the cheek. So many viewers called in, outraged, they had to shut the show down.

I smelled marijuana, saw kids with shaggy hair light up. Penny said the passion of the marchers made her high enough. She'd never tried pot because she wanted to stay alert and be useful. I recalled the ominous warning from Mr. Goldfarb, my ninth-grade social studies teacher. To my class full of bookworms, he'd ranted, "Drug pushers who hook kids on drugs destroy them. Drug addiction is a living death." I'd avoided pot until the night in Brooklyn with Don.

Loud cheers. On a high boulder, a bunch of guys were setting a fire. Someone yelled, "We're burning draft cards! Join us—we ain't gonna die to make old war mongers rich!"

"Right on!" Penny shouted. She'd read that the march organizer had stated that in Vietnam, "White Americans are exterminating a whole nation of colored people."

Over the loudspeaker came the thrilling call: "The Reverend Dr. Martin Luther King Jr. has begun to lead us to the United Nations. Time to march!" Announcers with walkie-talkies kept us updated. "Up front, King is flanked by other clergy and civil rights leaders, now linking arms with Dr. Spock and Harry Belafonte, taking our message to the world!"

I wanted to race but shuffled along with the packed crowd for an hour to get to the park exit on Fifty-ninth Street, where we slowed to a standstill. Penny and I grabbed a greasy hot dog and large pretzel before the street vendors sold out.

In the warming sun, we moved quietly along with nuns in habits, White men in suits and a Native American chief in a headdress complete with feathers and beads. Word spread that Pete Seeger, riding on a float with children, sang, "This Land

Is Your Land," and the Native chief looked amused. With a wry smile on his weathered face, he asked, "This land is *your* land?" Everybody who heard laughed. On other floats, girls and boys wearing daffodils held up a colorful sign, "Flower Power." We followed musicians playing a drum, guitar, and flute. The slim Brown boy on the silver flute wore a Hindu cap and danced as he led us cross town to the East River.

I spotted banners with the march logo, "Stop the War in Vietnam," and many others that represented the full religious and political spectrum in America. Penny said, "Yet, we're all united against this immoral war. Remarkable."

A shout from a White man in a crew-cut startled me. From behind the police barricades he yelled, "America, right or wrong!"

Penny retorted, "When America's right I support her, when she's wrong I correct her." A chanting war ensued.

He and his buddies yelled in her face, "Bomb Hanoi. Support our GIs."

Peace marchers countered with, "Support our troops, bring them home!"

"You fucking cowards! You should all be shot."

Penny joined the peace crowd in a nasty chant, "Hey, hey, LBJ, how many kids did you kill today?" I'd worked for LBJ's Great Society, but I got swept up chanting, too. A contingent approached bearing a blue and orange flag, identified themselves as National Liberation Front. *That's Viet Cong*, I thought. *That flag doesn't speak for me.* But I got called "a dirty traitor" by a contingent draped in red, white, and blue.

An older man in US army fatigues screamed at a dark-skinned musician, "Go home to where you came from, scumbag!" Penny and I determined to make it through the unruly crowd to the UN to hear Martin Luther King Jr.

Up ahead we saw the line of marchers sway to one side, as if retracting, and we wondered what was happening. A dazed guy pushing his way against the crowd brushed into us, his denim shirt drenched in red. Alarmed, I asked, "Are you bleeding?" In a choked voice he told us some jerk called him a "Red Commie" and dumped a bucket of red paint on him.

I looked around for cops to stop the violence, then immediately thought better. *Maybe the police on duty would side with the paint throwers against the protesters*, I thought. Faces grew fierce, drums louder, a flute more piercing. I slipped on a wet piece of sidewalk and fell under a forest of legs. The crowd relentlessly surging, I felt a rush of fear. *Will these boots crush me?*

Penny pulled me up. We felt as hungry as ever to hear Martin Luther King's call for peace at the United Nations. Upset by all the aggressive division, I asked myself the question I'd asked many times before, *Why can't people just find a way to get along?*

"Polynesian Girl"

Chapter 12
BLACK IS BEAUTIFUL

I imagined the beautiful dark girl before me a Polynesian Islander, her golden skin and features the legacy of mixed heritages. A kinky black braid snaked down her back to tickle the tender triangle above her buttocks. To match the rich colors of her skin, I merged coils of paint on my palette—from yellow ochre golds to burnt sienna and Van Dyck brown—and brushed them into the body's form sketched on my canvas. Her weight fell solidly on one foot, hips gracefully tilted, while her shoulders sloped in the opposite direction.

"A perfect S-curve," someone said behind me—a youthful voice, not my teacher. I turned to see a young man smiling at me. He wore a wool hat with interesting designs and colors, which I'd noticed many times from a distance—he and I were among the few people our age around the Art Students League. Often on the elevator or in the break room, I'd watched him talk with ease to artists and faculty, throwing his head back in laughter. His clothing intrigued me—he wore a *shawl* on his shoulder, which I'd wanted to ask him about but never did. Now he'd approached me. He lifted a slender arm to draw an "S" in the air, indicating the invisible curve from shoulder to hip often seen in classic Greek statues. *He speaks art language, my language*, I thought, which few people knew. "Sorry to bother you," he said, backing off. I'd been too impressed to say a word.

I found my voice and said, "Oh, no. I'm glad you see the way I see." Break time. I put down my brush, and we left the studio together. On the elevator down I observed the delicate bones of his facial structure, his eyes like almonds and his thin European nose. His skin glowed like the shiny amber in the "Polynesian" model, and under the flat-topped hat, his hair looked African American like hers. Seeing my interest in his hat, he said it was a Hindu hat from the Himalayas.

We entered the little room that served coffee and tea, and sandwiches—if you had the money. He told me his name was Carmen Jones. He said, "I know, everyone says Carmen is a girl's name. But my mama named me after my grandfather from Spain." I thought, *So I was right about his European nose.*

"I'm Janet Duffy," I said. He recognized my name as Irish and laughed, saying the Irish Day Parade had been a blast. "I'm Irish on one side," I said, "and Hungarian on the other."

"Far out," he said. "One of my favorite jazz musicians, Jarrett, is the same mix of Irish-Hungarian." I finally asked why he wore a shawl. Carmen said with a laugh, "It's called a *serape*, a blanket worn by men in Mexico." He wore it to honor his grandfather who'd migrated from Spain to Mexico where an Indian native bore him a child, a girl who grew up to be his mother. Carmen said his mama had moved to Kansas City, Missouri, and married a man, his pa, who was part Black and part American Indian.

I smiled and said, "Quite a mix."

"Yeah, people say I'm like a 'one-person United Nations.'"

United Nations, I thought. Carmen wears a *Hindu hat*. He's into *music*. I asked, "By any chance, did you play a flute at Martin Luther King's march to the UN?" He fell back and said I must be psychic. "No," I said, "I saw you there."

"You remember *me*? Out of the quarter million marchers? Far out!"

———————

The following Tuesday, we again went on break together. "Want some 'cawfee?'" Carmen said, teasing me about my New "Yawk" accent. He'd jumped at the chance to move here when the Art Students League offered him a work/study scholarship. "What I love about New York is the music scene. We have a good scene too in my hometown, Kansas City. Some call it 'Paris on the Plains.' It's where Bird was raised."

"Bird?"

"You know, the legendary Charlie 'Bird' Parker. He changed jazz, invented bebop. He played so freely, like he was flying, he's called 'Bird.' You're not into jazz?"

"I like jazz," I assured him. Rudy had recently lent me his Charles Lloyd album. "I'm listening to *Forest Flower*."

"My favorite album!" Charles Lloyd would play at Town Hall and Carmen had tickets to hear him and his Quartet. "Hardly anyone around here even *heard* of Charles Lloyd."

At the end of the night, I carried my supplies and "Polynesian Girl" to the exit and found Carmen waiting for me. He asked if I was heading west. "I can go east or west," I said. We walked west on 57th Street, famous for top galleries and exhibits, until we hit Broadway. Finding the evening delightful, we turned north to Central Park to walk among the trees beginning to sprout.

Carmen said, "This city is unreal. One minute we're bombarded with noisy traffic, and *bam!* now we're in the woods." Down a path we found a bench, and I set my "Girl" on it. He studied my painting, and noted, "The city lights make the cobalt blue background really vibrate." I observed the old streetlamps and high risers on Eighth Avenue and above them the glorious purple sky. Carmen laughed and said, "Yeah, mind-blowing technicolor. Brought to you by—air pollution."

"Yeah," I said, "things that seem wonderful might not be so good for you." He said he didn't mean to bring me down. I assured him I didn't feel down at all. I asked how he liked the art museums in New York. He said, he'd been meaning to visit the Museum of Modern Art, MOMA, just four blocks down from the League. We made a date to explore it on Saturday.

We surrounded ourselves with colors and light in a room filled with Monet's expansive murals, *Water Lilies*. Moving close, we faced jumbles of free brushstrokes and globs of paint. Stepping back, details came into focus. Carmen said, "Man, I feel like I'm sliding right into the blue pond."

His first day at MOMA, Carmen was eager to see all the masterpieces of European modern art from Cezanne, surrealists, and cubists, to the New York School that included abstract expressionists of the 1950s and Andy Warhol's Pop silkscreens of JFK and Marilyn Monroe. Carmen found one small work by a Black artist, Jacob Lawrence, and we encountered paintings by a woman, Georgia O'Keeffe, making us aware that the vast majority of art in the collection were by White males. Carmen and I agreed, soon it would be our time to be exhibited.

Carmen didn't want to miss "Guernica," Picasso's masterpiece of a little Spanish town bombed by fascists. Picasso's distortions and broken strokes captured the true emotional horror. He created a surreal scene in which the explosions, the women screaming, and horses neighing seemed almost audible. Picasso painted a detached eye at the top of the war scene. I said, "The eye is like a witness saying, 'We can't let this happen again.'"

"But war did happen again," Carmen said. "And again." He, like Rudy and other boys I knew, lived in fear they'd be drafted into the army and would be forced to bomb villages and kill innocents, just like in Guernica. He and I believed that the world needed fewer destroyers and more creators, like us.

Carmen brought his portfolio to the Art Students League the following Tuesday. Inside the black case were his charcoal portraits. The skill, details, and strong expressions impressed me, and I told him so. "You're both a musician *and* a talented artist."

Suddenly a wild-eyed guy rushed to our table, his blonde hair sticking out all over the place. He handed Carmen a print he called "mind-blowing," then turned to me to say, "Hi, I'm Fran," then rushed back to his painting. His spontaneous manner made me like him right away. It struck me how open he was about being homosexual.

"Fran is a trip." Carmen laughed. "He paints far-out abstract stuff, completely free of rules. Definitely different. The more I know him, the more I love him. He's my roommate." His words disheartened me. I thought, *If Fran is homosexual, and Carmen lives with him and loves him, maybe Carmen is not available.* I realized then I'd been hoping he might be more than my friend. Carmen looked at the print from Fran, a reproduction by Romare Bearden, a Black artist.

I said I'd seen Bearden's collages at City College, and Carmen asked if I went to college. I told him this term I was studying at the League and working. He asked my job. I said, "This year I've worked as an assistant to a mural painter, a clerk at a bookstore, in an office, and now a hospital."

"Wow, lots of changes." he said. "Cool about the painting, but I don't see you in an *office*."

"Me neither. I got the job through my boyfriend." Carmen's face fell. I wondered, *Does he feel disappointed that I might not be available?* I said, "But that guy and I broke up." Carmen seemed to be relieved.

I felt relieved, too, especially after the admission that Aviva had recently laid on me. Out of the blue she told me that Don had asked her out and she accepted. And he came on to her. Shocking. A twenty-four-year-old man, going after a fifteen-year-old girl. Aviva had apologized, looking so sad and lost. She said that afterwards she immediately regretted going out with him. Maureen worried I'd be angry with Aviva, but I wasn't. I completely blamed Don. I told Carmen, "The guy cheated on me."

"Bummer," Carmen said. "I relate. In Kansas City, my girlfriend . . ." I thought, *So he is not gay, he is into girls. Good. But is she still in the picture?* He said, "Some other cat turned her head around," and he looked so lonely I wanted to give him a hug.

Fran popped up again, this time to give a ticket to Carmen. "I can't make it to the Town Hall jazz concert this week," he said. "Sorry, man. Maybe you can find somebody else?"

A few days later, Carmen and I claimed our seats early at Town Hall, and looked around at the audience. Carmen said, "Mostly rich White folks. You see more of a mix at the clubs." I told him I'd never been to a jazz concert. He said, "You'll be blown away. Charles Lloyd and his Quartet do free-flow improvisation like no one else." He told me they were touring the world. "Next week, Russia. Last week, in San Francisco, hippies couldn't get enough of them."

I sat on the edge of my chair, eager to hear for myself. Carmen said, "It's important to be present in the moment." He told me he studied Eastern philosophy, like Lloyd and a lot of jazz musicians did. "Before I hear a concert," he said, "I like to prepare myself spiritually," and he sank into meditation.

Carmen opened his eyes. The concert began. I noticed Carmen wagging his head, and I did the same. Sounds hit one ear, then the other. A different experience.

Charles Lloyd played his sax first, then nodded to Keith Jarrett, signaling his turn to improvise. He played piano unlike anyone I'd ever heard. Hands on the keys, he jumped up and down on his piano seat, writhing, grimacing with emotion. He flipped me out when he rolled his head and threw himself around, using his body as an instrument. He stood up, lifted the piano top, and when he plucked the strings, the crowd exploded.

"He's a wild man," Carmen said at intermission, and tossed his head back in laughter. "Only twenty-two, a genius. Can you dig that?"

I did feel blown away. In the catalog I read that Keith Jarrett had a Hungarian mother and Irish father, a heritage that matched mine. I asked Carmen how that could be? He wore an Afro. I looked at the photograph of Jarrett and noticed he did in fact have light skin. "But looking at him on stage," I said, "I assumed he was Black."

Carmen laughed. "Everyone does. The Afro throws people off. Basically, the cat plays jazz like he's Black. Jarrett likes to say he's *working* on being Black. Funny, but, no, he ain't Black."

———

The next day, Friday, Carmen invited me to the opening of the faculty exhibit he'd helped hang. I spotted him, serape draped over his shoulder, standing alone in the gallery. I zoned in on the food table, and gobbled up crackers, chips, and cheese, which served as my supper. Then he showed me around. "Isn't this faculty far out?" he said. "Artists you see in top art magazines and museums right here, man, teaching us." Our teachers had been taught here at the League by famous artists like Georgia O'Keeffe, Hans Hoffman, and Rauschenberg. Carmen said, "New York's the grooviest city in the world!"

Just then he was called up to play his flute. The crowd went silent. He turned to me, "A solo," he said, with a flash of nervousness. But once his lips touched the mouthpiece, he projected confidence. He drew air into his lungs and blew life into his instrument, bending his lean body like a young green reed yielding to the wind.

After his solo, I said, "I like your style. Free-flowing." He invited me to hear more jazz uptown. "Tonight? It's so late."

"Man," he said, "the night's just getting *started*."

———

Carmen and I emerged into the warm night of Harlem from the subway station at 125th Street. Two White cops stared at me; the cops and I were the only White people visible for blocks. Carmen and I walked fast under the streetlights past people dressed up, absorbed in each other or listening to tinny transistor radios.

Carmen asked if I'd been to Harlem before. I said, "Yeah, but my first time at night." I told him about the kids at the Quaker House I'd introduced to an art museum.

"Dig it. Kids know art is fun." Carmen laughed. "You'll dig Olatunji's Center."

"Olatunji!" I'd loved hearing him drum at the World's Fair a couple years before.

"*Drums of Passion*! That record came out when I was ten," Carmen said. "My friends caught Olatunji on the *Ed Sullivan Show*, and we dug him. But his label, Columbia, wouldn't promote his record to the schools because the word 'passion' was 'off color,' like, too sexy for kids." I said I thought that was stupid. "Yeah," Carmen agreed, "especially since the man basically lives on such a high level." He told me Olatunji came from Nigeria, wanted to be a diplomat, and got a scholarship to Morehouse College, established after the Civil War to educate men freed from slavery. Olatunji found out that in Atlanta nobody, not even Black folks, knew a thing about Africa. "He took on a new mission—to teach us pride in our own origins."

At Olatunji's Center for African Culture, I saw an Afro on a beautiful young Black woman with a long neck like Queen Nefertiti, and for the first time saw a poster with the words, "Black Is Beautiful." We found excited children and a crowd made up, Carmen figured, mostly of Harlem locals, church people, and a few White liberal students and professors. He believed that Black middle-class folks could show up and teach their kids their African heritage.

Carmen was invited into the auditorium by musicians he knew, the band that would open for Olatunji. They offered us

Black Woman with Afro

front row seats but said that Olatunji's appearance was not guaranteed. *If* he came out—he didn't always perform. We waited in tense expectation. I saw a curtain on the side part. A man about forty appeared, wearing a hat decorated with African designs. The air quivered with reverential quiet as, confident and commanding, he walked to center stage and scanned our faces with a warm smile. He needed only to place a hand on his drum to cause an eruption of clapping and cheers. This was Olatunji! Carmen's eyes opened wide as if struck with a vision, and he called, "Baba!" Baba, his name of affection.

Radiant, Olatunji began. Every time his hands beat the drum, I felt my own heart beating. Other musicians joined him on stage with their instruments and shook rattles and chanted in African languages. With one last booming strike on the drum, Olatunji and his band went silent. No one moved or even took a breath.

A shout arose, "More!" The crowd clapped and stamped their feet, yelling, "More, Baba, more!" Olatunji graced us with an encore. The beat got faster, people couldn't sit still. I rose, filled with energy and joy, and Carmen got up to dance, too.

At the end, Baba stood still with eyes closed until we became quiet and ready to receive his words. Finally, as if he came from long ago and far away, he spoke. "I am the drum, you are the drum, and we are the drum. The whole world revolves in rhythm, and rhythm is the soul of life, for everything that we do in life is in rhythm."

———

Our spirits high, we floated away from Olatunji's Center. On the rocking D train, Carmen's body swayed back and forth, his long fingers tapping a beat on the pole to the *clickety clack* of the metal wheels on the track. I told him with regret that I had to get off at 59th Street to transfer to Queens.

"It's after midnight," he said. "Too late to go that far. I'm just a few minutes away—you could crash at my place." He added,

"I live with Fran," as if wild Fran made it safe. I felt tempted. I sensed the warm energy beaming off Carmen's sinewy body, and I leaned in, not wanting to part. But I remembered I had agreed to help Doc at the hospital the next morning. "On Saturday?" Carmen asked. I told him I worked at a Black hospital, and we offered free clinics.

"I dig you," Carmen said. "You work in the Black community. Baba tells us to serve our own people. Can I go with you?" We agreed I'd spend the night, and in the morning, we'd go to the hospital together. Laughing, we popped off the train. I found myself for the first time in the neighborhood known as Hell's Kitchen.

His building, a former factory, had been renovated for artists to occupy. At the entrance, Carmen told me not to worry, he'd bunk in with Fran so I could have a bed to myself, if that's what I wanted. I thought, *How cautious, so little pressure.* He opened the door to an enthralling display of huge, chaotic abstract paintings stacked up everywhere. "Fran's work," Carmen said. I saw paint-splattered tables and stools and an old couch, but no other furniture. To keep his promise, Carmen knocked on Fran's door. Fran sang back, "I'm with someone."

Carmen quietly asked if I wanted to see his room. I did. He put down his flute case next to a larger case. My eyes were drawn to the walls where he'd hung his small canvases—figures and portraits painted in shades of brown. I said the dramatic contrasts of light and dark reminded me of Rembrandt. He confirmed he "looked at Rembrandt a lot." I thought, *We share love for peace, beauty, and the arts.*

Inside a salvaged milk crate, he'd lined up books with strange titles like *I-Ching*, *Bhagavad Gita*, and *Egyptian Book of the Dead*. On top of the crate stood a small statue of a man's body with an elephant head. "It's Ganesha, a Hindu deity who removes obstacles. Fran gave it to me and told me if I meditate on the statue my life would change."

"Is it working?"

He looked at me, smiling. "Seems to be." He lit a stick of incense and the sweet fragrance relaxed me. Carmen removed a pile of jazz albums from his bed and said, "You take the bed, I'll sleep on the floor."

I thought, *How carefully he treats me, almost shy.* I felt bad for him, spread out on the cold floor. "There's room to share," I whispered.

He climbed up but hung so close to the edge of the bed that he risked falling off. I leaned over to give him a friendly kiss. He kissed me back. And that started it. Soulful kissing, tender touching, and falling together in easy rhythm until we reached a high point of desire. He asked sweetly if he should use protection—no complaints—but I said there was no need because I protected myself.

In the morning, Carmen showed me to the bathroom in the hall, which contained only a big metal industrial-size sink. No hot water. Splashing my face with cold water, I warmed up remembering our lovely night. New light shone through the translucent window and bounced off the wall. No mirror to apply makeup, but I felt confident in going natural.

Carmen kept his promise of joining me in Queens. "I don't want to be apart from you," he said, looking in my eyes. On his shoulder hung his purple serape, and from his closet he pulled out a peach-colored one and laid it on my shoulder. I admired its design and softness. He said it suited me, and he wanted me to keep it. In our purple and peach serapes, we walked out the door, a couple. Aromas rising from the many ethnic restaurants in Hell's Kitchen tantalized me. Smells of spices from last night's dinners blended in with aromas of fresh-baked rolls and aroused in me a hunger for life's variety more intense than ever before.

Chapter 13
NEW WORLDS

Now I took my turn giving Carmen a taste of my world: Queens. At Interfaith Hospital, he seemed happy to meet Doc. And Rudy and Socrates, who also volunteered to help folks get an exam.

At Freedom Place, I introduced Carmen to Stan, who gave me a scrutinizing look. I thought, *Maybe because I'm wearing no makeup?* He asked about my "shawl." I said it was a gift and nodded to Carmen, wrapped in his own serape. While Carmen acted friendly, Stan remained aloof. He pulled Carmen into the back room, and I thought with a smile, *I hope Stan won't challenge this boyfriend to an arm wrestle.* Carmen emerged looking unscathed and turned on. "Hey," he said, "Stan got funding for a youth program and wants us both to teach a class!"

"Great. What will we teach?"

"Art and music."

Later, over omelets at the Galaxy Diner, I expressed worry that neither one of us had taught before. Carmen said, "Basically, we're both artists. No problem. I'll take the music part." He planned to play the flute.

"Cool. Then what will the *kids* do?"

He asked, "Will they have instruments?" I didn't think so. Could he teach without them? He drummed on the table with his knife and fork. "Olatunji told us, *rhythm is everything.* You can drum on anything." He banged louder. "One element of music is volume!"

I laughed. "And some colors scream loud!"

"Yes, colors have sounds and sounds have color," he said, talking about the theories of Kandinsky, the mystical abstract painter and musician. I told him how Bill always painted to music, saying it moved his soul.

"Soul is what jazz is all about." Carmen described soul as invisible yet as solid and unchanging as a rock. "Like in Lloyd's Quartet, the bass is the soul. It keeps a constant beat, so the saxophonist is free to improvise, to roam all over the place, up and down, around the town. The beat is the ground the sax comes home to."

"Beautiful," I said. The consistency and variation he heard in music, I saw in art, especially the designs on the friezes of ancient Greek temples. Now Carmen asked me what the kids would do, and I thought out loud: "Perhaps create repeating patterns with paper cut-outs, alternating shapes that remain the same with shapes that change. Create a unified design where everything is interconnected."

"Everything is everything," he stated, making me crack up. He said he heard that line whenever he visited his mentor, a jazz musician into Eastern spirituality.

I was eager for him to meet Maureen. We walked next door and found her listening to the Blues Project and petting Felicia. She treated Carmen warmly, and he looked around our one room. I told him the deal with our parents. He nodded but seemed more interested in the long horizontal canvass I'd painted about a year before, all in blues, of infinity signs, circles and spirals, that evoked waves and galaxies. He commented on the abstract, free brush strokes. I said, "I'd been looking at van Gogh. And Jackson Pollock."

He said, "Looks like an eye in the center, like in 'Guernica.' All seeing, all knowing."

Maureen interrupted to tell me news about the guy, about thirty, who lived in the studio next to ours. He'd knocked on the door, told her he planned to be away for a month, and asked if we would water his plants. "In exchange," she said, "if we need extra room to relax, it's okay with him to use his place!" She held up his shiny key.

———————

Carmen and I wasted no time checking out the new space. "Wow," he said when we entered and saw the giant bed filling the room, surrounded by potted plants of all kinds—tough cactus, delicate orchids, and large rubber plants. Asparagus ferns and spider plants cascading from hanging baskets, crawling toward the sun, covered the picture window.

"I feel like I'm in a jungle," I said. We smelled something sweet and stuck our noses into cones of small purple flowers emanating intoxicating perfume.

"Just breathing in this place is getting me high." Carmen laughed. He found the guy's record collection and lit up like a child loose in a candy store. He delighted in the luxuries in the bathroom: fresh towels, a tub, and hot water. He asked, "Would it break the rules to bathe in the tub?"

"The guy said we could *relax*," I said, laughing. I took off my clothes, took a steamy shower, and emerged wrapped in a fluffy burgundy bath towel. Carmen had lined up some groovy albums. He took the towel off me to take his turn. Listening to him running the bath and humming, I dove onto the spacious bed, and when he came out, I stretched out like a cat and asked, "Is it breaking the rules to lie down here?"

He lay down beside me. In the soft afternoon light filtering in from the window through the plants, he stroked my nude body. He said, "If I were the painter and you were the model, I'd start with an azure blue glaze for the irises of your eyes. I would lay in undertones with earth green and pale yellow and paint your sweet, creamy skin with ivory white. I'd brush alizarin pinks into your cheeks, lips, and nipples."

In kind, as my finger followed the slim lines of his body, I said, "If I were the painter and you were the model, I'd squeeze out all my tubes onto my palette, mix the color of caramel candy, and spread it on my canvas with my tongue." I licked his ear and, giggling, we rolled around on the fluffy comforter.

"You're some chick. You're music to my ears." He dropped Jefferson Airplane's *Surrealistic Pillow* on the stereo. "I've always wanted somebody like you to love." Riding on the rippling rhythms and pounding voice of Grace Slick, we took off.

———

Awakening on Sunday morning after fifteen hours in bed, Carmen and I paraded in our colorful serapes down to Hollis to meet Bill. When he opened his door, I exclaimed, "You lost weight!" I hugged him saying I could now get my arms around his waist but fell short.

He joked that I had short arms. Carmen admired Bill's huge, still unfinished, Fire Island painting, and said, "I dig your work, man."

Bill wanted me to guess how many pounds he'd lost, and I said a hundred. "Come on. Thirty pounds! I lost weight, Duffy, because the doctor ordered me to. I was sick." I said I was sorry that I hadn't known. The last time we'd seen each other was in March. Bill said, "Yes, the day you brought Natasha."

"Yeah, the old-fashioned girl."

"Well, since then," Bill said, "I got serious about making changes for the better. I had to get rid of things weighing me down." Things weren't going good with his girlfriend, Gloria, so he'd moved in with his parents during his recovery. Carmen commented on a charcoal in progress on the easel. I said the model reminded me of Natasha. "It *is* Natasha," Bill said. My mouth hung open. "She'll be posing again today after school. It's for her I got my body in shape."

196

Carmen noticed my stupefaction. When we walked out, he asked, "What's up?"

"Natasha is one of my little sister's sixteen-year-old friends. I can't believe she's modeling for Bill! She was such a *prude*." I started to say, "Everything is—

"Everything," Carmen filled in.

"True. But for my life, it's like, 'Everything is . . . subject to change without notice.'"

———

Carmen returned to Hell's Kitchen, and over the week I found comfort in my routines at home and at my hospital job. On Friday evening, the beginning of a warm Memorial Day weekend, we met on Eighth Street and, wearing our serapes, strolled to the East Village, where Carmen had a friend named Marie.

We hit St. Marks Place where I spotted the Dom, the club where I'd danced with Don on a snowy winter night. Carmen pointed to the St. Marks Church and said he'd heard "Howl" there.

"'Howl'?"

"The poem by Allen Ginsberg. He read it himself."

We continued toward the East River, territory new to me, past Second Avenue and First Avenue to a park. The sign read "Avenue A." Carmen said, "We're in Alphabet City. Avenues A, B, C—they're cool. But forget about Avenue D, known as the Gaza Strip." His comparing it to the endless war in the Middle East made me think, *It must be really scary.*

We stopped only a block short of Avenue D, at Avenue C and Third Street. We climbed up a stone stoop where people were hanging out. On the first floor, Carmen knocked on a door and called out, "Hey, Marie. It's me." I heard metal click and clang as she unlocked, unbolted, and unchained the door. *Wow, a lot of security*, I thought. Marie, a fair-skinned woman with not a smudge of makeup, finally appeared, and Carmen introduced me.

He told Marie that he'd "sent a message," and asked if she'd received it. I wondered what kind of message. Marie said, "Sure. I sent my answer: Of course, you can bring Janet." She turned to smile at me with kind green eyes and invited us in. She'd draped sheets in doorjambs to separate rooms. Her dark place felt like a cave.

I asked about the "messages." Carmen said that they practiced mental telepathy. Fascinating. I'd been interested in ESP since sixth grade when I first experienced the Ouija board. Marie ran her fingers through her dull brown hair and said, "My Methodist Mammie and Poppy say telepathy is devil's talk."

"Mammie and Poppy?"

"That's what we call grandparents out in Wichita."

"Kansas?"

"Yes." She laughed. "Like, 'Toto, we ain't in Kansas no more.'" We all laughed. I told them my grandparents were Catholic, and that the medieval Church had burned women healers, who they feared were witches ruled by the Devil.

"Such ignorant hatred," Marie said. "Well, this weekend, we're gonna get away from hate and celebrate love." She told us about the love-in to be held the next day at Tompkins Square Park, the park we'd passed through. Excited to go, I wanted to call my sister to invite her, but Marie had no phone. I smiled. *No wonder she experiments with telepathy.*

Carmen said Marie was an astrologer. She held her hands over me to sense my "aura," whatever that was, and said it was purple, which indicates "spirituality." I knew nothing about astrology, but from horoscopes in the newspaper, I knew my sign, Pisces. She asked, "Do you relate to the Pisces symbol—two fish, swimming in opposite directions?"

"Boy, do I relate," I said. "I often feel conflicting impulses." She told me that "Pisces people" usually love water and are artistic. I laughed and said, "I do love rivers, lakes, and oceans. And art. I met Carmen at art school."

Carmen told me his sign: Libra with Scorpio rising. He said when Marie had delved deeper by doing his full natal chart, he'd been blown away. Marie shared, "In a nutshell, Carmen is affectionate and sensuous; he loves philosophy; and to manage tension, he meditates." It sounded accurate—I'd discovered those traits in him myself. "He's quite a charmer," Marie said. "A pied piper."

"Pied piper," I repeated. "Funny, he was playing his flute the first time I saw him, and I followed him all across the city."

She laughed. "You two, both in the arts, are a good match."

I needed the bathroom, and Marie showed me a closet. *Strange to find the toilet in a tiny closet*, I thought.

———

Carmen said, "Come on, babe, let's go out." He and Marie wanted to show me around the East Village. On the stoop a little white dog yapped at me, but got pulled back by two short old people, who Marie told me lived on the first floor and came from the Ukraine, a country that bordered Hungary. I admired the woman's colorful scarf from the region, and thought, *A good mix of people populated the neighborhood, so different from the all-White neighborhood of my childhood.* Here a variety of ethnicities—Jewish people and Gentiles, Black people, Puerto Ricans, and a sprinkle of White folks—seemed to live in "peaceful co-existence."

I looked up at the tenement buildings as we walked. The sun had long sunk, but heat radiated in the streets. From open windows, a cacophonous blend of festive music in different languages poured into the night air. We passed women busting out of tight clothes, kicking their bare legs to a Latin beat. "PRs use the streets like an extra room of their flats," Marie said, laughing.

"It's bursting with life here," I said. I finally found a pay phone that worked and called Maureen to invite her to the love-in the next day.

As Carmen, Marie, and I circled the block dodging panhandlers, a flashy car with darkened windows, painted with bright designs, sailed by going the opposite direction. A small gold statue of a naked woman adorned the hood, like figure heads placed on prows of ships to placate the sea gods. I wondered out loud which gods the drivers worshipped.

Marie answered my question: "Their god is Money." She called the cars "pimp mobiles." I saw them as devilish sharks swimming against the innocent currents of the neighborhood. Marie said I looked disturbed, and I was. *But good or bad*, I thought, *like Thoreau, I want to learn everything about the world.*

Marie invited Carmen and me to stay for the love-in the next day and a picnic on Memorial Day. "All in Tompkins Square Park," she said. "Should be fun."

———————

First up on Saturday morning, I tiptoed to the front room, found Marie stretching on a mattress on the floor, and searched the small refrigerator and yellow cupboards for something to eat. I'd take orange juice, cereal, anything.

Marie apologized, and turned up a few dry crackers. I ate a few with water and asked where I could wash my hair. In the kitchen where we sat, she cleared off clutter from a wide surface— actually a lid, which she lifted, revealing a porcelain bathtub. I turned the faucet to hot but got only cold water, getting why this place was called a "cold water flat." Feeling exposed in the middle of the kitchen, I removed my clothes and washed my hair and underpants with a scrap of soap—and took my quickest bath ever.

When my bare feet hit the splintered wood floor, Marie wrapped me in a worn grey towel. My panties still wet from washing, I pulled on my corduroys over bare buttocks. Marie dressed me for the love-in: a row of beads around my neck and ribbons in my damp curls.

My stomach growled for food. I woke Carmen, and the three of us headed out to the closest breakfast place, a dingy store-front that served fried eggs too dry and coffee too watery. The short-order cook threw in some home fries so greasy I barely got them down. The sound of bongo drums called us to boogie in Tompkins Square Park, already filling up with people: Ukrainians walking dogs, long-haired students wearing CCNY and NYU T-shirts, old Italian men knocking bocce balls together, and Puerto Rican mothers laying blankets on the lawn as their children ran in circles around trees. Carmen ran off to join the drummers.

I spotted Ruthie, her hair shining like cinnamon in the sun. I dashed up to hug her and Maureen and the other friend she brought, Rosita, a tall Black girl whose portrait I'd painted for a school art display. She said she loved my "cool beads." And Maureen liked me with my hair down. She asked for Carmen. I said, "Listen to the drums. The flute—that's him playing."

Marie brought us four Queens girls to a table with artists from the Jade Companions of the Flower Dance. "Lots of artists in the neighborhood," she said, "because they can afford the rent down here."

Ruth said, "Yes, the East Village is the *happening* scene. Janet, you're always right in the thick of things." We looked around at the growing crowd. Tall skinny men with tattoos all over their arms, short mamas with hoop earrings and scarves resembling fortune tellers, White boys in bright clothes so mismatched they looked like clowns. The spiked hair on a trio of Black guys appeared like shiny halos. A burly man with arm bands was training a dog as big as a pony.

Rosita said, "This love-in feels like a circus."

The drumming intensified. Following the unmistakable staccato sound of Carmen's flute, the girls and I found him playing with bongo drummers, circled by women with bare midriffs dancing with abandon. We too swayed to the beat. I felt my corduroy pants rubbing against my bare buttocks. The drummers launched a call and response, and Rosita joined in the gleeful shouts. I breathed in a cloud of pot and coughed. Maureen asked if I was sick. I admitted I had a little cough but kept dancing.

A piercing noise blasted from big black speakers, and we jumped to cover our ears. Carmen joined us and said it was feedback. The music stopped. Marie delivered good news that another band would set up better equipment. "The rumor is that the Grateful Dead is gonna play later, for free."

While we waited, excited, for the concert, a stringy-haired young man in a long robe shot onto the stage. No microphone set up, he shouted lines out, "'I saw the best minds of my generation destroyed by madness, . . .'"

"Oh, that's straight from 'Howl,'" Carmen said. Maureen knew "Howl," a poem that Allen Ginsberg, a beat poet with a full beard, had written about ten years before. Carmen said, "This clean-shaven guy ain't Ginsberg." He laughed. Nonetheless, the words sounded so powerful I strained to catch more: "Cold-water flats . . . poverty . . . tenement roofs, contemplating jazz . . . telepathy." I felt stunned.

I said to Carmen, "It's bizarre. Ginsberg described details of a life ten years ago that I'm living now." Carmen asked for specifics. "Things personal to me," I said, "Like the line about 'CCNY lecturers . . . expelled.' It echoes my self-expulsion from CCNY. How about the line, 'forget your underwear we're free'? That freaks me out the most—I left my panties off today, and I feel free!"

Carmen said, "You're not wearing panties?"

Chapter 14
CLASH

The rest of the Memorial Day holiday did not turn out as expected. My cough grew worse. On Wednesday morning, I dragged myself to a phone booth to call Maureen and Interfaith Hospital to relay that I was sick, then conked out at Marie's. Late Thursday afternoon, I managed to get home to Queens to rest. I couldn't wait to tell Maureen the unimaginable things I'd witnessed in the park.

She wasn't home, so I looked for her at Mom's. Dad startled me by answering the door. He grabbed both my hands and twisted my forearms up.

"Dad! What are you doing?"

"Looking for tracks."

I didn't even know what "tracks" meant. He told me, "Needle marks." According to him, the East Village—the 9th Precinct—was "a pit of heroin traffic," one of the toughest places in the city.

Oh my God, he thinks I left home to shoot up. "You don't know me," I said and tried to pull my arms back. He said the city is full of creeps lying in wait to hook stupid girls. "I'm not stupid," I said. He told me sometimes pimps drug girls without their knowing. "Let me go! You know nothing about me." I got into a coughing fit, and he finally released my arms.

Tompkins Sq. Park, Memorial Day, 1967

"Look at you. You're sick." It sounded like an accusation.

I said, "I just want to find Maureen." He opened the door and I plopped down in a chair, coughing.

His tone switched back to a growl. "You're thin as a rail. You're not taking care of yourself." I shook my head and said that I took care of myself as best I could. I slumped forward, coughing, holding my hand to my mouth. "No, you don't," he said. "Look at your shoes."

"*Shoes?* What's your obsession with my goddamn shoes?" I heard the toilet flush. I turned, hoping to see Maureen, but Mom appeared. Her face showed relief at seeing me. I smelled her sweet scent as she hugged me. I asked, "Why aren't you at work?"

"I left early. Let's sit." She pointed to the coffee table where *Newsday*, the Long Island daily, lay open to an article about Memorial Day with a photograph of young people linking arms. One of the people looked like . . . me! "Don't tell me you haven't seen this?" Mom said in her nervous way. "They report that protesters were singing Hare Krishna." She faced me squarely. "Janet, did you join a cult?"

Another ridiculous question, I thought, weary. "No, Mother, I am not in a cult. Where's Maureen?"

Mom said, "Why? You don't care where she is when you take off for days and leave her all by herself." That hurt. Mom told me Maureen preferred to stay with Aviva's family. Zap—a different kind of hurt, mixed with guilt. I coughed until my eyes teared. "Oh, you sound terrible," Mom said, looking worried.

Dad said quietly, "How about you stay for dinner and afterwards we take you to the doctor?"

———————

In the backseat of Dad's car, I felt safe enough to nap while my parents sat together up front, reminding me of the times they took me to the family doctor when I was a child. We rang a bell, and a woman with a pinched faced answered, wearing no white jacket or stethoscope. Dad handed her the copy of Long Island *Newsday*. Why? I caught on that this woman would examine not my chest, but my head. The plaque on her office wall confirmed she was a head shrinker. Dad had been right to call me stupid— stupid to trust my parents.

The psychiatrist, with hair rolled in the style of the 1940s, took me into her cramped consultation room where we sat opposite each other. She said, "Your parents are concerned about you."

"When did that happen? I musta missed it," I said, coughing, heart thumping.

"They think you need therapy."

"*They* need therapy," I said, shaking. "They can't even decide if they want to be married." She held up the photo of me in *Newsday* and asked where it was taken. I said, "At the Tombs."

"The Tombs?"

"The place where cops were throwing innocent people."

Her crooked smile revealed that she thought I sounded irrational. She asked, "What were you doing at the Tombs?"

Everything that happened rushed into my head, and I spilled it out. Memorial Day began as we'd planned. Carmen, Marie, and I strolled over to Tompkins Square Park, where we found families from the neighborhood as well as hippies and tourists spread out on picnic blankets listening to the usual Puerto Ricans playing bongos. I said, "I was with my friends in the park, having fun. Out of nowhere, I saw police pull up in vans. Cops arrested people randomly for no good reason."

"No good reason?" The shrink said as she cocked her head. I sat back, coughing. She showed me an article in the *New York Times*. Looking concerned, she said many people were hurt and arrested. "Janet, were you clashing with police?"

"No."

She peeked over the rim of her cat-eyeglasses. "Did you call police 'fascists?'"

"No. I'm telling you, I was sitting peacefully in the sun, with friends, little kids, old people, when we suddenly heard sirens and vans screech up. Police charged out like we were criminals. They wore riot gear—helmets, face guards, bullet proof vests, shields, guns. It didn't seem like America; more like Nazi Germany."

"So, you do think they're fascists."

I asked her, "What would you think if you saw cops in shields break up a picnic, swing clubs at unarmed people, handcuff them, and throw them in paddy wagons?" I told her my friends and I felt so helpless. We'd just witnessed an injustice and felt we had to do something. Word rippled out that the arrested people were being taken downtown to the Tombs, which sounded scary. All we could think to do was join the crowd and walk miles downtown.

The shrink asked, "What did you expect to do?"

"Talk to the judge, speak up for the people who got wrongly arrested."

Her narrow grey eyes glanced sideways at the photo in *Newsday*. "So this is you, protesting police action."

I laughed. "Yes. I just told you I'd walked miles to protest."

With her nose held high, she asked, "Would you say that your protesting against the police has anything to do with rebellion against your father, a police officer?"

"No," I said. I hadn't been thinking of my father, but about the third-grade schoolteacher with flowers in her hair who'd been taken away from a picnic in a paddy wagon.

"You just wanted to set the record straight," the psychiatrist said with gobs of sarcasm. I nodded, tired. She stated accusingly, "You linked arms. Were you chanting Hare Krishna?" I thought, *Is that a crime?*

I said, "Someone started the Hare Krishna chant."

I had no part in Hare Krishna. I'd avoided the followers who popped up in inappropriate places and were called "freaks." But I'd learned about their Hindu mantra. *Hare* is the divine feminine, and *Krishna*, the one infinite source. They were chanting,

"Lord, please engage us in loving service." I thought, *Does this shrink have any clue about the irony of her condemnation?*

I said, "To keep our spirits up, a few of us spontaneously joined arms and we swayed as we sang, 'We Shall Overcome.' That's what happened, that's all. If my parents think I'm in a cult ..." I stopped to cough.

"Well, what is one to think? You locked arms with longhaired hippies, and you were draped in an Oriental robe."

"Not Oriental, Spanish," I corrected her. "Not a robe, a serape. From my boyfriend Carmen, to show his love."

She sucked in her breath, scratched her nose, and fell back into her stuffed armchair. Eyes squinting, she said, "Your parents told me you'd been a very studious and well-behaved young girl. They struggle to understand how you changed." It looked to me like she was struggling to fake some compassion. She then showed off book knowledge as she explained that adolescents have not yet developed the pre-frontal part of the brain and often act on impulse. Sometimes they rebel against authority or grow angry at parents who divorce. "I ask you again to consider," she said, "are you trying to punish your father by conducting yourself improperly, by sleeping with a boy, a Negro boy?"

I jumped up. Trembling with anger, I said, "Who are you to tell me what to do with my own body?" I blasted out a cough and pushed through the door.

———

Dad drove, shoulders resolute. He broke the silence to scold me in the back seat. "You wouldn't even *talk* to the doctor?"

"I talked a lot! But she didn't listen. Didn't even try to understand. She judged."

"She charges fifty bucks an hour!" I reminded him that a psychiatrist was his idea, not mine. He turned away from the wheel to scowl at me.

Mom yelled, "Eddy, watch the road!"

Red in the face, he said, "Who's the son of a bitch you spend weekends with?" Mom cautioned him to calm down.

"His name is Carmen. He's my boyfriend." I said, "We love each other. He's very talented and spiritual."

"Spiritual! You're so damn gullible." He twisted his head, almost snarling. "Do you think he cares about you? All he wants is to get into your pants!"

"That's how *you* think," I yelled.

He swung his hand to swat me, but Mom caught his hand. A car honked.

"Watch the road, Eddy!"

———————

Dad pulled up to our building, I dashed upstairs, and once inside my apartment, breathing hard, I quickly turned around to double lock the door. "What are you doing?" Maureen asked, making me jump. "What are you scared of?" I coughed. "What's the matter with you?"

I collapsed on the couch and said, "I don't feel safe. Dad is being violent." She sat next to me to listen. "He hates that I have a Black boyfriend. He never even met him. I guess he's not as free from the 'poison of prejudice' as he thought."

I exploded in a coughing fit that made Maureen worry I had that "bark" back again.

"I know," I said, "I'm physically sick, and our parents took me to a psychiatrist. Dad is out of control. If Mom didn't stop him, he would have bashed me." My mind reeled back to a couple years before, Dad slamming all three of us hard across the face to prove he was in control. I told Maureen I felt afraid he might come after me that evening. Her eyes widened. "Hey, don't you worry, Mutzie, you're fine. It's *me* he's after." The coughing left me nauseated. I said, "I'm too sick to go back to the city. I just want to crawl under the covers, but I don't feel safe here."

She suggested an emergency room. I thought I'd try Doc's hospital. She asked if it cared only for Black patients. I told her, "No, it's just that most White people wouldn't think of going to a Black-run hospital." I packed a paper bag with a few pairs of underpants, a book, and my journal, and walked the fifteen minutes to Interfaith.

The night nurse at the desk observed me. One deep barking cough got her to hit the switchboard. A Polish intern took me for an examination and determined I had a fever and bronchial pneumonia. He administered a shot and led me to a private room—quiet, clean, and safe.

I slept that night and most of the next day, and then sat up to write in my journal. A nurse informed me I had visitors—my parents. I immediately reacted by tensing up. But calmed myself remembering how I'd once been a beloved child.

They entered my room looking flustered. Mom fixed her startled eyes on Black nurses in starched white uniforms as they dispersed medicines and buzzed in the hall. She said, "Janet, we didn't realize you were so sick." I thought, *did you not hear my cough?* Mom continued, "We would have driven you to a hospital."

"This is a hospital."

Dad said, "So this is where you work?"

I felt relieved when Dr. Matthew pulled them out of the room. When they returned, they looked at me funny. I asked what Doc had told them.

"You're very sick, but will recover soon," Mom said, trying to sound cheerful but her wavering voice gave away her doubts. Dad studied me with troubled eyes. I hoped their new concern arose out of Doc giving them hell for ignoring my cough. Mom saw my journal. I read to them my latest entry:

I am struggling through a forest of reactions to reach the center . . . the center as clear as the reflection of the sun in a wood's pond. I want to be no other person than the Me that I am. The awareness of this Me is all that there is.

Mom admired my words, but Dad rightly understood it as a "declaration of independence." He sat by my bed, swiping his hands on his pants as if ants were crawling up his legs. Then he stood and shifted his weight from one foot to the other while his face shifted expressions from discomfort to troubled. Feet spread wide, he stuck his chin out as if ready to argue, then gave up. He moved to the door and looked up and down the hall.

Jon, the Jamaican orderly, popped in with my dinner tray. I greeted him warmly as he propped me up to eat. He smiled and said, "How you doin' today, Duffy? Happy your parents here?" Mom sat carefully watching him until he left. I told Mom that the night before, Jon and I talked and laughed about life in Jamaica (our town) and Jamaica (his island). Before he left, he looked at me with curious eyes, studying my face. His voice caught in his throat. He finally said, "You is a angel."

Mom said, "He probably never saw a White girl so close up before." Then she added, like she had to convince herself, "The doctor and the staff seem competent. It seems like a good hospital."

"I know," I said.

"Janet, you'll be all right. Your father and I have to go away for a week." My mouth fell open. Dad re-entered my room. I asked if they had a problem. She said they had a vacation booked in Bermuda.

I stared at them, speechless.

"We can't cancel it." I kept silent. Flustered, Mom explained that she and my father needed private time alone to relax in the sun. "So we can, you know, patch things up." She tossed him a look of affection, which he didn't catch. She said, "We hope to remarry."

Dad challenged me, "Any objections to that?" I had objected in the fall to living with him as a family after the divorce. Now I had zero objections. If they were to go off again to chase their pipe dream, to try to "patch up" their hopeless marriage, I just wanted them to go quickly. I felt my ribs tighten like armor to guard my heart. I stared straight ahead of me as if they didn't exist.

They waited, but I wouldn't speak. I shut my eyes. I felt Mom kiss my forehead and heard her say, "I love you." I listened to their footsteps recede down the corridor and the ding of the elevator bell. My heart felt like a stick of driftwood, but the little girl inside still wished she could float down the hall and go home with them.

Yes, once upon a time I believed I was a beloved child. If they loved me, would they leave me sick and alone? Had I killed their love by pushing Mom away when she asked my advice, by repelling Dad when he needed forgiveness?

I heard Jon lift the metal cover on my food tray, and I opened my eyes. He said, "Duffy, you okay? You hardly ate a bite." I felt too worthless to eat. "And why tears in your blue eyes?" I hardly realized I was crying. I slowly slid like a glacier into a stiff position flat on my back.

———

During the night, I tossed, and my feelings flipped from frozen to fury. Alone all the next day, in a room with no window, outrage played tug-of-war with sadness in my heart. Maureen popped up in the doorway, and I cheered up and propped myself up. Carmen came with her. He said he'd phoned my sister, and she told him about my hospitalization. "Babe, I flipped out."

Stan arrived, surprising me and setting off a cough. He nodded at Maureen and Carmen. He told me Doc had informed him. "Is he treating you well?" I nodded with a smile. Stan handed me a note from Rudy. "He couldn't visit. He's in class, a college boy now." I smiled. Stan pulled out the clip from *Newsday* with the photo of me protesting. "What's up with this?" I waved the paper away and held my hand to my throat—I couldn't talk.

Carmen said, "I'll fill you in, man." He told Stan that the photographer focused on Hare Krishna while the real story was the outrageous police bust. "Damn right, we protested that." I remembered guards had finally allowed us upstairs to the courtroom but stuck us high up in the peanut gallery. "We burned to give our side of the story," Carmen said. "At last, the judge called in one of the arrested people."

"A beautiful woman in a long skirt, flowers in her long blond hair," I said.

"Babe, save your voice." He went on. "The judge asked her occupation. She told him, 'Elementary school teacher.' Laughter in the courtroom. Dig it. The judge shook his head and, zap, he let her go. We scored."

Stan said, "I heard about it, an announcement on the radio. An apology for 'excessive force,' issued from the mayor himself."

I said, "The 'Knight in Shining Armor' rides again."

Stan smiled at my reference to Mayor Lindsay saving Doc from eviction. He turned serious and asked, "Have your parents come to visit?" My stomach muscles tightened. I said yes, but that they had to go away. His brows furrowed. Maureen told him their plans. Stan said with anger, "Their daughter is in the hospital and they went on *vacation*?"

I broke out into a coughing fit. The nurse entered to announce the end of visiting hour. Carmen sat on the edge of my bed and held my hand. "Babe, I hate seeing you with the blues. I get that you feel angry. To get well, you gotta let it go. Rise to a higher vibration." He told me to take long deep breaths, which I did and felt a bit better. He said he'd teach me to meditate and promised he'd come out from the city again the next day.

Maureen told him, "Look, if you want to stay over, you can use that apartment next door." Carmen's face brightened. He said, "Cool. And babe, guess what?" He told me about a vacant pad in Marie's building. "Maybe you and I could rent it."

"Sounds good," I said.

Stan frowned, straightened his back, and addressed Carmen. "I have to tell you about this young woman you're holding. You need to understand what you have here." His voice broke up as he said, "She is a jewel of youth."

I felt astonished. No one—Stan, or anyone else—had ever said such a beautiful thing to me or about me. Carmen said to Stan, "I know man. Don't worry, I'll take care of my chick."

And he did. Carmen stayed in the apartment next door to ours for a week and visited me every day until Doc released me. I thanked Doc but told him I had to leave my job at Interfaith.

Chapter 15
RUNAWAY

At the mouth of the incinerator, I held an armful of childhood drawings, pink diaries, and prize report cards and I
spoke to them: "I'll miss you, but I have no home to keep you
in anymore."

But I couldn't dump them. I turned back to my apartment
hanging onto my treasures. Carmen said it would help if I med-
itated, like he'd taught me in the hospital. I closed my eyes and
sank deep, swallowed up in silence. Coming back to ordinary
reality, I heard Carmen say, "Babe, you were, like, in a trance."

I felt my eyes wet and wiped them. I said, "It's hard."

"Right. To be free, you gotta let go."

I gathered my stuff again, marched through the hall, and
did it! The belch of the incinerator churned up emotions, and I
howled with regret. I stood steely still until the gobbling noise
stopped, signaling the fire had fully ingested the remnants of
my past, and a wave of peace washed over me. I felt lighter, and
yes, freer.

Carmen hugged me. He turned on the radio and a new Beatles
song was playing: "She's Leaving Home." Listening, I felt less
alone and said, "It's weird. It's like these songs pop up at the exact
moment I'm living through the stuff myself."

Carmen said, "That's *synchronicity*, babe. A sign you're on the right track."

I remembered my parents—due back from Bermuda soon. My breathing became shallow, my sense of peace fled, and a blaze of rage shook my body. *They'd abandoned me.* I resolved that when they came back, they would find me gone.

Maureen came home from school and cried when she saw my packed bags. "Janet, I understand how you feel. I want to leave home too."

My heart ripped. But I felt compelled to go. "Mutzie, don't worry. Mom and Dad will be back—you're still a child—they have to take care of you."

———

Carmen picked up a couple suitcases jam packed with my remaining stuff—clothes, books, drawings, and a few of my paintings. I carried my paint box and easel, and we headed by subway to Marie's. She kindly let me deposit my stuff behind her pile of dirty laundry until the next day when Carmen and I would claim the vacant pad upstairs for ourselves. This evening we'd go out to a club—Slugs'. We'd celebrate my emancipation!

Marie took me shopping on the north side of Tompkins Square Park for a special accessory to wear. But at a shop window, my eye was drawn to a long sheath with a pattern of black and white triangles on a burnt orange background. Marie said it was batik, hand painted in Indonesia. I hesitated, not having purchased any clothes in a year, but she pulled me into the store, saying, "You can at least try it on."

I pulled the sheath over my head, the silk lining whispering softly as it slipped over my body down to my feet. I saw in the mirror—a perfect fit. "Beautiful," Marie said.

Beauty is what I needed to start my new life. The dress cost a good chunk of my small savings. But I had to have it. The artful, sensuous sheath represented my newfound identity.

Back at Marie's, Carmen said, "I'm excited. It's Monday."

"So?"

"On Mondays Sun Ra plays at Slugs'. We'll see him tonight. He's far out!" Carmen held up *The Egyptian Book of the Dead*, a book Sun Ra recommends to followers. I looked through it, full of translations of hieroglyphics from the pyramids, like those I'd seen on mummies at the Metropolitan Museum of Art, and in history books Penny had shown me about the Egyptian king, Akhenaten, a sun worshipper.

"Glad you're digging this, babe." He pointed to a picture of Ra, the sun god, whose name Sun Ra claimed. He said, "Ra gathers the world together." He read a passage: "'Having sprung from formless water, he takes his shape in fire. . . . And for as long as the sun is singing, may the strings of my soul hum like a lyre.'"

I said, "You must love all the music metaphors."

Carmen told me it was all about understanding your life. He pointed out Maat, the goddess of truth and justice. She weighs your heart at the time of death. If the scale balances, you led a good life and can pass into the afterlife.

I said, "It's cool that Egyptians worshipped goddesses as well as gods."

"Dig it, this is ancient wisdom from Africa. Sun Ra encourages Blacks in America to take pride in our African spirituality and history."

"Like Olatunji does," I said.

"Exactly." Carmen said we needed to rest and prepare for Sun Ra, because he played into the night. He got ready to meditate, and I asked him to teach me to go deeper. He said, "Okay. Start by saying a prayer." I didn't know any prayers. He said, "Oh. Just talk to God."

"What do you mean by God?"

He said, "Whatever you believe. Names don't matter." I told him I thought of God as nature, the life force. He said, "Perfect.

In Egypt they called the life force, 'ka.' Connect to it." I asked how to do that. "Babe, you gotta get outta your mind."

"That sounds scary."

"Okay, let's go step by step. What are you thinking right now?" I said I couldn't wait to see Sun Ra. He said, "Stop thinking of the future." Thoughts of my old apartment came up. He said, "Think of right now." He found a candle and lit it. "Focus your mind on the flame, a symbol of the sun. Become aware of your breath. Your breath will take you to something bigger than you, the real you, where we are all connected." *Everything is everything*, I thought. Carmen said, "Feel connection to the One that endures, that is all knowledge, bliss, and love."

———————

After dark, leaving panties and bra off, I slid my bare body into the silky Indonesian sheath, seeing the black and white triangles in the design as pyramids. I put on dangling earrings and colored my lips with bright lipstick to match the orange in my dress. I lined my eyes with the heavy black kohl worn in Egypt and draped my peach colored serape over my shoulder.

Marie said I looked like Queen Cleopatra. I smiled and said I preferred to resemble Nut, the Egyptian sky goddess. "She swallowed the Sun at night and re-birthed him every morning."

"Girl," she said, "You've been listening to Carmen too much for your own good."

Carmen and I started down Third Street toward Slugs' Saloon on the corner of Avenue D, shops still open. Mid-block we came across a huddle of bikers revving up and guarding their motorcycles. I moved next to Carmen. "Hell's Angels," he said. "Just duck around them." I took small steps because the sheath was tight and pleasurable as it rose and fell against my body. A biker with bulging biceps and a bandana wrapped around stringy hair turned to gaze at me. "Just keep walking," Carmen said low. "They don't bother you as long as you don't mess with their bikes."

When we made it to Slugs, I exhaled with relief, but inside it was so dark I couldn't see a thing except a brick wall and a drum set up in the back. I watched my feet as I stepped gingerly in my sandals through the sawdust scattered on the floor.

Carmen led me toward a wicker chair around a wood table, where a mustached young White guy, sitting with his girlfriend, said with a smile, "I like the *vibes* here, man." At the next table sat a group of young mixed couples. A Spanish-looking guy, wearing a crucifix on a glittery gold chain, rested his head on the shoulder of a White girl with a beehive hairdo. A Black guy, looking collegiate in a V-neck sweater, sat next to a freckled Irish-looking girl in a plain white shirt. Suddenly the white in her shirt transformed into brilliant electric blue. Carmen explained it as "day glow," the effect from the stage lights they'd just turned on. He said, "Look at your dress."

A dance of electrified triangles fell in a pattern down my floor-length sheath, mesmerizing me. I felt its soft silk as I shifted my legs to face the stage. I looked up, stunned to see a man glowing in yellow and orange robes appear on stage. He looked out into the audience, and his eyes landed directly on me. His attentive glance made me feel like a different person—the woman I truly was, free, artistic, and feminine.

Carmen caught us locking eyes. "Sun Ra and my woman, making eyes, far out, man." He laughed and kissed my eyes, then excitedly pointed out the instruments on stage from all over the world—drums from Africa, the shennai from India, shekeras from South America. When the full "Orkestra" began to play otherworldly sounds, Carmen tuned in, blissed out, and—like he'd done in the presence of Lloyd, Jarrett, and Olatunji—he closed his eyes for a moment of worship.

The waiter, after convincing the bartender that our proof of age was not forged—we both really were eighteen—finally brought our drinks. The buzz of the beer, the dizzying atmosphere, the gold shine on the saxophone, and the mystical music all made me feel aboard a magical high-flying spaceship. On my napkin I scribbled a poem for Carmen:

> *Lover, you are a splash*
> *of exuberance on a dark street,*
> *a kiss on the eyelid,*
> *an orgasm of the Indian shennai,*
> *and the violent frenzy*
> *of the saxophone's*
> *eager rapid tongue and biting teeth.*

———

The time had come for Carmen and me to start our life together. Minus the money I paid for my Indonesian sheath, I had enough to pay the fifty-three dollars for rent. Because of my skin color I was designated to be the one to walk to the rental office on 14th Street to secure our apartment and sign the contract. When I returned, I held up the brass key. Carmen said, "Give me five, babe!" We threw open the door to our new place.

The nauseous smell of debris strewn on a splintered floor hit me. I stepped back in disgust and said, "I guess you get what you pay for." Just like Marie's, ours was a railroad flat with rooms lined up like a train of box cars. It had the same bathtub next to a stove in a small kitchen, but our kitchen connected to a large open space with a dusty window, barred with a black iron gate, that looked out past a fire escape to a scruffy backyard. Walking the other way through the kitchen, we found two small rooms but no clothes closets. A tiny door opened to toilet and sink, both stinking. Distressed, I leaned against the wall.

"Don't worry," Carmen said. "We'll get it together. This is the best pad on Third Street."

"Why?" I asked.

"Because it's *our* pad." He kissed me, and I mustered a smile.

We opened the window for air; we took out the trash; we borrowed from Marie mops, brooms, sponges, and soap. After scouring everything, we carried up a mattress she'd pulled off her old Castro convertible and placed it in the large room by the window.

Carmen lay down with his arms crossed behind his head. "Wow babe, our own pad." I rolled down onto the mattress, and we took off our clothes. He fondled my curls with his long fingers then used the fringe of my peach serape to caress my body from my neck to my toes.

I said, "I've never experienced foreplay with a serape before." We laughed.

"We'll be a groovy artist couple," he said.

"Yeah, like Jackson Pollack and Lee Krasner," I said. He imagined us more like Ike and Tina Turner, who'd sung "A Fool in Love." For afterplay, he produced melodic notes on his flute that set me off dreaming.

The heat burned my sandals as I hit the sidewalk the next morning to the East Village hardware store to purchase cleansers and paint. I got everything Carmen and I needed to turn our place into a home. I lugged the bags up the four floors just as Carmen was skipping down the stairs, humming, pausing only to tell me he had a job to finish at the Art Students League uptown.

Surprised to be on my own, I dug in anyway, starting on the bathtub. My mind drifted to the porcelain tub in my childhood house on Gettysburg Street, from where I could see through a curtained window to the playhouse in the backyard. I scoured the tub in jerky motions hoping for the same spanking white, but no luck.

When Carmen returned for lunch, I felt glad to have help. But he left again, saying, "I gotta check in with a dude who might get me a gig." Good news. I wished him luck and got back to scouring until the heat became unbearable. I walked to a bodega a few blocks away to pick up sliced meats for dinner, shopping for one meal at a time because we had no refrigerator. I made sandwiches and waited for Carmen.

Evening brought no relief from the heat. I ate my sandwich on the roof, hoping for a breeze, and looked down at the yard. Not one lousy tree. I remembered that in Queens Village at that this time of year, early June, I'd see many slender trees in bloom. I descended to our pad, and there, Carmen startled me. He said, "I got the gig!"

"Congratulations. We can use the money!"

He said, "No bread for this gig." I sank against the tub counter. He said the freebie could lead to the break he needed. He chattered about the cool musicians he'd jammed with. He seemed spacey, and then I smelled something on him. Pot. He pulled away, "Anything to eat, babe?" I pointed to the sandwich I'd left for him, now wilted, but he ate quickly. Cheeks puffed, he said something I couldn't understand about "Oscar."

"Oscar who?" I asked.

"Oscar *Mayer*." He pointed to the plastic food wrappings, laughing. I asked what's funny. He said, "*Levy's* Rye with *Hellman's*? Mayonnaise dribbled onto his chin. "I feel like I'm in *Queens*, man," like it was hilarious. "Brand name food, eaten in nuclear families in lily-white suburbs all over middle-class American."

"You gobbled it up I noticed," I snapped. "If it's too *middle-class* for you, buy your own damn food." I heard music starting up in the park and flew down the stairs to head to Tompkins Square.

The cooler air calmed me as I walked to the bandstand. The rock music sounded groovy. A boy in granny glasses and an NYU T-shirt told me the band was Global Image. Clouds of sweet weed filled the air, and through the swarm of students and hippies, from many feet away, I caught a glimpse of black hair swinging and the back of a man dancing in his own world. I moved closer. When the set ended, the man stopped, opened his eyes, and caught me staring at him. Don.

His face lit up as he spontaneously engulfed me in his strong arms. "What are you doing here?" I told him I had a pad on Third Street. "You do?" he said, excited. I told him I lived with my boyfriend. His brown eyes turned down. He put his hands on my shoulders, looked straight at me, and asked, "Are you happy?"

My eyes started to tear, and I blurted out without thinking, "It's not what I expected." I cupped my hands over my mouth. "I don't know why I told you that."

"You can trust me," he said.

"*Trust* you? No, I don't think so, not after . . ."

We had it out over Aviva. He admitted he'd been wrong, he'd made a mistake, and he didn't blame me for being pissed. He looked sheepish and said, "I miss you so much." He spoke with such sadness that I felt sad too. He said that both of us cherished freedom.

"At the moment, I don't feel so free."

He said softly, "Janet, listen, remember all the plans we made about going away on an adventure? I promised to show you Provincetown."

I nodded, my eyes scrunching up.

"Well, I'm leaving on Monday for Provincetown," Don said with joy. "I have a cottage there, we're forming a little commune, a few of us, so close to the beach you can hear the waves and smell the salt air."

It sounded fantastic. "Good for you," I said.

"If it's not working out with this new guy, I mean, you and I can still do what we dreamed about, right? Can you give me another chance? I want you to come with me."

Don floored me. "I can't," I stuttered. "I'm almost out of money."

He assured me I didn't have to worry about money now; he'd earn tons of money as a waiter in Provincetown. "It's a mecca for artists, and you could do portraits. Will you come with me?" His words reminded me of when he first tempted me to come to Sheridan Square, to stay with him. This time, I shook my head no. "Okay," he said, "if we can't be lovers again, the least I can do is to keep my promise to show you Provincetown."

I didn't know the way up or down. I said, "I'd love to go away to the beach. But I just moved in with someone I thought I loved. I should try to work it out."

Don blew my mind when he said, "Bring him, too!"

No way, I thought. I knew I could not handle going away with two boys, an ex-boyfriend and a current one. Crazy. And Carmen would certainly find the idea ridiculous and completely reject it.

PART V: SUMMER, 1967

Chapter 16
PROVINCETOWN

In the heat of midday, the summer solstice a week or so away, I felt so damn hot. I longed to feel the cool ocean breezes. I waited with trepidation on my stoop on Third Street. A white convertible pulled up: Don at the wheel like a white knight, and Grace Slick blasting "White Rabbit" from the car radio. He hopped out with that look of glee I knew well, giddy with the romantic daring of it all. He yelled out, "We're free!" He unburdened me of my bags and easel and stuffed them into the trunk.

Carmen, too, tossed his bags and instrument cases into the back seat, where he and I squeezed in together.

A few days before, when I'd returned to the pad to tell Carmen I was going to Provincetown with Don, his almond eyes filled with sorrow. He said, "Babe, I'm sorry. It's all new for me living with a chick. I'll change." I noticed he had made a minor improvement—constructing a bookshelf with planks and bricks. "Please don't leave me," he said with such love and sorrow, I thought, *Should I invite him?*

Don passed a joint to the back seat, which Carmen smoked. I felt high enough as the three of us charged north up FDR Drive, car top down, breeze blowing, singing our heads off, throwing all logic to the wind.

Crossing the bridge out of Manhattan on that gorgeous day, I caught a last glimpse of the Manhattan skyline and turned east to look beyond the flat Sound, throwing a kiss goodbye to Queens.

———————

As the sun began to sink in the sky, the smell of cool salty air signaled we were near the sea. Arriving in Provincetown, Don pointed ahead in the dark to what he called the "main drag of P-town." Carmen said that "drag" was a good word—his friend Fran had told him that P-town was a gay paradise.

We turned left on a sandy road and pulled up beside a tiny cottage at the end of a line of tiny cottages. The interior looked like a dollhouse with its miniature kitchen, sitting area, and two bedrooms; Don claimed one and went out. Carmen and I put our bags in the second room, ours for just one night, until Don's other renter showed up. We spread out on the double bed that filled the small room and conked out.

Hungry for breakfast, early next morning Carmen and I ambled past tall reeds and cottages up the sandy path to town. In the simplest place, we ordered the simplest meal. I softly sang an old Shaker song: "Tis the Gift to Be Simple." Paying the check, we learned even simple things were expensive in P-town.

We walked down the main street, wondering if we could afford a room in one of the cute bed-and-breakfast places. We stopped at one with a vacancy sign. At the reception desk, the owner, a casually dressed man about thirty with longish hair, welcomed us with a smile. He showed us a room with a thick rug, an antique desk with gold drawer handles, and a quaint painting of men fishing on the Cape. He asked, "How many nights?"

I said, "Three," and paid cash for the first night. He gave us two keys and left.

Carmen said. "Are you crazy?"

I told him I had it in my savings. "We'll stay just one night— let's enjoy it."

We filled up the beautiful big bathtub with hot water, squirted in scented soap, and jumped giggling into the bubbles. We slowly washed each other all over. The soap made us slip and slide up and down as we found a way to make love, laughing and splashing until water spilled out of the tub.

Shining and satisfied, we ventured out to explore the main street, Commercial Street, and found portrait artists working in many shops. I said to Carmen, "Hey, I'm good at portraits. Maybe I can get a gig." I stopped in one storefront to ask. The owner, the resident artist himself, waved me right out the door saying, "The last thing P-town needs is another damn portrait artist."

We found a kinder reception at a small boutique where handcrafted jewelry studded with shells and stones attracted me. Chimes rang as we stepped inside where a dark-haired young woman had set up a crib for her baby girl, now caught in a crying jag. Carmen took out his silver flute, which he took with him everywhere. A toot or two startled the baby, and she halted mid-sob. She listened with round brown eyes, hypnotized by the sounds.

Bells jingled as the shop door opened, and a blonde boy sauntered in, saying, "I heard a flute." He carried a guitar case and wore a sand-colored sweatshirt and a red bandana around his neck. The baby cried again; Carmen's flute again quieted her. "Sounds soothe the savage beast," the boy said, laughing. "I'm Billy. I can help." On his guitar he gently strummed along with Carmen's flute.

Chimes again caused me to turn. I saw a girl in a gauzy India-style blouse enter, and outside the shop, another girl adorned with beads and ribbons sitting on a pile of sleeping bags. We all bade the baby and mom goodbye. Billy said, "Meet my birds, Sherry and Annabel."

Each one of us had come to be by the sea, and we set off together to Cape Cod Bay, where the breeze kicked up sand that tickled our skin. I threw my head back and breathed in the salty air. Sherry, the beaded girl, said, "Oh, my God. The ocean! Nothing like this in Akron, Ohio."

Carmen said, "Not in Kansas City either." I told them that Jones Beach was near, and rivers surrounded the place I grew up, New York City.

"New York City!" The girls fell back in awe. I said we'd just left the city, and Billy said he'd love to go there sometime. "Yes, but right now," Annabel yelled as she ripped off her lime green socks, "I want to swim in the ocean!" I laughed watching Sherry and Annabel dash to the bay, dip their feet in the waves and shriek, "The water's freezing!"

"Hey, it's freakin' cold at night, too," Billy said to Carmen and me. They'd brought sleeping bags to camp on the beach but found the gear a pain to lug around all day. He threw towels to the girls to dry off, and, his blonde hair flopping over his forehead, he asked, "Do you know any cheap places to crash?"

I told him about the B&B room we'd booked for a few nights. I floated the idea that we share it and split the bill. Carmen said, "Cool. But there's only one bed."

"The floor is all we need," Billy said, and the girls nodded. He pulled out his grub, saying, "Let's break bread on the deal." And like in a Bible story, we shared a loaf of bread and a chunk of cheese.

Annabel asked me how I'd landed up in P-town. I told her that I'd run away from my parents who pissed me off. She told me she'd left Ohio to see the East Coast, but she had no problem with her folks. I felt a sharp pain in my heart, wishing I could say the same. I missed Maureen. I wondered how Barbara and Nanny were, and if my parents worried about me. I decided I'd write postcards later to all my family and friends.

Gulls swooped over us, their calls sounding like mocking laughter. Carmen answered them—ha, ha, ha—with sharp notes on his flute. He said, "P-town is a groovy town, I hope I find a gig playing here."

Billy said that he had a meeting with a club owner the next day, to talk about performing. "Maybe he can find a spot for you, too."

———————

We parted with the Ohio trio around dinnertime and headed for the Lobster Pot where Don worked—he'd promised us a deal. Pleased to see us, he beckoned us to sit at one of his tables on the dock. He brought us two fresh lobsters, which tasted heavenly—affordable since Don charged half price. I said, "It's good to have a friend." Carmen questioned if *friend* was all Don meant to me. I answered, "Perfectly sure."

At our B&B, we found our three new friends waiting for us with all their gear. No one at reception, Carmen and I snuck them up one by one. I noticed the queen bed had two thick mattresses. We pulled off the top mattress for the girls, and Billy rolled out his sleeping bag for himself. That night the five of us slept peacefully like kids in one big family.

In the morning, after we shared the last of the bread and cheese, Carmen went off with Billy and his "birds" to see about getting gigs, and I walked down the sandy path to fetch my sketch pad. Don opened his cottage door, got my pad, then pointed to the bikes and said I was free to borrow one. He was on his way to work, but he first took me next door to meet his friends. "Chuck and his girlfriend, Bev—they're part of our little commune."

At their door we heard lively lyrics, ". . . Lovely Rita," and knocked. Chuck, wearing a macramé necklace on his bare chest, opened up and said, "I'm blown away by Sgt. Pepper's."

Seeing I looked perplexed, Don said, "The new Beatles album. Chuck, you gotta play it for Janet," and he took off for work on his bicycle.

Chuck said, "Bev is out working. We take turns working." He said money is a necessary evil, but they live simply and share their earnings, so not everyone needs a full-time job. That sounded like a great idea. He said, "I'm off today, and I'll be glad to play the album for you, Janet."

He showed me the album cover for *Sgt. Pepper's Lonely Hearts Club Band*—a collage in bright colors. We sat on the love seat to examine details: many faces of American idols—Marlon Brando, James Dean, Bob Dylan, Laurel and Hardy, Marilyn Monroe. I wondered most about the two portrayals of the Beatles themselves. One of the original Fab Four wearing brown suits and ties, the other image of them transformed into a fantasy band decked out in electric-colored costumes.

"Everything changed after George went to meet Ravi Sankar in India," Chuck said, pointing out bearded gurus on the cover. I thought, *Carmen's got to see this.*

Chuck lowered the needle onto the vinyl. The tunes struck me as playful and upbeat, each song so different from the other. But I couldn't make much sense of the lyrics. I asked if the Beatles were high when they wrote the songs.

"Likely," Chuck said, lighting up a joint. I watched his shaggy hair fall over his face as he sucked in the pot. I thought, *I should get up and go out and sketch, like I'd planned. It's too early for this happy-go-lucky mood.* Then he passed the joint to me.

I shook my head. "I'm not into pot. I can't get high."

Chuck looked quizzical. "I can teach you how." I reluctantly took the joint. "Take a deep inhale. Now hold it. Good. Let it out. Relax."

Relax? I wanted to go sketch. Thoughts intruded: *What am I doing in P-town? Why did I book a fancy hotel when we're almost broke?*

"Let everything go," he said. "Again, inhale, hold, exhale." I listened to the songs, catching snippets about being late, rushing for the bus, falling into dreaming. *I can relate to those lyrics,* I thought. The tingling sounds in "Within You and Without You," the Indian drums mingling with symphonic violins enchanted me. "Just be here now," Chuck whispered, and I rolled back onto the pillow feeling wonderfully content.

Then the words in "She's Leaving Home" hit me. *Oh, the girl is so lonely*, I thought. Her sad story crushed the sweet imaginings of my mind. Her parents felt perplexed. I thought, *Maybe I'd been thoughtless to my parents. I need to get up and call my family right now.* But I couldn't budge. The mesmerizing sounds bouncing off the cottage walls flooded my mind with images of diamonds, sunsets, empty halls, and police officers.

"How are you feeling now?" Chuck asked.

I said, "Hungry." He laughed and got up to get crackers. "Thanks, Chuck." Chuck. A song from childhood popped up, "The Name Game." My sisters and I used to fool around and bastardize the lyrics, which now rolled around in my brain: *Chuck Chuck bo buck banana fanna fo fuck, Chuck.*

I opened my eyes to a glaring Medusa in my face, her black hair curling like snakes. Chuck said, "Bev!" *Oh, his woman is home from work*, I thought. I imagined what this scene looked like from her angle—a strange girl curled up on the divan munching crackers with her man, Chuck, bare-chested, both of us high as hell.

I watched her lips round to say "Hell. Oh." She looked grave, like in a graveyard, but we were in a comedy.

I grinned and slurred my words. "Hi. With help from . . ." Noise from her clanging pots scared me. I thought, *She's not exactly the lovey-dovey* commune *type.* I giggled.

She glared at Chuck and me, and over her head, like a bubble in a cartoon, I saw the words, "What the fuck are you doing?"

I'm getting away, that's what I'm doing. Bev can have her man Chuck in their phony commune, I thought as I took the bike from the yard outside Don's cottage, put my sketchbook in the basket and, still high and humming "Lucy in the Sky," found myself flying down the highway. *Route 6 is wider than Gettysburg Street where I rode my blue bike as a little girl, maybe the last time I've bicycled? I'll surely find a beautiful spot near Provincetown to draw.*

I buzzed past trees, saw a big field open up. *Perfect.* I laid down my bike and grabbed my pad. The roar of engines. Two guys passing on motorcycles jerked their heads to look at me. I slid down the slippery grass and hid under a bush until the noise of the motorcycles faded. I looked around. I noticed something plopped in the middle of the green field, something large, white, and still. I approached and found a large gull, lying on her side. I wondered, *Is she hurt?* I fell to my knees to check, saw no sign of death—no blood or decay, no gnats in her eyes. But she was dead, no doubt about that. No movement of heart or breath. Her feathers so fluffy, she appeared the epitome of peace.

A roar. The two bikers passed again, going the opposite way. *Whoa.* I thought, *Are they just riding back and forth, or are they coming for me?* When I no longer heard them, I sat cross-legged to study the bird: *Beak closed, eyes shut, and wings broken, she can't squawk, see, or fly. She's just an empty form now, the life gone. Where did the life go?*

The bikers returned. I watched them stop and prop up their bikes, shake their long hair and start down the slippery slope toward me. My heart beat harder, my breath raced. *My God*, I thought, *Are they Hell's Angels? They, like dogs, will see me as prey if I show fear.* I told myself, *Keep your eyes on the pad.* Peripherally, I caught sight of lots of black leather.

"Oh, it's a bird with a bird," I heard one guy say.

Another guy asked me, "Is it hurt, dearie?"

Dearie? These blokes had British accents; they sounded like the Beatles. I wanted to laugh, but not now. The bikers sat on either side of me and moved close. Holy shit. My head still down, on my left I perceived dangling gold chains; on my right a heavily tattooed arm raised and waving in front of my face. I heard the question, "Hey, girl, what are you . . ." The arm jerked back and one of them yelled, "Fuck! It's a dead bird! What the hell are you doin'—a witch ritual or some bloody thing?"

"Bugger off!" The guy wearing chains told tattooed man. "She's an artist, you idiot—she's drawin' the bird."

"The bird is fuckin' dead!"

"Brilliant. Then it won't fly off then, will it, you moron? A dead bird stays still so she can draw it."

I would have cracked up if I wasn't so scared. I kept sketching. Without forethought, words poured out of my mouth like a torrent. "The bird's body is dead, but the spirit of the bird is not dead, and I honor the spirit of the bird. I am capturing the form of the bird, but her spirit cannot be captured. It's the same spirit within all of us, within you and without you, it's the spirit within me, within you, and we all go to the same place after we die, to the eternal spirit, and that spirit is watching over us right now."

I never looked up, but sensed their bodies pulling back. The tattooed guy said, "Fucking crazy shit, man." I heard keys jingle and boots stomp the soft grass as they fled up the slope. "Creepy as all bloody hell."

I heard the bikes rev up, fade into the distance, and a smile crept along my face. *I scared the blokes off*, I thought. I slumped and stayed low until my body stopped shaking.

———————

Feeling wobbly, somehow, I peddled the bicycle back to Don's cottage. Back at our B&B, I found no one around, just bedding, bags, and clothes strewn all over the floor. The roar of the engines and images—gold chains, tattoos, and leather—ran through my head. Thinking about what the bikers could have done with me, I scrubbed my skin red in a hot bath, trying to wash the incident out of my mind. I told myself, *I am lucky I escaped*. I patted myself dry with a soft towel, then dropped it to scrounge among the backpacks for some bread or cheese. I tripped over the mattress on the floor.

A knock on the door.

"It's me." A deep voice. Don. I rose to crack open the door. Don told me he saw Carmen walking to the beach. "He told me where you guys were staying." I asked why he came. He said he'd seen me return his bike and thought I looked upset. "I want to know if you're all right. Let me in." I said no—I had to get dressed. He pushed open the door, stepped in, and shut the door behind him. Smiling, he took a long look at my body. "You don't have to get dressed for me. I know what you look like nude."

"You better go."

He took a step toward me, tripped and fell on the mattress on the floor. "What the . . .?" While he was down, I slipped into shorts and a T-shirt. He said that he'd met the three waifs who were crashing with us. "Is it fun sleeping all together?"

I said, "Get off the bed and go."

He reached for me. "Remember the great sex we had?"

"Don! I have a new boyfriend now, remember?" He reminded me I'd been ready to dump Carmen the week before. I said, "We had a fight, and we made up." He said he and I should make up, he missed me. "Get off it. I know you see other girls." He admitted that but said it was me he loved. "Look," I said. "I don't two-time. I can't bounce back and forth between lovers like you do."

He said, "I feel hot," and opened his shirt, exposing his muscular tan chest.

I felt upset. *Why is life so peculiar?* I told him to go before Carmen came back and got the wrong idea. I stared at him and said, "You're a liar. You didn't come here because you felt concerned about me. You came for something else. And, since you won't leave, I will."

———————

I fled barefoot down the elegant stairs to the lobby and ducked into the first open door to hide—the B&B Cafe. Well-dressed people sat at tables with white tablecloths eating dishes with enticing aromas. I sat down in my T-shirt and shorts at the empty table in a corner, thirsty, hungry, and shaken. A gentleman in a black bow tie and white shirt came over, but I felt so distracted I couldn't understand a word he said. Very politely, in what sounded like a Spanish accent, he kept saying, "*Noomba, noomba.*" Did he want to dance? Then I understood he was the waiter and wanted my room number. I didn't remember it.

He smiled and said, "The key?"

Damn. I'd run out without it. I shrugged and said, "Please, just a cup of tea." I hesitated. "Is it free for guests?"

He looked at me with curiosity, then said, "No charge for you, Miss." He brought me tea in a delicate porcelain cup decorated with flowers.

"So beautiful," I said.

He later returned with a smile, poured me a refill and left me the whole teapot. I lost count of refills, of minutes, of my surroundings. I finally looked up, surprised to see the dining room empty, except for the waiter, who stood by the door, rocking on his feet, perhaps ready to go home. All the tea made me need the ladies' room. When I returned, the waiter had gone. I saw he'd left me a big, buttered roll with seeds on top. *How kind*, I thought, as I gobbled it up.

I told the receptionist I'd locked myself out of my room and asked to borrow a key. The friendly owner appeared; he'd heard my request and said, "I'll be glad to open your door for you."

Uh-oh. He'd see our room in disarray. As we climbed the stairs, he smiled at me and asked, "How are you enjoying your stay?" My stomach churned. I had to keep him out. I schemed that when we got to the door, I'd grab the key and just slip in. We got to the door, and he turned the key—I couldn't stop him. And I couldn't block his view through the open door. His jaw dropped. He exclaimed, "What do you think this is, a crash pad?"

———

I searched the beach for Carmen. A long mournful wail I recognized as his saxophone drew me to the water's edge. His sax spurted notes sounding like a mating call, the sea his object of seduction, his music rising and falling with the roll of the waves. Feeling pained, from new wounds and wounds long suppressed, I slumped in the sand.

Carmen noticed me and said, "Hey, you're grooving on my sax." He looked into my eyes. "Babe, are you high?"

"I got high yesterday. Now I'm low. Carmen—"

"You're Pisces. High, low, like the tides, you ebb and flow. I want to play some more." He walked away.

I squatted on the edge to watch the ocean spill itself on the sand, then retreat, repeating the cycle again and again. In the damp sand, I drew a thin line with a ragged piece of driftwood, a long continuous line, dug deep, which became a brow, circled around an eyelid, spilled down the bridge of a nose to the nostrils, connected to thin lips and a strong chin, and trailed off down the throat.

"Cool drawing," a man said, standing over me. I looked up and saw the first Black person, other than Carmen, I'd seen in P-town. His face was smooth as ebony, and I could see his nipples through a tight mesh shirt. He turned his head upside down to look at my scratching, and with a melodic voice, said, "Oh, groovy, it looks like a face. Who is it?"

"Nobody," I said. Just then I realized Carmen had stopped playing and was looking at the sand too. He said it looked like I'd done a self-portrait. He was right. With my fist, I pushed sand into the crevices and erased the face. "Look, Carmen—"

He stopped me to introduce the man as Henry, a singer he'd bumped into when looking for a gig. "This is my woman. She's an artist."

"Oh, my," Henry said with a charming smile, "a musician and an artist—such a sweet couple." He told me he performed in P-town for the summer.

I asked Carmen if he'd heard about getting a paid gig. He said not yet. I finally blurted out, "Carmen, we got kicked out of the B&B."

"Say what?"

"Evicted." I immediately turned to the singer. "Henry, do you, by any chance, know of any place we could crash tonight?"

Chapter 17
BOSTON

Carmen and I spent almost all our cash to buy tickets and caught the last bus from Provincetown to Boston. Henry the singer told us his apartment sat empty in Boston. He said, "Brother and sister, you're welcome to stay there."

We arrived during rush hour at the main station bustling with well-dressed, mostly White, people. A woman politely pointed the way to Cambridge. Carmen and I descended underground to the "T," a mass transit system—so different from NYC. A clean train running on quiet wheels, full of color-coded maps, and signs in the playful Peter Max style, felt more like a ride in a theme park.

Knowing nothing but the address of Henry's place, we emerged in Cambridge trusting we were going in the right direction, our baggage feeling heavier by the minute. Passing a church, I felt a wave of fatigue at the same time as an overwhelming urge to pee. I dropped my easel and prayed to keep control of myself.

Carmen saw that I'd stopped. "What's up, babe?"

"The church steeple inspires me. I want to do a quick sketch."

"Babe, quit playing. Come on, I'm beat."

While I squeezed and strained to keep from losing it, we took wrong turns and had to retrace our steps. Finally, we found Henry's place—an old fashioned, brick, three-story house.

Forgetting our fatigue, we skipped up the porch steps to the entrance where Carmen inserted the key Henry had given him. It didn't work. I paced back and forth, desperate for relief.

At last Carmen succeeded in jiggling the door open, and we lugged our bags up to the third floor. The key to Henry's apartment did work, and I made it, barely, to the bathroom in time. Henry had left his apartment empty except for a futon in the living room, and a table, chairs, and pots and pans in the kitchen. I found a few blankets in the closet and spread them on the floor for our bed. Carmen crashed right down, and I wanted to flop down next to him, but hunger pressed me. Carmen gave me the six dollars we had left, and I walked back to a grocery we'd passed to purchase some food.

My choices did not please Carmen. "Peanut *butter*?" He told me peanuts in shells were much cheaper. And jelly? Useless. We'd argued once about meals, but now he was right. "We gotta make our dollars stretch, babe." I asked what to buy. He said, "Rice and beans. Eggs." I agreed but that night we enjoyed peanut butter and jelly sandwiches, sitting on the floor, like I did as a kid. Just before we toppled over, dead tired, I said that the next day we needed to go out and get jobs. And he promised to fix the door downstairs so we could get back in.

———

In the morning, a warm day, I took my one quarter, bought a paper for fifteen cents, and sat on a bench in a Cambridge park. I read about the damage just ten days before from rioting in "the Negro section of Boston," sparked by police busting women who'd blocked welfare workers from leaving their office building. I thought, *These stories of rebellion are everywhere.* Even in "civilized" Boston, mothers had to demonstrate to get aid to feed their children. I could relate—*To eat you need money.*

I turned to the classified section and saw a job for waitressing, which could pay okay if tips were good. From a phone booth, with my remaining dime, I called the restaurant and a man picked up. I said, "About your ad . . ." He told me to call back later and hung up! I'd just wasted, literally, *my last cent*. I slumped down on a bench and stared at other listings. An ad for a college secretary looked good—I could type really well—but to call I needed another dime.

I looked around the park, blooming all over with flowers, and saw a young White couple stroll by. I figured they were graduates of one of the dozens of colleges in Boston, feeling some envy. Though I was not dressed as clean-cut as they, I thought that in my sandals and linen dress I looked presentable enough, and they would not see me as a common beggar.

"I'm looking for work," I said, smiling and holding up the classified page where I'd circled an ad. "I see a job I want to apply for. I wonder if you could lend me a dime to make a call."

The guy stared at me as if expecting an explanation, like my wallet was lost, forgotten, or stolen. Since I offered none, he looked at me like I was an annoying panhandler. Though humiliated, I kept my head high and looked him straight in the eye. The boy slowly reached into his pocket and pulled out a quarter.

I called the number for the secretary job and a man gladly told me how to get to the office by bus. I said, "Can you please give me directions by foot?" He paused. He told me it was a long walk. I said, "I'm a good walker."

———

It started to rain. I saw no place to take shelter, but the rain felt warm and calmed my distress. I soon found the place and knocked, and a large White man opened the door with a smile. His mouth dropped. "Oh, you're drenched!" he said, but let me in. I asked for the bathroom, where I dried off with paper towels.

His professionally dressed daughter brought me some coffee, which she pronounced with a Boston accent, *kah-fee*. Acting as cheerful as her dad, she offered a biscuit and I gobbled it up.

She sat me at a typewriter with text to type and, in two minutes, snatched the paper away. Her dad said, "You're fast! And you made only minor errors. Try again." My third test: speed excellent, zero errors. He stapled my test to my application, and said, "I booked you for an interview at the college first thing Monday morning."

Monday! I panicked. I thought, *This is Friday—how will we get by all weekend?*

He studied my face. "You need this job, don't you?" I nodded. At the door, we saw the sun shining. He said, "For the interview, you won't show up all soaking wet, will you?" I laughed and shook my head. "You're a good typist, you have an excellent academic record, and some office experience. I'll recommend you." I felt relieved. He asked if he could give me a little fatherly advice. "Put those sandals away and wear regular shoes."

I owned no other shoes.

———————

Back at Henry's about five o'clock, I found the front door ajar, and trudged upstairs, discouraged. I told Carmen I'd lined up a job interview. "But," I said, "I need—"

He interrupted to announce, "I found a job!" I perked up. He said, "I saw a job posted on a door up the street, walked in, and got the gig right away." I said I hadn't noticed a club nearby. "No club. A store. I sweep the floor." *Oh, what a downer for someone with his talent,* I thought. But his face brightened. "I worked today," he said. "I get paid at the end of every day." He pulled out of his pocket a ten-dollar bill and waved it in the air.

I snatched it, saying, "I need shoes."

I found a bargain store near the underground where I purchased plain black pumps for $6.99. With the three dollars left over I bought stockings, as well as the groceries Carmen suggested. For dinner I cooked rice and beans, which—he was right—tasted good and filled us up. Carmen boiled eggs. "For breakfast tomorrow?" I asked. No, for celebration that night.

Later, he lit candles and set them before us as we sat cross-legged on the floor. He said, "Elisi taught me a Cherokee ritual I want to show you, babe." We began by slowly inhaling and exhaling while letting go of worries. He said, "If you're in the right state of mind, the high lasts longer. You use less peyote."

"Peyote?"

He said that medicine men used it in rituals during spirit quests to gain wisdom. "Do you want to try it?"

I hesitated but said, "Sure. I want to be wiser." He gave me some leaves to chew, then spit out. He struck a match and lit up the peyote, smoked it and held his breath. He passed it to me, and I did the same. We slowly blew the smoke out together.

He said, "Focus your eyes on the flame to center your mind. Let all other thoughts go." It sounded easy, but I couldn't do it. Carmen took out a treasured book he'd been carrying, the *I Ching* (translated, "The Book of Changes"). He said, "I use it when I need guidance." He tossed some coins, and on scrap paper made long and short dashes that formed patterns he called hexagrams. He referred to charts on the last pages and found that our pattern matched "Dwelling People," and he read the entry out loud.

Exhausted and high, I only caught bits: ". . . distress . . . sad at heart, humiliated, turned around or upside down." Those few words closely described some dark feelings I held within. Carmen shared the phrases regarding relationships: "Man and woman . . . creative . . . hold together, live and work together within doors . . . Whatever you want to do is possible, act on your desires, do what you need to do, the way is open, the spirits are with you . . ." Intrigued, my mood rose.

"Right on, isn't it, babe?"

Yes, I thought, assured we'd find a way. I leaned back and asked where he got the peyote.

"I got a package just before we left New York. From Elisi, my grandmother."

"You're kidding—you got peyote from your *grandmother*?"

"She turned me on years ago."

I laughed. In a million years, I could never picture my own grandmother giving me dope to smoke.

"Yeah," he said, "Elisi and Grandpa, they had a thing going. They'd smoke, then go up to their room, and in the morning, they'd come down together, singing." He brought out the boiled eggs. "Elisi gave me wise Cherokee counsel: For good sex, eat eggs before." I thought, *He has a wild grandmother.* Laughing, we ate the boiled eggs, savoring them slowly, feeling our energy rise. As we lay down, he quoted the *I Ching*, "It's auspicious to act on your desires."

———

We slept well but did not wake up together in the morning singing. Alone, I heard Carmen talking to someone in the kitchen. I dressed quickly and smelled the pot before I found him smoking a joint with another Black guy. They continued talking, but I couldn't catch the drift.

When the man left, Carmen said, "He's a narc."

"A narc?

"He's on the narcotics squad."

"My God!" I said. "The neighbors must have called!" Carmen said the narc was looking for Henry. "And you let him in? What about the peyote?"

"He knew we had it. He could smell it—these narcs have noses like police dogs."

My hands clenched my chair. "What's going to happen to us?" Carmen seemed almost amused at my alarm.

"Nothing," Carmen assured me. "The narc promised he wouldn't bust us. He's cool. He smokes too. Like all narcs, he has a continuous supply. He's the one who rolled the joint."

———

I showed up early at the college for my interview on Monday, a hot and humid day, feeling grateful for the air-conditioning in the waiting room, where a young White woman in pink already sat waiting, looking cool. I'd perspired on the long walk over, and my stockings clung to my legs. My plain linen mini dress was a little short, but in fashion. I'd fixed my hair and makeup to look most professional and chose earrings that dangled least. I thought I'd break in my new $6.99 black pumps on the walk, but, instead, they broke in my feet. I slipped them off for a little relief.

While the woman in pink sat absorbed in her magazine, I studied her. Her pearl earrings and frosted hair, teased and pulled back in a neat bun, looked in style—1950s style. Wearing a straight skirt, she tucked in her legs. It was her shoes—spanking white patent leather to match her boxy purse—that made me realize with a sinking feeling that she'd win out.

A good-looking middle-aged man, sporting a light-blue seersucker jacket and tie, came to the door and called me in first. He smiled, shook my hand, and pointed to a cushioned chair in front of his huge desk. I sat on the edge, my back upright. He said, "Please, make yourself comfortable." He leaned back in his leather chair trying hard to appear casual. In fact, he had the authority to decide what I would do all day and what he would pay. He looked down at my application on his desk, then asked pleasantly, "What kind of student were you?"

On reflex, I answered "An A student." I stopped. I didn't want him to suspect I might want to leave in September to go back to college (which had been my original intent when I took a break).

"Your favorite subject?"

"Art." *Another bad answer*, I thought. People stereotype artists as unpredictable—not a good fit for the drudgery of office work. *Here, my "gifts" may become drawbacks.*

"Well, I see you're an excellent typist." Then he launched into the complete run-down on the job: eight thirty to five, five days a week, a half hour lunch, two fifteen-minute breaks, seventy-five dollars a week, twenty-three percent deducted for federal, state, and payroll taxes. He ended with, "Two weeks vacation a year to start."

Hell, I thought, *when will I ever find time to paint?*

"Vacation increases to one month vacation a year after ten years . . ."

Ten years! I thought. He went on to say I'd get a bonus after twenty-five years, and a gold watch when I was sixty-five years old. I thought, *God, my whole life contracted away. All I want is wages so I can eat.*

———————

After the interview I wandered, not knowing where I was going, and passed an imposing building with a classical façade—a library. I thought, *A library would be a lovely place to work.* My legs started for the personnel office, but my heart stopped me, repulsed by the process of picking through my unconventional past to fit boxes on another form. The courtyard drew me.

Along gravel paths, I circled around a fountain, where all colors of the spectrum danced in the water's mist, brilliantly back lit by the sun. Drawn to it, I put my hand in the spray and felt spurts from the pump that cycled the water around. I fell into a meditation as my eyes followed the water, its force diminishing the higher it rose until it peaked; pulled by mother earth, it fell in careless descent back into the shady pool of its origins. The water reflected the green of the cultivated shrubbery boxed around marble edges. A dry patch of wild grass grew out of place. It leaned toward the sun; its browning blades hung over like drooping eyelashes. The passive water again easily got sucked into the pump, rose again—and at its shining height, some lucky droplets escaped into the air.

———————

I moved inside the library and came upon a listening room full of records, lined up in alphabetical order. I pulled down an album by Bach and made a mental note to return it to the same numbered section and shelf. I entered Cubicle 4 and placed the album on the turntable. Bach's brilliant fugue flooded the box, transcending all measure. I tried to recall what my high school music teacher had urged us to listen for—exposition, counterpoint, voice, repeating voices, connecting episodes. Exalted, I heard a key return, just before the end, to the opening—

The door of my cubicle opened, interrupting my reverie. A priggish boy and I faced off for a moment, then he donned his spectacles as if to gain authority. He told me, "You have to sign the book. And I need your identity card."

"Identity . . . I don't have one. No ID, I mean. I'm not a student."

"A license then."

"I don't drive."

"Okay, your address."

I'd forgotten. I blurted, "Cambridge."

He rolled his eyes and said, "You can't stay."

"Can I just finish listening to this fugue?"

Frowning, he said, "Ten minutes," and slammed the door on me.

Chapter 18
BOSTON, ON THE EDGE

I hit the hot pavement again the next day, clutching the classified section listing the restaurant's number. I called again,
and this time the manager answered and told me to come over to
apply. Hamburger Haven—I got there quickly and smelled the
coffee and burgers on the sizzling grill. A middle-aged woman
with dyed red hair said, "I'm Karen, the manager. We're looking
for a counter-girl. Ninety cents an hour, but tips are your own."
She smiled and added in a motherly tone, "Plus you get a free
meal every evening you work." I pictured diving into piles of
food. She asked if I could work from five to midnight. I thought,
No problem.

She told me, to start, I could wear a plain white blouse and
black skirt. I thought, *How in the world will I get that clothing?* I
said, "Fine."

"You'll also need waitress shoes." She told me, for now, I
could wear sneakers, which I didn't have. I asked if the shoes I
had on were all right. She looked down at my feet pinched in the
black pumps, and up to my pleading face. She nodded and said,
"You start tomorrow. At five."

I checked Henry's closet and, luckily, I did find some women's clothes. Carmen speculated that maybe Henry and his friends cross dressed. I said, "Look, a white blouse!" In the light, however, it looked beige, too big, and too jazzy. It had to do. I still had to buy a black skirt.

Carmen said, "I get paid ten dollars again tomorrow."

"What time?"

"Every day, five o'clock."

I groaned. "I'm supposed to *report* at five o'clock!"

———

From a phone booth the next evening, I called Karen, who gave me until six o'clock. Just before five, I paced back and forth outside the window watching Carmen finish his work, jarred by the image of him in thin baggy pants pushing a broad broom across a polished floor. A passerby, someone like my bigoted Irish Aunt Florence, living nearby in Boston, would never imagine this boy to be a talented artist and musician with knowledge of Eastern philosophy.

Carmen slapped his day's earnings in my palm, and I rushed to the bargain store where I rifled through racks until I found a black skirt under ten dollars. It hung below my knees, but no time to shop for another. Wearing the too-long skirt and ill-fitting blouse, I paid and dashed down the street feeling like a refugee.

I hope I didn't miss the free meal, I thought as I charged, breathless, into Hamburger Haven. Karen shot me an apron and said, "Other girls covered for you. They filled up your salt shakers and ketchup bottles." She hurried me to the circular counter and left me alone to deal with people already calling out orders.

The loudest guy got my attention. He yelled, "Coke!" and pointed to the soda fountain. After a few tries, I figured out how to press the lever to fill the glass. "Ice!" he demanded. I added ice and some Coke spilled out. "You're supposed to add ice before the soda."

A woman shouted, "Dr. Pepper!" I knew to add ice first, then soda. Good. Another customer ordered a tall Coke with cherry, and while I squirted flavor into her glass, people shouted at me from all directions:

"Straw!" one called.

"Napkin!" another demanded.

My hands began shaking, and Karen arrived to show me where to find straws and napkins. I wrote down food orders. Karen said, "Honey, you gotta *call* the orders to the cooks." She pointed to the rear, where over a ledge the kitchen was visible, and I saw two cooks in puffy white hats.

I called out in their general direction, "Two cheeseburgers and fries, one well-done, the other rare! And coffee light!"

"One at a time," Karen said. "And tell them the code."

"Code?" She pulled out the long list. I found the hamburger code and called it in.

"But *kah-fee*," she said, "you pour yourself at the counter." I got busy pouring coffees, sodas, drinks, and yelling out codes. Karen intervened. She said, "Can't you hear the cooks? They're announcing your codes—go get your meals!"

I retrieved the platters from under the red light on the kitchen counter, returned, and asked, "Now, who gets cheeseburgers?"

"Here," a woman said.

"I was ahead of that woman," a guy said with annoyance. "Why are you serving her first?"

"Sorry." Another thing to track—*who sat down first, who sat down second.*

Karen added more duties. "In between orders, don't forget to wipe the counters, fill the ketchup and creamers, wash the glasses." She'd been writing the checks but told me, "Write your own checks now. Check the price and compute the tax." Careful to be correct, I computed slowly, which displeased the customers. On the counter they left no quarters for me, not even a dime. After the rush, Karen asked me, "Will you need your wages tonight, honey?" I nodded and thought, *She knows*, probably because of my funny looking clothes. She said, "Now it's your break. Time to eat."

I hungrily took a menu. My mouth watered at the descriptions—sliced turkey breast with mashed potatoes and gravy, green beans almondine on the side. An experienced waitress with sausage curls atop her head, Irene, told me, "Oh, no we don't get to order anything we want. You get a hamburger, fries, and a Coke."

Whatever. I salivated as I headed for the counter to get my platter, but saw only a thin burger, tiny pickle, slice of tomato, and one leaf of lettuce. I thought, *This is my only meal of the day—it's not enough!* I asked a cook, Dmitri, a Greek man with a handlebar mustache, "May I please have a slice of cheese on the burger and a little extra lettuce?" He quietly slipped them on my platter. I also asked him to switch my Coke for a milk shake. "Chocolate, please." He shook his head at first, indicating shakes were not included, but he winked and shook it up for me.

Irene said to follow her downstairs to the basement where workers ate. Her manner was pleasant. She asked if she could give me a tip. I nodded and thought, *It may be the only tip I'll ever get.*

She said, "People who sit at the counter want to be served real fast."

Jeez, I got that much. I would have rolled my eyes, but I closed them to appreciate the wonderful sensations in my mouth—tastes of melted cheese on fatty beef, ketchup on a sweet roll, and chocolate foam. I paid attention, as Carmen had shown me, to chewing and swallowing—and felt my tummy full for the first time in a long time.

———

In the morning after Carmen left for work, I picked up my skirt to shorten the hem and saw smears of ketchup and grease on it. I washed and hung it up in the bathtub to dry. Hours later, I pulled back the shower curtain, horrified to find the skirt shrunken and curled up into a thousand wrinkles. I could not believe my eyes. I read the label: *crepe, dry clean only.* Too late, I remembered Mom's advice: always check fabrics for care instructions.

Well, I'd just have to iron out the wrinkles. I searched all the closets and cabinets but turned up no iron. I thought that a neighbor would surely lend me an iron, I knocked on the downstairs door. A little blue-eyed girl opened it.

I smiled brightly and said hello. I explained I lived upstairs and said, "Please tell your mother I'd like to speak with her." She said to wait a minute and shut the door.

After many minutes, the child cracked open the door and asked, "What do you want?"

I felt ridiculous pitching my case to a girl of about eight years old, but asked, "Could I please borrow her iron? I'll bring it right back."

Again, the girl closed the door. When it cracked opened again, I expected to see the mother's face, but it was the girl again, who said quickly, "My mother says no," and slammed the door in my face.

What a mean mother, I thought. *What am I going to do?* I trudged back up the stairs. *I can't wear the skirt as it is so I must improvise something.* I asked myself what women did before the invention of irons? I spread the skirt over a bath towel on the kitchen table, boiled water, then lifted the heavy pot and set it down on the flattened skirt, expecting it to smooth the wrinkles. No go. After several tries, I gave up, and yelled out in frustration, "I need a goddamn iron but can't afford one!"

I could not be late for work again and, having no choice, I pulled on the skirt—not only wrinkled but shrunk. Yesterday, it was too long; today too short. I thought, *Crappy crepe!* Unable to control looking weird at work, I turned to an important decision I had to make at the restaurant. Should I ask Dmitri for *a cheeseburger or a bacon burger?*

About to leave, I heard noises downstairs: a man's gruff voice, and the entrance door opening and closing. I peeped out the window and saw a man in working clothes talking to a woman in a floppy housedress (*probably the mean woman who wouldn't help me*). She pointed to the front door and shot glances up to the third-floor window from which I peered down. I ducked. To get to work I'd have to make it past her. I mentally commanded, *Go inside, lady!*

When I could no longer see or hear her, I grabbed one of Henry's shawls to cover my short, tight skirt so I wouldn't look like a prostitute and took mincing steps to the bottom of the stairs, where I bumped into the kneeling workman fixing the lock. I said, in my most feminine and educated voice, "Good evening. I have an apartment here. Is there a problem?"

He looked up at me. "Oh," he said with an Irish lilt, "Got a call sayin' somebody be tamperin' w' the door." He turned a screw, "Lots of riff-raff around here these days, hippies, coloreds. You know, after the riot nearby in Roxbury. But don't worry Miss, I fixed it. No one can get in now without their proper key." As he left, he looked at my face, my White Irish face, and smiled.

"Thank you," I said with a sweet, White smile, but felt paralyzed, wondering what the hell to do. *Carmen and I will be locked out.* I rummaged in my bag for scrap paper, folded it, and slipped it between the door and jamb to keep it open. I prayed that no one would notice this for an hour, until Carmen got home.

I walked as fast as I could with the tight skirt hugging my thighs. The little girl saw me and said, "Chop chop," as she mimicked me stepping like a stereotyped Chinese woman with bound feet. *Nasty*, I thought. *The apple doesn't fall far from the miserable tree.*

I reached Carmen. As he leaned on a broom, I said, "This can't go on. With luck we might get back into Henry's to stay tonight, but they're watching us, and we have to get out before we get arrested or something."

He got glum, "Where would we go, babe?"

I hurried toward the subway station, and at the crosswalk waiting for the light to change, I noticed a girl with red hair. When she turned, I recognized her—a friend from my church youth group! Though our faith rarely addressed the supernatural, meeting her felt like a miracle.

"Betty," I exclaimed. "I'm so happy to see you!" The past blasted through my mind: good times in our youth group, partying, marching for civil rights, singing folk songs, laughing. Betty made jokes out of everything. She was my sister Barbara's friend, a couple years older than me. Noting her T-shirt and jeans, I asked, "Are you in college here?"

"Yes, Boston University," she said, looking me up and down with a quizzical face. "I have the same question for *you*," she said. "What are *you* doing in Boston? And what kind of *get-up* are you in?" Betty—always so direct.

I told her I was staying in Cambridge, because that sounded good. "And I have a job in town."

"Barbara told me you were studying at City College." I told her I'd *started* studying at City but took a break. "To drop out and turn on?" she said in a sarcastic tone. I admitted I'd run away from home. She pinched her brows together making her look just like her fussy Jewish mother. She shook her head. "That's dumb."

"Listen, Betty," I said, trying not to sound desperate, "I'm moving out of my apartment. Do you happen to you know anywhere I can stay for a few nights?"

"Starting when?"

"Tonight."

———

I opened the door at Hamburger Haven and customers turned from the counter to look down at my weird skirt. Face flushed, I dreaded taking up my spot in the middle of them. I almost walked back out, but feeling the sudden urge to pee, I rushed downstairs to the bathroom. A sense of relief passed over me—from emptying my bladder, and from knowing I had a bed at Betty's the following night.

But that night, when I left at midnight, I had to go back to Henry's. My mind conjured an image of a locked door blocking me. I worried. *If we can't get into the apartment tonight, where will we sleep? Will we lose our stuff? Will the police bust Carmen for his peyote? Will they lock me up, too?*

I reached the house and crept up the path. Past a tree, I glimpsed in the shadows a figure moving. I freaked out. "It's me," Carmen whispered. "I've been waiting for you for hours." He hadn't dared to pry the door ajar, afraid that lady might call the cops.

"I thought you were a cop," I said, wringing my hands as he jiggled the lock with a pin. We slowly snuck up the stairs to the apartment, and he plopped down, looking blue. I told him I had some news.

"Man, what *now?*"

"I found us another place to stay!"

"Are you messing with me?"

"It happened like magic."

Nervous and excited, the next morning we dragged our stuff to Betty's place to move in just as she moved out. She introduced her roommate, Beatrice, who studied the flute at the Conservatory. She noticed Carmen's flute case, and immediately they hit it off talking music. Betty showed us to the large room with three narrow mattresses on the floor. "That's my bed," she said, pointing. "I pay for it, so you can take it."

"What, your bed is like a piece of real estate you can rent out?" I said, and we all laughed. Betty wished us good luck, and when she left for home in Queens, part of me wished to follow.

Beatrice pointed to another bed, one belonging to a girl who'd moved out, saying we could use that one, too. To give us privacy, she moved her mattress to the living room. Soon

Beatrice and Carmen took out their flutes and played a duet. "Carmen, you're so *good*," Beatrice said, and encouraged him to apply to the Conservatory. She invited us to stay as long as we liked.

"By any chance," I asked, "do you have an *iron?*"

———

Later, with my ironed skirt all smoothed out, I felt better showing up at Hamburger Haven. But Karen greeted me with the announcement: "You're not working the counter anymore." I lowered my head. I figured she'd heard too many customer complaints, and I was fired. She smiled and said, "You're promoted!"

I began "working the booths," a whole different experience. Couples took more time to eat. Customers didn't shout at me; in fact, some shared small talk or kidded me about my New *Yawk* accent. A man who saw me peering over his shoulder as he read *TIME* magazine said he was a history professor and gladly talked to me about Israel's six-day war and the first Negro appointed to the Supreme Court. He left a good tip.

However, people at tables ordered larger and more complicated meals, and I had trouble remembering them. I grew nervous. Pressure on my bladder caused me to dash down to the bathroom frequently, which the other waitresses clearly noticed but no one said a word.

———

I had Friday night off. Carmen arrived home with his ten bucks and said, "Tonight we're gonna hit the town!" I needed sneakers, but agreed we needed a "date" more. He found a jazz club with a low cover charge that also featured a good band.

In the largely Black audience, we sat down near the piano and ordered white wine. In the mellow atmosphere I felt relaxed. I noticed a few other interracial tables—most were hip and young, but one mature White woman caught my eye. With black hair cut short and sharp and wearing an elegant black-and-white-striped dress, she looked conservative and out of place, though she sat with a handsome Black man. The emcee called up the band, and the guy stood up! Two other Black men stood up, brass horns in hand, and the three men took the stage. The elegant woman followed them and took her seat at the piano! She blew my mind. *No way*, I thought. *She plays in the band!* She flashed a wide smile at me, and I laughed, chiding myself for falling into the easy trap of stereotyping.

The jazz, the wine, the soft light, and the good company all created a sweet heat within me. I forgot my worries. I reached for Carmen's knee, noticing his sax case lay on his lap—he carried it everywhere, always hoping for a chance to play. I enjoyed watching him get absorbed listening to the jazz. At the saxophone solo, he got so enthusiastic he could hardly keep seated. During break he said, "Dig how the cat played the music in his *head*, taking his sax way out."

"For me, he went too far off. I got lost."

Carmen said, "That's jazz, man. Nothing is rehearsed. The cats start off with a motif, totally in tune with each other. Then one takes off, improvises, goes farther and farther out."

"It put me on edge."

"Yeah, damn right. Puts us all on edge. Then the cats get back to the motif, and man, they lead us back home."

"What if you can't find your way back home?"

He said, "You will if you totally tune in, trust the beat of the bass." He smiled. "Jazz teaches you about *life*. You gotta be in the moment, ready for anything, babe." He pronounced every syllable of the word, "Im-prov-i-sa-tion." *The two of us*, I thought, *we improvise our way out of the junk thrown at us and pick ourselves back up*. He said, "Trust the beat, babe, it's the constant the other instruments weave around."

"Carmen, I'm getting it." I took his hand. "You're my bass, the beat I weave around."

———

At one in the morning, we stood to leave the club, and asked the hostess about the train. She said, "You missed the midnight train—nothing now until the morning."

I said to Carmen, "Shit. In New York, the subway runs day and night. I can't believe we're stuck."

"We ain't stuck," he said. "We just gotta go by foot."

I asked, "How far?"

He didn't know or care. He said he felt so "jazzed up" he could walk all night. He seemed to need less sleep, less food, less security than I did. I envied that—it made him free. We climbed the bridge over the Charles River. The water running underneath looked black in the dark. A white seagull floated down and landed upon a lamp post with such grace that she inspired Carmen to stop and play his sax—not a soul around to listen except the gull and me. I felt so exhausted that not even the sharp sounds of the sax kept me from dozing off. Upon opening my heavy eyes, astonishment filled me as layers of rose and gold shimmered in the dawning sky.

Fatigued, we climbed to Betty's door. Carmen slapped his pockets and said, "Shit, where's the key?" I felt urine trickle down my bare legs—hot, fast and silent. I prayed he wouldn't look down and see the puddle at my feet, that he wouldn't smell anything. He did locate the key, *glory be*, and unlocked the door. I later cleaned up my mess, in secret, leaving Carmen in the dark about what was really going on with me.

In my journal over the next week, I wrote how the urgency to urinate at odd times continued and made me jittery. Walking calmed me down. I'd finally purchased sneakers and took long walks by the Charles River, where I'd stop to journal. One pleasant afternoon I followed a tree-lined path along the banks and got lost in gazing at the river.

I suddenly looked up, fearing I'd lost track of time. I had no watch, saw no clock towers. I sprinted on the river path as fast as I could back to Betty's but had wandered farther than usual. I suddenly had to go really bad. No public toilet around, no restaurants, no bushes to hide under. On the bridge over the river, as two trains racing in opposite directions crossed in a noisy blur, I lost it. Relieved physically, but distressed mentally, I stared at my new sneakers and thought, *I'll wash them, and I'll just have to work in wet sneakers.*

I carried cold dread that I might someday lose control of my bladder at work at Hamburger Haven. On the first day of July, it happened. I flew to the bathroom, crashed into the stall but couldn't pull down my hose fast enough—the pee filled my panties and ran down my stockings and into my sneakers. I pulled everything off and stood half naked at the sink, hoping no one else would enter. I rinsed off my sneakers, set them aside, dabbed the stockings, squirted soap on my panties, scrubbed them and wrung them out, wiped my legs with a soapy paper towel, and pulled up my wet panties followed by damp pantyhose that clung to my skin. I tugged, praying the nylon wouldn't run. With paper towels I dabbed my sneakers and slipped them back on.

I reapplied lipstick and rouge and walked back upstairs as if nothing had happened. I coolly picked up an order from the kitchen counter and placed it on the table in front of an elderly woman, who whined she'd waited too long, and her hamburger was cold. I had no excuse to offer.

At break-time, I went outside to the public phone booth and tried to reach Maureen by dialing the number to our apartment. The number was disconnected. I tried my parents' phone but got a message they had a new number. I rummaged through my bag to find a scrap of paper and a pen to write down the new number. Shaking, I called the operator, who dialed "collect" for me. I heard my father answer, and the operator ask if he would "accept a call from Janet." To my relief, he said yes.

"How are you, Janet?" Dad sounded glad to hear from me. I said I was fine and asked about him and Mom and Maureen. He said, "Just honky dory." I asked why he got a new number, and he said, "Your mother and I moved to a bigger apartment, in the same building. To take Maureen in."

Feeling guilt, I asked for Maureen. She wasn't home. I asked, "Did you get my letters?"

"Got them, thanks. They were forwarded. So you like Provincetown?"

I said, "Now I'm in Boston."

"Boy," Dad said, "you sure are getting around. I don't know how you do it. It's good to be foot loose and fancy free while you're young and full of piss and vinegar."

"Yeah," I said. *Piss for sure*, I thought. "Well, I just wanted to call and see how you all are." My throat choked up. He thanked me for calling and said to keep in touch. I hung up, still shaking, and headed straight through the doors of Hamburger Haven. I approached Karen at the cash register and lied, "I just found out my father is very sick," followed by the truth, "I have to quit because I need to go back home right away."

Chapter 19
THE SUMMER OF LOVE

irst time ever I'd stuck my thumb out to hitch—standing on the Thruway, I worried who would pick up a White girl and a Black boy loaded with baggage. But soon a guy in a van decorated with peace signs and flowers heading to New York picked us up. Young with ginger hair, he asked what attracted us to Boston, and Carmen answered, "Adventure." We said we'd stuck together through thick and thin, which moved the guy so much he offered to drop us home at our *door*, on the corner of Third Street and Avenue B.

We found Marie at home, and she greeted us with hugs. We left our bags with her and scooted a few blocks down to eat at Junior's Cave, where she sometimes waitressed. Between two flashy parked cars, we entered the cave-like darkness and made our way to a table.

"Babe," Carmen said, holding my hand. "We sure had a wild three weeks."

"It felt like a year," I said, releasing a breath. "I'm so glad to be back in New York." I went to wash my hands and noted, *Hey, I'm not in a mad rush to pee.* I figured maybe I felt less nervous because I had my own pad and bed to lay my head that night.

I noticed a flyer announcing fireworks that night in Tomkins Square Park, for the Fourth of July. *My favorite holiday*, I thought. *I can celebrate independence—my country's and my own.*

A Black man with a sinewy body approached our table. A thin beard accented his hard jaw. Carmen called him Junior and said, "This is my woman." I saw no warmth in the vacant eyes he set on me.

"Vanilla flavor," Junior said and lifted his chin to Carmen. "Gonna share the wealth, bro?" When I pulled back, he laughed with an open mouth, flashing a gold tooth. I glued my eyes to the menu. Carmen asked what's up in the kitchen, and Junior said, "Corn bread, collards, and chitlins."

"What are chitlins?" I asked.

"The large intestines of a pig." Junior succeeded in arousing my disgust, and exploded in laughter as he pointed at my face. He returned to the kitchen.

Carmen said, "Don't worry, babe, it's soul food. It tastes good." He looked around at the people hanging out and recognized some musicians. "Here to cop some dope. Whatever you want—pot, coke, uppers, downers—get it at Junior's." Carmen identified guys with big arms and tattoos as regulars at the Cave—pimps and drug pushers. My stomach tightened. I thought about the warning issued by my ninth-grade teacher who'd called drug addiction "a living death."

"Why did you bring me here?" I challenged Carmen, just as a beautiful young White woman with fine long hair and a full round belly placed plates on our table and left without a smile. Carmen said, "That's Junior's woman," before he dug into the chitlins. I ate only the corn bread and collards.

———

"Disgusting," I said later on Third Street as we lugged our stuff up four flights of stairs. "Junior knocked up that girl, and he was coming on to *me*?"

"Not really coming on," Carmen said, sweating. "More like messing with your head."

"Don't defend him," I said as I unlocked the door. A blast of hellish heat hit us. We dropped our bags and pried open the back window but felt no breeze. Through the window and walls, I heard sounds of humanity: a baby crying, a toilet flushing, water running, drummers playing, lovers grunting, and bedsprings creaking. A woman's voice from a neighboring pad penetrated my ears, "Just let me tell you a coupla mother fuckin' things . . ."

I looked down to the splintered floor and recoiled in horror—an army of dark mustard-brown insects shaped like tanks feasted on a moldy piece of bread on the floor, a scrap we must have left when we'd vacated.

"They invade more in summer heat," Carmen explained. He knew about cockroaches from the flats in Kansas City; I'd never had to live with them. He swept the roach-covered bread into a dustpan and dumped it into a garbage bag.

Repelled, I said, "If we're gonna live here, we gotta exterminate the roaches. And we need to sand the floor and paint it."

"Yeah, when we get some dough," he said.

"We can start by cleaning at least." Though fatigued from our move down from Boston, I felt motivated to spray Windex on the tall back window. But no matter how much I wiped it, the grime and bird shit on the outside remained, blocking the light. I said, "Only curtains will hide the crap." Carmen said he was going to the park. "You're leaving?" I asked, taken aback. "You're ducking out on me all over again?"

"Look, you want paint, curtains—we need bread to pay for it. I'll try to line up a gig."

I handed him the garbage bag full of roaches to take outside to the bin.

———

Stifling heat, the smell of dust, and the crackle of cockroaches behind the walls quickly drove me out to follow Carmen to Tompkins Square Park. I found Carmen playing his flute with bongo players, and Marie in the circle of stoned admirers around them. Among the usual old Ukrainian couples walking dogs, and Puerto Ricans and Blacks in dashikis, I noticed new groups— young White students and hippie types. Marie told me how things had changed since news of the Memorial Day police raid in the park went national. She said the Lower East Side of New York, newly termed the "East Village," was now hip, the East Coast version of "the Summer of Love" that first erupted on the West Coast in Haight-Ashbury. Months before, I'd hoped to go to San Francisco. I thought, *Now San Francisco has come to me.*

A loud bang made me turn to see men in undershirts with kids about twelve years old setting off illegal firecrackers. I asked myself, *Is this what passes down here for a fireworks display?* The musicians stopped and passed around a hat. I thought, *Is this what Carmen means by a gig?* He saw me but didn't come to me. He began playing again, seeming right at home. I thought, *What the hell am I doing here? I don't fit.*

———

I needed a friend. I thought of Vera, who'd told me at Vassar that she and Ken would be in the city this summer taking courses at Barnard and Columbia. I'd kept their phone number in my wallet, and dialed it in a nearby phone booth, which stunk of urine. No matter—the phone was broken anyway. I traipsed blocks through the East Village before I found a phone that didn't eat my dime and actually emitted a dial tone. The phone rang, then, Vera's voice. "Darling, it's so good to hear from you."

"You, too!" I said with a squeak, swallowing to keep from choking up. "Hey, I'm living in the Lower East Side, and I thought I'd ride up to the Upper West Side and visit . . . if you're free . . . like now?"

————

"You lost weight," Vera said, opening the door with a brilliant smile and hug. I commented on her dangling earrings, which she said I'd inspired her to wear. I smelled pea soup already boiling on the stove, like old times. While we ate, she told me Ken was studying Sanskrit and that she took classes with "the world's foremost authorities" on Tibetan Buddhism. I told her that my boyfriend, Carmen, also read ancient spiritual texts.

Interested, Vera asked how we met. We caught up about our very different "journeys" over the past several months. Later she made café au lait and said she'd been a Francophile since we studied AP French together. That seemed like another lifetime. Remembering it stirred my longing to be a student again.

I asked about Ken, and she said with a blissful smile that they were still in love, which made me think she'd found a way to admit she'd deceived him about when she'd started college. But she said with sorrowful eyes that she'd felt too ashamed to initiate that honest conversation. "I waited too long and now that little lie has grown into a monster." She feared that she'd taken the wrong path and couldn't turn around. I shared the fear of being lost, unable to get back on track.

Vera invited me to spend the night—Ken was at a conference and we could talk in privacy. I hesitated because we had no phone in our pad and Carmen would worry. She wanted to hear more about him. I described him as "interesting, smart, creative." I told her our struggles had bonded us and I hoped that, sharing a pad in the East Village, we'd fulfill our dream of living artists' lives. "But now . . . I'm honestly not sure."

"He's so young," she said in a motherly tone, though she was only two years older. "Both of you, only eighteen. Give it time, my darling." She convinced me to stay the night on the couch.

————

Early the next morning, I opened the door of our pad and saw Carmen asleep on a new mattress he'd placed by the window. I saw he'd softened the harsh bare light bulb by covering it with a paper bag—a no-cost lampshade. There was something in the way he lay there, thin and alone on the splintered floor, that drew me closer. He woke, and his face lit up. "Babe, where were you?"

The air in our pad felt stultifying. I apologized for leaving without notice and said, "Let's talk on the roof." We climbed up there, and, standing on the hot black tar paper, he said, with his usual high spirit, that the roof served as an extra room. I scanned the neighboring rooftops. Under sooty chimneys, I saw men in ripped Grateful Dead T-shirts smoking while noisy kids circled around them.

I addressed what had upset me the night before. "It was Independence Day. You took off for the park, leaving me to clean our pad by myself, then when I found you, you hardly noticed me."

"Babe," he said, "I was *working*." He pulled out eleven one-dollar bills—his haul from the hat.

"That's not enough to fix our pad," I said. "We need real jobs!" He promised he'd get everything we needed to make it "real hip." He took me downstairs to show me the mattress he'd found. I didn't dare ask where he found it. "We're flat broke," I said. I told him I'd gone to visit Vera, and she fed me and even gave me subway fare. "I felt bad having to ask her for a lousy fifteen cents." I leaned against the tub counter and lifted a hand to my head. "So how can we afford to fix our pad?"

"Here's how. Look!" Carmen pulled some more bills from his pocket. He told me he'd called his mama, and she wired him money from his savings account in Kansas City. "A hundred dollars!" I perked up. He picked up a sketchbook and started drawing a floor plan. We leaned together against the tub imagining what our space could be. We agreed on the colors to paint the rooms and where our art would hang on the walls.

He planted my easel in the small back room and said, "Take this space for your studio. I want to see you painting again." He told me that in the park, he'd met a brother who ran a gallery. "I told him you're an artist," Carmen said. "He wants to see your work for a show he's putting together." I felt excited. I asked Carmen where he would practice his music. "Up on the roof," he said. We laughed, toppled over on the mattress, and balled.

The next morning, with change in my pocket, I left early for the kiosk on St. Marks Place where I bought the *New York Times*. I turned to "A" in the classified section, searching for "artist." Most wanted "cut-and-paste" artists. But—I couldn't believe it—I saw an ad for a "painter." And not a house painter.

A man with a gentle voice answered my call and asked if I had experience painting for needlepoint. *Needlepoint?* I thought. *What is that?* But I said, "I can paint anything. I'm a painter!" He laughed and asked what kind of painting I did. I said, "Murals, portraits, figures. And I can copy anything." He gave me the location of his shop: on Madison Avenue at 66th Street. *Wow*, I thought, *I have my foot in a fancy door!*

I shot up to the Upper East Side, where residents adorned windows with flower boxes, and found "Mazaltov's Needlepoint Shop." I knew from Vera that "*mazaltov*" in Hebrew meant "congratulations"—I took it as a positive sign. I observed passersby: mature people dressed in fabrics too heavy for summer, and younger women in light minis wearing fashionable pointy shoes. Feeling okay in my mini but awkward about my sandals, I pumped myself up as I strode inside, thinking, *Hey, sandals are what artists wear.*

A nice-looking man in dark rimmed glasses and thinning brown hair greeted me. He wore no tie, just a loose white shirt over a slight paunch. He smiled and said, "Hi, I'm Mazaltov," his expression as gentle as his voice. He said that my "positive attitude and confidence" on the phone intrigued him. He asked about my experience.

I talked about painting "Willoughby" with Bill at Squire's Restaurants and our mural in Westbury featured in *Better Homes and Gardens*. He raised his eyebrows and said, "Impressive." He asked about school. I said I'd started at City College, but preferred taking classes at the Art Students League and working.

"So this would be your 'day job'?" he said, smiling. I nodded. He showed me a needlepoint canvas and asked if I could paint on it. It had holes for needles to pull wool through.

"It's a canvas," I said. "I can paint on any surface because . . . I'm a painter!" Laughing, he hired me.

———

Back at our pad, I found Carmen up on the roof trying to cool off. Excited about my job, I told him I'd start the very next day. Carmen slapped me five and said he'd go look for work the next day.

"I can't believe my luck," I said. "I found work painting!" He asked if I'd create my own designs. I explained that I'd paint designs the clients selected for wall hangings or pillows. "They apparently like pleasant subjects like butterflies, birds, flowers, and cute cats and dogs."

"You messin' with me?"

I felt bummed. I said, "Look, I don't care *what* I paint. The point is, I'm *painting* and getting *paid* for it." He asked how much, and I said ninety dollars a week. He said that Marie made more than that from tips waitressing. That pissed me off. "For one thing," I said, "I stink at waitressing. It stressed me out. Plus, poor Marie has to work for that creepy Junior in the Cave, while I work for a *mensch*, a gentleman, in a private apartment above the shop, with a kitchenette, and I can make tea or coffee anytime I want, for free. And the view out my window is not of pimp mobiles but of fashionable shops on Madison Avenue."

Carmen grudgingly said, "Cool," as he wiped sweat off his brow.

"You're damn right it's *cool*. Did I mention that my studio is air-conditioned?"

One other artist, Candy, worked beside me in the studio above Mazaltov's shop and generously showed me the ropes my first week. She was a quiet person, like me. We liked to concentrate on painting while we listened to classical music on the radio— just like Bill and I had.

In a large room next to ours, lively women spoke in a foreign language as they did their handiwork for Mazaltov's clients. They laughed and chatted continuously as they completed projects in needlepoint and other sorts of embroidery that looked similar to what Nanny and my great aunts had created. Candy wondered what language they spoke. I said it sounded like Hungarian, the language I'd heard Nanny and her sisters use with each other as they cooked and sewed. I relayed the story of my Aunt Ilona, who'd been employed as a lady's maid. "She'd worked near Madison Avenue, too."

Candy said, "Far out."

"In fact, just a few blocks north of where we're now sitting, my Aunt Ilona held a responsible position with a wealthy family, the Vogels, who took her with them everywhere. They traveled to Europe every summer and gave Ilona the opportunity to visit relatives in Budapest."

Candy said she had Irish heritage. I said, "Me, too. My father's side is Irish." Candy loosened up and confided she was living with a guy, a Puerto Rican, on the West Side of Manhattan in the Chelsea area. I told her about Carmen. Discovering that we were both secretly living downtown in interracial relationships, we developed trust and talked freely to each other.

I told Candy that sometimes when I'm heading uptown, the

downtown people make me feel that I'm crossing into enemy territory. "Hippies, panhandlers, and the homeless who sleep in Tompkins Square Park all night," I said. "Just this morning, I was rushing through the park and a strung-out dude yelled, 'Hey, you look like you work for the fuckin' Establishment.'" Candy called the remark a paranoid put-down. "The priceless part," I said, "was the next thing out of the guy's mouth: 'Got any change?'" We laughed. But deep down we knew that we *were* leading double lives, and sometimes navigating the class line felt tricky.

On payday at the end of the day, I brought my finished needlepoint designs down to the retail shop and waited for Mazaltov. At the bench beside me, the conservatively dressed accountant prepared paychecks. I observed her lacquered nails, perfect coiffed hair, and spectacular alligator shoes. *Put a bonnet on her head,* I thought, *and she'd resemble an aristocratic lady in Bill's mural, "Willoughby."* She informed me my records were incomplete, and asked for my phone number.

"I have no phone." She looked at me with piercing, uncomprehending eyes. She asked my address. Learning I lived on Third Street and Avenue B, her mouth, coated in tangerine lipstick, flattened into a frown. Mazaltov walked in, apparently having overheard our exchange, and said, "The East Village is full of artists, the new hip neighborhood." In front of the all the ladies, he smiled at me and personally handed me my check. Again, for all to hear, he said, "In the next few weeks, Janet, I want you to come up with your own designs. I'm very pleased with your work."

———

On the subway home, I thought of what I could buy with my first check—I needed proper shoes and a dress for work. I couldn't wait to tell Carmen I would be creating designs, but in our pad, I found him slumped on the bathtub counter. He said, "Someone stole my flute." His voice cracked. "I've had it since ninth grade."

I felt bad for him and sympathized as he looked about to cry. "I put it down for just a second on a park bench . . ."

The park? I was surprised he'd played in the park on a day he had promised to spend looking for work. He said, "You got paid today?" I showed him my check for sixty-nine dollars. "Babe, I need this money to buy a new flute."

Chapter 20
THE REAL GREAT SOCIETY

On Saturday at a pawn shop, of all places, Carmen found a fine new flute that cost me almost all of my first paycheck. To make up, he took me to meet the cool guy who'd just set up a gallery right off Tompkins Square Park. The corner storefront gleamed with floor-to-ceiling picture windows over which hung a sign, "Creative Space Gallery." Inside, Carmen spotted a burly man with a scar on his face and introduced us. "This is Ramon," he said. "Founder of the gallery."

Ramon gripped my hand, his arms powerful, his eyes like dark coals. With his chin up, he said the gallery was just a part of his grander plan. He and his gang rented the entire building and offered all kinds of programs—all affordable for this community. "Take any course for just five bucks!" He showed me a bulletin board. I noticed an acting course taught by an Off-Broadway actor and film star and signed right up.

Ramon laughed at my enthusiasm and invited Carmen and me upstairs, where he and his gang lived. The industrial elevator rose, and doors clanked open upon a huge space with walls painted pitch black. Ramon said, "Welcome to our inner sanctum," I felt disoriented, but followed Ramon in taking off our shoes and moving to the center, a hub with many side rooms, in which I saw guys lying about. They padded barefoot to the central space to join us, striking me as men who wanted others to fear them. But they smiled when Ramon lit a candle, introduced Carmen and me, and invited us all to sit on pillows in a circle on the floor. It seemed like a ritual, their way of incorporating strangers. Ramon brought out a glass contraption filled with water with long tubes that they called a hookah. Carmen sucked on a tube; I passed.

Latin music reverberated from tall speakers that surrounded us on all sides. The guys, now lying back on elbows, laughed among themselves. Ramon pointed to them and said, "See these thugs? We all met in prison. We bonded. No one knew what the hell we'd do when we was free." He told us how during TV time in prison, he'd watched LBJ drawl about the Great Society and aid for Black communities. "A light bulb went off in my head," he said. "The next time we all met in mess hall, I sprung my idea. Ain't that right?"

"Right on, brother," they mumbled.

Ramon said, "I told 'em, soon's we get out we gonna set up our own *community* center. And that's just what we did. We got ourselves an application—our chicks typed it up. I dictated: 'The kids in the ghetto you want to train, we know them and all their tricks. They're restless, need a place to express themselves. We'll get tutors, teach 'em music and art, plus survival skills. We'll keep 'em off the streets, outta trouble. We'll cut down crime. And no more riots.'" I thought his idea very similar to the music and art program Carmen and I had tried to launch with Stan. I asked Ramon if they got the grant. He proudly said, "LBJ and the Great Society folks fell all over themselves gettin' bread to this poor Black community right here, man! We're callin' our organization the *Real* Great Society!" I laughed.

Descending in the elevator, Carmen reminded Ramon they'd talked about my art. Downstairs, Ramon said to me, "My gallery here is puttin' on the first ever art show for local artists. About fuckin' time, right?" He called over the one in charge of the exhibit, Bostic, a handsome and assured Black man. Bostic greeted Carmen and said to me, "Sure, I'll look at your work, sister. Hey, why don't you two come by my pad tonight for some grub and meet my woman?"

———————

High in spirits, Carmen and I carried two of my paintings to Bostic's pad closer off Avenue A and 5th Street. Suzie, a White woman with long, blond hair, greeted us wearing hip hugger bell bottoms. Bostic showed us his library with books on history, and Suzie showed us the pad, which she kept clean, organized, and decorated with Bostic's abstract art. Furniture was minimal, but enough for comfort. An interracial couple—*Challenging,* I thought, *but it looks like they're making it work.* I said, "I'm impressed how you transformed your railroad flat into a *home.*" She tended to a pot on the stove, and I sat with the men on cushions on the floor while breathing in aromas from the kitchen of spiced pork, rice, and beans.

Bostic lit a joint, passed it to Carmen, and slipped on a record, *Bird in Paradise,* by Charlie "Bird" Parker. Carmen flipped and said, "He's my man! Best alto sax ever. I was born in his hometown, Kansas City, dig that. He left for New York and made it big."

I knew Carmen dreamed of making it, like Bird. Bostic said Bird died too young. I asked the cause of death. "Heroin." *How tragic,* I thought. Talents and youthful ambitions sabotaged by drugs.

With a sweet smile, Suzie called us to dinner. We talked about how hard it was for artists to make a living. Even getting grants from foundations were suspect because they were, in Bostic's opinion, only corporate schemes for tax deductions and more profit. We were all artists except Suzie, who worked full time as a secretary, supporting Bostic's art. *She works,* I thought, *and plays the wifey role—cleaning, cooking. And him? He's doing "his thing."*

After dinner Bostic asked to see the oil paintings I'd brought— two nudes— the *Polynesian Girl* of a Black model, and the other of a White female model. He said he'd include them both for the upcoming exhibit at Creative Space Gallery at the Real Great Society. *Wow!* I thought. *A lucky week for me.*

Bostic rolled another joint, and said to me, "So you work at a fancy shop uptown. Don't you feel like you're selling out?"

His question surprised me. "No," I said. "We need the money. It's not like I design ads for corporations or anything. I'm not pushing crap products." He said that I was catering to ladies married to capitalists and war mongers. I felt stung.

"Guess how much desire I have to go uptown," he said. "Zero." Not even for museums and galleries, he added, because they showed nothing about him or his culture. Carmen and I agreed the art world needed more representation of Blacks and women. Bostic said, "White culture is so flat. Cookie-press. It bores me to death."

"Tomorrow," I announced, "I'll be taking a daring trip, to Queens, land of the dangerous cookie-press." All turned to face me, like, is this chick for real? Truly, my own discontent with White suburbia had driven me out, but Bostic's view—so narrow it sounded paranoid—irritated me. I said, "I hope to escape being flattened into a cookie."

––––––––

I called Mom. I realized I'd missed her birthday and apologized. Happy to hear from me, she invited me home for dinner. Maureen greeted me at the door, dark kohl lining her eyes in the striking Cleopatra look, and showed me her room in the new apartment. She said Dad was on the outs and living elsewhere. No one knew his address. When Mom arrived home from work, I gave her a small box of chocolates for her birthday, which we sampled while waiting for Barbara and her husband Maurice to arrive.

Mom took a call and looked upset. It was from Queens General Hospital—Dad had suffered a heart attack. Mom quickly alerted Barbara to meet us at the hospital. In the waiting room, tasteless sugar cookies left out by heavy nurses reminded me of the image of Queens as a giant cookie-cutter. Mom said she worried because this was Dad's second heart attack. "All the alcohol and smoking—it's taking a toll on his heart." When nurses allowed us into his room, his pale face stunned me. Seeing the IV tubes and hearing the buzz of machines, I felt a jolt of pity. I put my hand over my nose to block the hospital odors of foul breath, sick bodies, sanitizers. We couldn't hug Dad, so we took turns touching his hand. I thought, *Poor guy. He worked a tough job he hated for us, and now he's recently orphaned, divorced, and estranged. But at least we're all together now.*

Dad tried to sit up. Mom put pillows under his head, asking softly, "Ed, what do the doctors say?"

"Too much stress," he said, then looked straight at me. Had I caused him stress when I'd objected to his return to the family fold after the divorce? And when I'd run away from him full of rage? As if he read my mind, Dad shook his head and smiled stoically, true to his fatherly vow to never lay on his girls the guilt his Catholic mother had laid on him.

———————

Back at Mom's apartment I sat with Maureen in her room. She told me that she and Mom argued constantly. Her cheeks looked rounder, and I worried that stress made her crave the comfort of junk foods. I told her with regret, "I'm so sorry I had to leave you."

She hugged me, saying, "I know," then added, "Believe, me I understand!" I looked for our little kitten Felicia and her bottom lip trembled. She grumbled, "Mom made me give her away." In the compact apartment, Mom overheard us and came to explain there was no room for a litter box. She said I looked "too thin."

Maureen snapped, "I thought *thin* was your thing?" My stomach tightened to hear them spatting. The phone rang; Mom jumped. We dreaded bad news from the hospital. But it was Barbara, saying she'd picked up a cake, for Mom and Maurice—they'd both had birthdays recently.

I recalled Maurice would soon be forty-one, and said, "He's about your age, Mom." She looked bothered and moved to the sitting room. I followed to ask, "What's up?"

She said that she didn't like the way Maurice looked at her. "He corners me in conversation and gets too close, and sometimes I notice. . ." she whispered, gesturing with her hand over her groin, "he's *hard*."

Later, I said to Maureen, "I see that at home, everything is reliably the same —as dysfunctional as ever."

When Barbara and Maurice arrived, I told everybody about my new art job and the art exhibit. "Art runs in *zis* family," Maurice said with a thick French accent. "Like *Mozzer*, like daughter." Mom ignored his reference to her. I invited everybody to the art opening, including Nanny. I asked where she was. Mom guessed she'd arrive soon. Barbara said she only had to climb up the stairs.

"What?" I asked. "Where is Nanny living?" Maureen explained Nanny had taken a one-bedroom in this same building.

Maurice said, "You move out, Grandma moves in, it's like *zat* game, musical chairs . . ."

I asked, perplexed, "What happened to Nanny's house in Queens Village?"

"Sold," Mom said.

I felt a blow to my heart. Only months before, Nanny had sold her vacation house, the lake house, which I sorely missed. Now her main home in Queens Village—where we girls played on stone steps, wandered in Grandpa's garden, and even lived in for two years while Mom went to art school—*that's gone, too?* Barbara said,

"Too much to keep up, all alone." I thought it might be good that Nanny left the house where Pauline's death haunted her.

We heard a knock on the door. I moved to answer it, ready to embrace Nanny, who always loved me without question. But she charged in like a hurricane, flattening me. "So Janet! You left home. To do what? Live with a *man*? A *schwartze*? Janet, are you . . .? Tell me, are you a *prostitute*?"

"Stop! That's enough," Mom said.

My sisters pulled me into Maureen's room. Barbara said, "Don't be upset. Nanny is just Old World. Love, sex, marriage—everything's different now. She grew up in Hungary before the world wars . . ."

"Before the hippies," Maureen said. "Even before the *flappers*."

———

At Creative Space Gallery on Friday evening, I volunteered to help Bostic and Suzie receive art for the exhibit. I looked out for my mother and sisters, who'd promised to come for a preview. Through the glass wall, I spotted the dazzle of Mom's golden beehive hairdo and my sisters' Queen Cleopatra look. As they walked down the street, guys strained to catch an eyeful, and, like bees to honey, panhandlers began to hover. I rushed up the block to meet my family and shepherd them to the gallery. I asked about their walk over from St. Mark's Place and whether they'd liked the cool boutiques—the Indian shop, the artisan earrings, the handmade candles.

Barbara shook her head. "No. After seeing a pawn shop, and learning what's sold in a head shop, Mom got turned off."

Maureen pointed out Tompkins Square Park, where she and friends had joined me in May for the love-in. Mom asked me in a huffy tone, "Is this the park where the riot took place? The day you got your picture in the paper?"

To distract, Barbara pointed to the sign over the entrance to the gallery, "RGS: The *Real* Great Society," and said she thought the name clever. I told my family that the Great Society in DC funded the art courses. Just then I saw Andy, an artist in the community, carrying a large wood carving in African style. I held the door open, we all entered, and I directed Andy to Suzie. The early evening sun streamed in and bathed the space in rosy light. My family studied all the people buzzing around. Maureen asked, "Where's Carmen?" Good question. I figured he'd probably use one of his usual excuses for not showing up: either he had to practice his sax, or he was looking for a gig. Mom looked relieved, not really wanting to meet him.

"Over there," I said. "That guy, Ramon. He runs the place." Maureen commented on the bulging biceps on Ramon and the guys around him. I didn't tell them they were ex-cons. I said they had set up RGS and were damn proud of it. I showed my family the community bulletin board announcement: "Take any class for five dollars." I told them I'd taken an architecture class with a young professor from Cooper Union. I wanted to impress on my mother and sisters that I was not only okay down in the Lower East Side, but I was living the artist life I wanted.

Mom asked to see my paintings, and I took my family to where my two nudes hung. Maureen remembered I'd painted them at the League. Suzie and Bostic approached us, and I introduced everybody. They handed me a gift for volunteering: free tickets to a concert—Indian musicians in the Ravi Sankar tradition. I felt honored and excited. Suzie, charmed by Mom, took her around the gallery.

I told my sisters that Suzie and Bostic were a couple, role models to Carmen and me. "And Bostic is taking a course with me on improvisation."

"Jazz Improvisation?" Barbara asked, impressed.

"Actually, I took it because Carmen is into jazz improv," I said. "But the course I'm taking is Improv for Actors. See that man over there with the grey beard?" I identified him as Arnold Johnson, an off-Broadway actor, who starred in a movie Robert Downey was currently filming in the city, *Putney Swope*. Barbara agreed it was cool the teacher was an actor in a movie. I said, "In class last night he got Bostic and me onto the stage to improvise a scene."

"From which play?"

"No play. In improv we have to make the whole thing up. Arnold directed us to do something with our hands. I mimed doing needlepoint." All three of us laughed because none of us could even sew. "Bostic mimed peeling an apple with a knife, then Arnold told us to start talking. I felt so awkward! No script. Neither of us could think of a word. Arthur told me to just say whatever popped into my mind. I blurted out, 'I'm pregnant!'"

Barbara's mouth dropped.

I gave the gist of the dialog that followed:

Bostic: What do you expect me to do about it?
Me: We could get married.
Bostic: Not my style, but I'll give you money to take care of it.

"No!" Barbara said with a shocked face, "Don't tell me!"

"Not in real life," I assured her. "We were just improvising!"

"Oh, what a relief." Barbara took me aside to whisper, "Remember my friend Linda? Her boyfriend paid for her to fly to Puerto Rico, the only place where abortion is legal. In the United States, there are only three options: have the baby, adoption, or a back alley abortion." I recalled horrifying pictures I'd seen in teen magazines of women lying dead in pools of blood. Barbara asked me, "Have you thought about what you would do if you did get pregnant?"

My stomach flipped at the possibility. "Don't worry," I said. "I'm still on the Pill."

Mom wanted to get to the subway before dark, and I walked them back to the station at St. Marks Place. We passed a tattooed guy with sunken cheeks, who said to us, "You ladies look like queens."

"Queens from Queens," I said smiling.

He opened his mouth, full of gaps where teeth had either been pulled or punched out, and repeated, "Queens from Queens, queens from Queens."

Mom asked, "Janet, why did you talk to that strange person?"

Looking through the eyes of my mother, I surveyed the people around us. A barrel-chested man allowed his dog to poke his snout up their dresses—*vicariously getting a sniff himself*, I thought. An old lady, having a heated conversation with herself, bumped into us. I noticed more pimps and pushers than usual, and on this day it seemed hippies outdid themselves with bizarre costumes, complete with fringe and feather headdresses. A guy with long hair flying, wearing a gauzy tutu and swinging his arms like the tooth fairy, blazed right by us on roller skates. Some Puerto Ricans, expressing their feeling that their old territory had been "invaded," heckled the hippies and the gay people, telling them, "Go back where you came from." Mom definitely appeared ready to head back home.

I returned to the RGS art gallery. Carmen's former roommate surprised me by stumbling in with arms wrapped around two huge expressionistic paintings. Fran grinned when he saw me. After I registered him, I looked closely at one work. "You're known for your wild brushstrokes," I said. "Surprising shapes and unexpected colors. Yet somehow I sense an underlying consistency." His head bobbed. He said he'd created an "all-over" texture by building up plaster on the ground of the canvas. I said it worked to unify the whole thing.

"Yes!" Fran exclaimed. "Below all the chaos is underlying peace." His idol was the obscure Mark Tobey, who'd influenced Jackson Pollock, who later became famous. Fran said Tobey worked in a quieter way on small canvasses. He shared Tobey's aim: to find wholeness by balancing opposites, like East/West, religion/science, image/word. I told Fran that my world, too, seemed charged with contradictions and paradoxes. I liked the Taoist symbol of yin-yang—it helped me see how opposites feed into each other. Fran told me Tobey followed the nineteenth century Persian Baha'i revelation that "Everything is one."

"Now you sound like Carmen: 'Everything is everything.'" Carmen, just entering the gallery, overheard his old friend and me reciting his motto, and cracked up.

When Fran departed, Ramon closed up shop, and again invited Carmen and me up to the inner sanctum. Once upstairs, seated on cushions, he played music he called "psychedelic," signaling his men to emerge from their rooms. He took out the hookah. After a few inhalations, Ramon said to Carmen, "That guy with the wild hair and wild paintings—you joked with him. You're tight with him?"

Carmen said, "Fran? I used to live with him."

"Live with him? The guy's a fruitcake. You hugged him, Carmen. Are you fuckin' queer?" Carmen's eyes and mouth opened, expressing the same shock I was feeling. Ramon laughed and the guys around him laughed. He said, "Just messin' witchoo."

The hookah made the rounds, and the guys sucked on the tubes. Ramon said, "Hey, Carmen, I heard you wailin' on your sax the other day in the park. You know, my man, we know dudes who run clubs all over the city."

Carmen perked up and asked, "You got a lead?"

"Yeah, man. But you gotta change your name. Carmen's a girl's name, man." The guys snickered. "From now on, we're gonna call you Carmine." Carmen nodded. I wondered, along with his name, what else would change?

The news of riots in Detroit spread through the Lower East Side like one of the fires there raging out of control. Carmen and I hightailed it down to the Real Great Society and were ushered upstairs, where we found Ramon and his guys hanging with Bostic, Suzie, and Marie, all fixed on a large TV. In the morning twilight on Sunday, July 23rd, police had arrested eighty-five people at a party in Detroit. Suzie expressed distress that police busted a party to honor vets. "Two Black vets home from Vietnam! True, it was an unlicensed bar, but . . ."

"Cops provoked the riot by using excessive fucking force," Bostic interrupted. "That's the way cops operate in poor Black neighborhoods."

Many of us, just months before, had witnessed police busting up the Memorial Day picnic in our park. I thought, *My father's anger at me for joining Carmen in protesting that police injustice provoked me to run away and radically changed the direction of my life.*

Candy and I followed the news of Detroit on the radio at Mazaltov's that week. The governor called in the National Guard to stop the looting, and the mayor announced a nine o'clock curfew, which was ignored. On Wednesday, police hunting for snipers killed three Black teens point-blank. By Thursday, reports circulated about raging fires and mass arrests. Even the ladies in the shop below talked about Detroit, but Candy and I shared dismay that their main concern was not the dozens dead, not the thousands of hurt people—but the damage to *property*.

In our pad in the evening, I updated Carmen on the news. He said, "It's too much. And it's too fucking hot up here. Let's get outta this pad. I gotta jam."

———

I rarely went along with Carmen at night, but not wanting to be alone, I followed him. I watched him, determined to jam, work his way through Tompkins Square Park, sax in hand, heading for the sounds of drums. He first picked up a drummer, then recruited a bass player. Now the search was on for a piano player.

Through air thick and hot as dog's breath, the bunch of us traipsed up and down the Lower East Side searching for a cat named Jamal. No one but this guy "Jamal" would do. Finally, we reached a club between Avenues C and D, in the Gaza Strip. *The Gaza Strip?* Carmen had warned me of its danger, but that's where they found Jamal rapping at the bar with a bunch of other musicians. We perched on stools beside them and tuned in to their conversation. One of the musicians, Sam, lowered his head with grief and said, "My horn was stolen, man."

"Shit, man, me too," another musician said. "My favorite drum—gone!"

Carmen looked bummed out.

"Musicians are under attack down here," Sam said. "Smells like a fuckin' conspiracy." Dumfounded, I piped in to ask who would target musicians. "Who?" Sam replied. "Don't know. Lots of desperate people around." His sad brown eyes met my blue eyes. He said, "Somebody, some group, is attackin' us brothers for sure. And they ain't stoppin' at just the instruments. They goin' for the cats' chicks, too—especially White chicks." His words frightened me. He looked around at the circle of musicians and said, "We gotta protect our chicks."

Jamal cut everybody off. "Look you cats, if you came here to jam—let's fuckin' do it."

Cool. I wanted to hear them jam. I wanted to get my mind off riots and crime, hoping their fears were exaggerated. I couldn't wait for Jamal to lead us to his piano. But he had no piano. A new search was begun for a piano. We walked around dozens of blocks, stopping here, asking questions there, chasing one false lead after another. But still no piano.

Exhausted, I told Carmen, "It's almost midnight. I gotta work in the morning. Can we go home now?"

He said, "No, babe, the cats are just gettin' going. But go and do what you gotta do."

"You mean I should go home alone?" I said, stunned. "After what Sam had just told us? I'm afraid. Can you at least walk me partway?"

"No," he said flatly.

Jamal called, "Let's go, Carmine." *Carmine*, emphasis on *mine*. I knew at that moment that Carmen, the gentle boy I loved was no longer mine.

Chapter 21
AROUND

My legs stiff with fear, I scurried down streets past cruising pimp mobiles and abandoned cars stripped of hubcaps. To calm down I played in my head the soothing voice of Mrs. Rousson reading the 23rd Psalm, *"Yea, though I walk through the valley of the shadow of death, I will fear no evil . . ."* Shirtless men atop a roof passed bottles back and forth. Through windows devoid of curtains, blank eyes fell on me. Fierce fury crowded out fright and propelled me to my door, where I stopped dead. *God damn to hell. Carmen's got the key.*

Laughter and rock music rolled out from behind another door. I knocked, and a guy in an undershirt opened up and stepped out, a cloud of sweet smoke drifting out with him. I said I lived across the hall. "Oh yeah, I know you guys." The smell of alcohol on his breath made me step back. "Your man, Carmen—he plays the sax. I'm Jeremiah." I told him I couldn't get into our pad. He said, "Well, come in, hang with us, join the party." He hesitated. "But . . . I don't want you to get the wrong idea."

"About what?" He opened the door wide and I saw all the stuff he'd crammed into his pad: TVs, stereos, speakers, cameras, radios, and . . . musical instruments.

"You could think we musta stole it all, right?" I said nothing, recalling Sam's complaint of stolen instruments. "But, no, we didn't. So, you'd ask, how'd it get here? It's the weirdest fuckin' thing. My brother and I come home today and the door was open a crack—somebody broke in, probably a junkie. So what did we expect? All our cash—gone, to be cleaned fuckin' out, right?" I shrugged. "Instead, we find all this shit piled up here in our pad. Some assholes broke in, not to *steal* our stuff but to *leave* their stuff. Can you fuckin' believe it?"

"Funny," I said, not knowing what to believe.

"Me and my brothers, we figure guys had cops on their asses and they had to dump their hot goods!" He laughed so hard he snorted. The guys inside were snorting and laughing too. "So join the party. We got weed, we got—"

"Jeremiah, look, I wonder if you can help me. I'm locked out."

"You is locked out?" He strode across the hall, rattled the locked door and looked at the window above the door. He said, "No problem," dashed to his pad, and returned with a baseball bat. Before I could say a word, he smashed the window.

At the sound of shattering glass, the guys at the party laughed and lazily called out, "Hey, waz happenin'?" I figured the neighbors would hear the racket and show up, maybe call the cops. But no one dared.

His brother lifted him to the cracked window, where Jeremiah picked out the shards stuck in the frame and slowly heaved himself through, skillfully avoiding cutting his belly or back on the broken glass. I heard a *thud* when he landed. Jeremiah undid all the locks and opened the door, beaming at all the guys now standing in the hall, cheering.

I said, "You're amazing—you did it."

He stuck his chest out and said, "That's how I do. Burglar by trade."

Burglar? Horrified that I'd just invited a professional burglar to break into my place, I smiled, thanked him, and stared up at the yawning hole. He looked up too and waited. For what? I offered to pay him. With his hands up, palms out he said, "No, Miss, neighbors is like family, glad to help out," and he left.

Inside, I swept up the glass and locked the door with the police lock, out of habit. Stupid, I thought. What's the point? Any creep can now crawl in through the hole above the door and get in, no problem. Again, I ran the phrase through my mind, ". . . fear no evil."

Alone all night, I hardly slept but stumbled to work in the morning. On a break, the fluffiness of the bathroom rug tempted me to lie on the floor . . . for just a minute. The next thing I knew, Candy was standing over me asking if I was okay. I'd conked out. At the end of the day, dragging myself across Tompkins Square Park, focused on one thing—getting to sleep on my mattress—I saw Carmen on a bench with Fran. I didn't stop.

Carmen caught up to me and said, "Hey, babe, I worried about you."

"Bull," I said and kept walking.

He followed me. He said, "I grooved all night. But when I saw the smashed window and found you missing, I flipped. The guys across the hall filled me in."

"Good, then I don't have to." I picked up my pace. He followed, promising to fix the window. I heard meowing and stopped to see a skinny kitten under a bush. Carmen said she must be lost. "Or abandoned," I said. I picked her up and said, "I'll take her home and feed her."

Carmen abruptly turned and said, "I'll catch up with you later." I thought, *He must have spotted a "cat" with more interesting things to offer.*

Fran, who'd been trailing us, walked me home. His eyes looked hurt. He said, "You know, Carmen's changed. He's so thin his pants are falling off. He's not as friendly. And he's always high, so restless, like always looking for the next fix."

A fix. Fran opened my eyes. Why hadn't I figured that out? Jamming all night with jazz musicians, hanging with Ramon and the ex-cons—their new boy, Carmine, was hooked on drugs.

———

Over the weekend the kitten stopped eating altogether; she was so weak all she did was sleep. On Monday morning I gave Carmen ten dollars and said, "Take her to the vet today, okay?" He promised.

I found the kitten dead that evening. When I arrived home from work, there she was, lying stiff in the middle of the kitchen floor. I wrapped her up in a pillowcase, took her downstairs, and searched for a place to bury her in the back yard. There was too much dog poop, and I had no shovel to dig a grave anyway. I had to leave her in a trash can, which broke my heart. Upstairs in our pad, I told Carmen that the kitten died, and started to cry.

"Too bad," he said. "Here, feel better, take a toke."

"Pot?" I stepped back. "I gave you ten bucks for the vet. Did you use it to buy pot?" He said no. I asked, "What did the vet say?"

"Worms."

"Did he treat her?"

"Too late to fix."

"Yes," I agreed, glaring at him. "Too late to fix."

———

Everything needed fixing. When I opened our small fridge the next evening to unload groceries, it smelled of rot and emitted no cold air. *Damn. I just bought it. It's already broke?* The stink and heat stole my appetite. Later, I slapped mayo, ham, and cheese on bread to consume alone, but prepared none of this "White suburban food" for Carmen. I took my sloppy sandwich up to the roof where it was a couple degrees cooler.

Ah, the smoggy pit of the Lower East Side. Above, I could barely make out the distant skyscrapers of midtown Manhattan, but I could clearly see the chrome Chrysler Building, a corporate temple, reflecting the gold of the setting sun. Somewhere in the city, Carmen must be gearing up to enjoy the nightlife.

When the light faded, I descended to make tea, but couldn't get the stove lit. *Anyway*, I thought, *who needs the extra heat?* I decided to read and flicked on the switch, but no light. The radio—nothing. *Oh, I get it, nothing will work because the electricity is out. Who will fix it?* Too bummed to think about it, I readied for sleep and automatically leaned to plug in my alarm clock. No go. Now I worried, *How will I wake up on time?* All night I slept in fits, regularly checking the window to gauge the light. When it appeared to be morning, I had to climb to the roof to confirm the hour. Across many rooftops, blocks away, the clock on the church tower alerted me it was time for me to wake up. *Yes, time to wake up.*

By the time the art show opened on August 5th in the Creative Space at the Real Great Society, I rarely saw or spoke to Carmen. Nothing he promised to fix was fixed. Over our door, the dangerous gaping hole remained. I'd given Carmen money to pay the bill, but we still had no electricity.

For the art reception, I put on my only fancy dress, my Indonesian sheath, and hoped to see the people I'd invited—Stan and the gang, Penny, Vera. None of my friends appeared. But Carmen showed up in a dashiki he'd borrowed from Bostic. I noticed that the sturdy sculptor, Andy, also wore a dashiki. He stood erect but looked small next to his tall African masks and wood sculptures. He strode over to ask Carmen, "Is this your chick, man?" I didn't like the possession implied in the question, but Carmen nodded and told me Andy was his "soul brother." Andy said assertively, "Brother? I could be your old man."

Ramon tapped Carmen's shoulder. "Carmine, got something for you." They ducked upstairs. I wondered, *What shit is he turning Carmen onto now?* Andy guided me over to his sculpture. I told him I loved the African masks at the Metropolitan Museum of Art, the Rockefeller collection.

"Rockefeller?" Andy's face stiffened like one of his masks.

I clarified. "The collection of African and Primitive Art."

"Primitive?" His lips puffed with contempt as he spit out the word.

I immediately apologized. "I just mean to say, your work is *powerful*, as good as anything in a museum." He smiled, pointed to my figurative nudes, and asked who posed for me. I told him I'd used models. He asked if they posed at my studio. I said, "No, at the Art Students League. Even if I could afford a model, my 'studio' is just a small room that's too damn hot. And too dark since the electricity is out."

"I got light in my studio," he said. "It's big. You can spread out. Come any time."

"How nice of you," I said. I did have something in mind to paint—a performance. I'd used the ticket Suzie had given me to attend the concert of Indian music, and the colors and shapes of the costumes and instruments stimulated my imagination. I told Andy, "I'm dying to put the images in my head on canvas, but . . . it's frustrating."

"Don't be frustrated. Come to my place."

Grateful for Andy's invitation, I arrived late afternoon the very next Saturday at his studio. He set up my easel, paint box, and canvas in a corner. "You're so generous," I said, opening my bottle of sweet-smelling linseed oil, eager to get to work. Andy suggested coffee. Bill and I had always started with coffee before we painted "Willoughby." But, not able to get Andy's instant coffee with evaporated milk down my throat, I put the cup down and unfolded my sketches of the Indian musicians in concert. Andy picked up his carving tools. His presence did not keep me from sinking into the deep concentration I'd experienced when painting side by side with Bill.

I grew excited because for the first time, rather than work from a model, I worked from memories and imagination. I painted musicians with shiny black hair, sitting cross-legged in white pants and orange jackets, breathing into golden flutes and drumming on tablas. With the rhythm of chiseling wood in the background, my vision took form on the canvas. I grew ecstatic and oblivious of time.

A sudden halt in the banging and knocking caused me to look up—stunned to see that Andy had stripped off his clothes and stood completely naked. His smile broad and wicked, as if he enjoyed my eyes on him. His strong body looked strikingly similar to the small Black male fertility statues in museums with their flat feet, short legs, and long penis hanging to the knees. "I work better naked," he said, standing defiant, sharp tools in hand. "It makes me feel free."

I felt much less free. I jerked my eyes away and slapped my paint box closed.

"Wait. Draw me. I'll model for you. No charge." Grinning, he struck a pose, pelvis stuck out to show off his erection. With one hand I grabbed the wet oil painting and with the other I tucked my easel under my armpit and snatched the handle of my paint box. As he was hopping into pants, I escaped out the door.

"Stop," he yelled as he chased me to the bottom of the stairs. "Let's be friends. I'll help you carry your stuff." I refused his help. I made it to the street and walked into the hellishly hot, moonless night. We passed a bar, and Andy must have noticed my head turn at the tantalizing smell of burgers on the grill. He said, "Let's get some grub." I said no. I had to put my things down a minute to get a better grip. I smelled the stink of evaporated milk on his breath. He said, "Come on, girl. You paint them nude models. You tellin' me you never strip your own clothes and paint naked?" He snatched my painting, saying, "I'll carry it." I demanded it back, but he wouldn't let go, and stalked me all the way to Third Street.

At my stoop, I swerved around and demanded, "Andy, give me my painting now."

"I'll take it up for you." I said no. That Carmen was home. He said, "So what? He my bro. I wanna see your studio. I let you see mine." I shook my head no, reached for my painting, then thought, *I can do another damn painting*. I charged up the stairs aiming to reach the fourth floor before him and mentally prepared quick moves at the door: unlock it, slip in, and shut the bastard out.

But the little guy wormed himself in.

"Get out," I shouted. He demanded to see my studio. Standing my ground in the kitchen, I pointed to the adjacent little room. "That's it." For what seemed like an interminable time, we stood in the small dark kitchen face to face. He flattered me, tried to coax me, said we could have some fun. When I said nothing, he turned nasty and called me uptight, bigoted, not a real woman, nothing but a scared rabbit.

He undid his pants. He said, "Back in my studio I was just lettin' my nuts hang out. Yo' eyes popped out your head, girl, act like you never seen a man *naked* before. Maybe you never did see a *man* before—little Carmen, he just a *boy*." He looked around. "Where is Carmen? You said he be home."

"He will be."

"Where is he?"

I said nothing.

"It's Saturday night and you don't know where your man is? Carmen's out havin' hisself some fun. We is home—we can have fun, too."

"Andy," I said, "You're right. It *is* Saturday night. Time to go *out*." I inched to the door. "I'll be your date. Let's go back to the bar and eat some burgers."

He huffed. Arms crossed, he plopped against the sink in the kitchen. "How 'bout you *make* me somethin' to eat." I reminded him I had no electricity and had no food in the fridge. I offered to treat. He asked if I liked ice cream.

"Sure. Good idea, let's go for ice cream." I made a move for the door.

He blocked me and asked, "You like chocolate?"

I said, "Sure, let's go."

He said, "I got a chocolate popsicle for you, right here." He exposed his penis. "I'm fixin' to taste me some sweet vanilla tonight. Some creamy vanilla." My heart beating in alarm, I kept my eyes fixed, staring at him straight and hard as if my eyes could smack him against the wall. Fondling his penis he said, "You wanna eat? Eat me."

I heard noises downstairs. "I hear Carmen coming!" I said.

He packed his penis in his pants and leaned against the wall near the door. We waited, listening. The footsteps stopped on a lower landing, a door opened and closed, and my hopes sank. He sneered, "Ain't him. You don't recognize your own man's footsteps. I'd know the footsteps of my woman all the way down the block. I'll tell you where your man is. He's got himself a Black chick who ain't uptight like you. Carmen's havin' him some fun. Fuckin' her good. You don't know a fuckin' thing."

I kept staring him down. The man possessed physical strength. My only possession the force of will that streamed through my eyes, focused on squashing him like a cockroach against the wall. Finally, he gave up and with a barrage of curses, slithered out. I locked all the bolts on the door behind him and collapsed.

That Saturday night, Carmen never did come home.

———————

Too disgusted and afraid to stay alone in my pad, I walked like a sleepless zombie the next day to a phone booth to call Vera. She surprised me by saying she was moving back to Vassar. I took the subway to the Upper Westside to say goodbye. When I arrived, she expressed worry about the circles under my eyes. I helped her fold clothes for her suitcase and pictured her on Vassar's country campus, again feeling envy, then guilt for feeling envy.

She insisted on feeding me pea soup, and over cafe au lait, I asked why she was returning so early. Vera's face sank as told me she'd finally revealed her lie to Ian, admitting she'd been wrong. But he took it badly. She told me, "The longer a mistake goes uncorrected, the worse the consequences." I thought, *Yes, too late to fix*. I felt a flood of sadness—for Vera and Ian, for myself and Carmen, for my parents and all people who fail in love. As I moved to leave, she asked me to carry out the stack of papers from the Sunday *New York Times*. I saw that the magazine featured Martin Luther King Jr. and tucked it under my sticky armpit to read on the subway.

———————

In oppressive heat, I trudged up to my pad and at the top of the stairs I felt slapped at the sight: Carmen passing a joint to a pretty Black girl wearing a scarf around her head. I thought, *Is this the girl Andy had sneered about?* Carmen introduced her as Jasmine. I searched his stoned eyes and drawn face for the Carmen I had loved, the gentle boy with dancing eyes who'd introduced me to jazz and meditation, who played the flute for me as we traveled, my partner in survival. That Carmen was absent. I felt a strange indifference. He looked at me with similar indifference and asked, "Where were you today?"

My frustration and anger exploded. "Where were *you* all last *night*?"

"Babe, I play jazz remember? We get it on at night."

"I needed you." I told him about Andy's assault. His only comment was that it didn't sound like something Andy would do. I felt abandoned and incensed but noises from our pad distracted me. Carmen said Jasmine had brought friends from Brooklyn.

What I saw inside made my head spin: chattering girls with hair dyed red or jet black draped themselves around the tub counter, while a bunch of boys in giddy panic whacked cockroaches. They spoke to me freely. One boy with multiple piercings talked about how he'd dropped out of school and had hepatitis; a heavily made-up Asian girl said she had gonorrhea. I asked her age. She said, "Oh, we're all sixteen." I thought, *These sad kids are still in high school? Too young to be so messed up.* They got busy wrapping straps around their arms. Needles came out.

Oh, no. I froze. *Not heroin. Not in my home.* An image of ashen-faced zombies crashed into my brain as I recalled the ominous warning from a ninth-grade teacher who'd ranted, "Drug pushers who hook kids on drugs destroy them. Drug addicts are the living dead."

Dizzy, I moved into the small back room and, feeling nauseous, slouched against a wall, weeping. I asked myself, *What could make kids so unhappy that they risk their lives?* I screamed to them, to Carmen, to myself, "You have to get out of here. You have to get out of here." I sank to the floor. Next thing I felt myself being lifted and Carmen walking me to the mattress by the gated window. Jasmine gone, the strung-out kids gone. I shut my eyes but could not shut out images of the living dead occupying my head.

I felt Carmen's hands, waking me for sex. It was light. I asked, "What day is it?" He told me, Monday. I said I had to go to work.

"Come on."

Afterwards, the blood all over the sheets stunned me. Carmen asked if I was having my period, but I wasn't. He said, "Fucking weird." I stood wide-eyed, looking down at the stains, bewildered at all the blood that had poured out of me. I had no idea why. I remembered I had not bled the first time I made love. I thought, *Maybe my hymen just broke now for the first time.* But it felt more like something deep inside me just gave out and broke.

I could not leave all that blood to dry and cake up and further foul our pad. I asked Carmen to wash the sheets, but he pouted, like doing laundry was woman's work. *So much for equality,* I thought. *I'll have to be late for work while Carmen goes off somewhere to play. I've been allowing myself to be used. No more.*

In the stifling hot Laundromat, I watched the sheets churn in the washer, and the water turn red to pink, then rinse all traces away like there'd never been any blood. I myself wished to be rinsed clean of my many mistakes. I transferred the sheets to the rumbling dryer and, mesmerized by the spinning, my mind conceived a poem.

After
Thoughts of you crawl in my intestines
gnawing at my gut like sandpaper.
Abandonment pricked a wound.
The raw pulp of my heart passed
out of me like a menstrual clot,
like something unborn, bleeding sharply.

Back on Third Street, Carmen gone, I dressed up in the freshest clothes I owned, and reported to Mazaltov at his office in the shop. I apologized for being late, saying I'd had an emergency. He listened with kind eyes. I said I could make up the hours in the evening. "Fine, I trust you," Mazaltov said. "Here's the key, just lock up when you leave."

At five o'clock, Candy and all the tapestry ladies left for home. I made myself a cup of tea and painted alone in the quiet sanctuary. After a couple hours, hunger urged me to think about picking up groceries and taking them down to Third Street. Then I thought, *What for? No air conditioning. No company. And no electricity, so no reading, no radio, no light.* In the dark all I'd hear would be cockroaches crawling in the kitchen.

Instead, I walked next door to Gristedes, an upscale grocery where the "ladies" shopped. At the deli counter I treated myself, ordering chicken breast on seeded roll with all the works—tomato, lettuce, cheese, and a fat dill pickle. With the privilege of possessing a key, I ascended to the safe and cool needlepoint studio where I enjoyed eating my expensive comfort food. I pulled from my bag the *New York Times Magazine* I'd taken from Vera the morning before and spread open the article by Bayard Rustin, who'd organized with Rev. Martin Luther King Jr., the 1963 march in DC. The title, "A Negro Leader Defines the Way Out of Exploding Ghetto," made me think that I, too, needed to find my way out of the ghetto, the one I cornered myself into.

Sensing a man in the doorway made me gasp. *Oh, Mazaltov.* He said, "I saw the lights were still on." I showed him the design on needlepoint I'd completed and explained I'd taken a dinner break. "That's fine, Janet." Glancing over my shoulder, he said, "I read that article, too." Rustin called the riots in Detroit, "the worst destruction in our cities since the Civil War."

Mazaltov said, "Such a shame." He'd read a letter to the editor by Martin Luther King, Jr. and conveyed his interpretation of King's view: Negro looters had to pay for crimes they'd committed, and so did policy makers for their crimes, like failing to pass a bill to "control the rats that bite babies in the ghetto." Mazaltov and I agreed that Dr. King was "the conscience of our times."

He suddenly changed topics. "Janet, if you like, I'd enjoy your company for dinner on Friday." I'd seen Mazaltov only as a kind boss and felt too startled to say anything except, "Thank you." He and I walked out together.

I couldn't talk to Vera about it, because she'd left town, but I imagined her counsel if I asked her about Mazaltov. I could hear her say, "Janet darling, he likes you and is trying to help you. Accept the opportunity."

But I did decline Mazaltov's invitation. I imagined telling Vera why. "Surely, over dinner, he would ask more about me, and I feel too humiliated about my life to talk about it."

Late coming home from work, I found Carmen sitting slumped on the tub in the dark, brooding. He said, "My sax was stolen."

"Oh, too bad."

"I had that sax since I was eleven years old," he said, almost crying like a little boy.

I couldn't muster up sympathy. Instead, I blurted, "The burglar came in through the window over the door you never fixed."

He said "Look, I'm really broken up right now. And you're *blaming* me?"

"Carmen! You broke your promise. You left a hole big enough for a burglar to get through and that's what happened. All these weeks you left me to sleep here *alone*—did you care what would happen to me if someone fucking broke in? Now I'm supposed to feel sorry you lost your horn?"

He snorted and uttered words that laid me flat. "Babe, you're not music to my ears anymore." And he walked out.

———

On my path through Tompkins Square Park the next morning on my way to Mazaltov's, I saw a woman in a purple hat. I thought, *Too early in the morning to be decked out party style; too hot for purple plastic boots reaching so high up her thighs they almost touch the edge of her skirt so short it reveals the cheeks of her buttocks.*

She flipped her long black hair, stopped to look at me through dark shades, and startled me by saying, "Hello, Janet."

"How do you know my name?" She lowered her sunglasses and my mouth dropped. "Marie?" I asked, flabbergasted. "You dyed your hair black?" She said it was a *fall*, phony hair. I asked about her purple outfit. "You're going out somewhere special?"

Her chest caved in, and she said, "Going nowhere." She was coming back from working all night. She started sniffling. Then I knew.

"Oh, Marie, why?"

"For love," she said, trying to explain. "How do you test

if your love is true?" I wanted to know. "How much will you sacrifice for your man," she asked. "Are you willing to do the ultimate—to prostitute yourself?"

I recoiled. *What a twisted question!* I said, "No. Someone who loved you would never ask that of you." Horrified, I hurried away.

Later that week, habitually cutting across the park on my way to work, I came across another friend, Suzie. She, like Marie, wore large dark sunglasses. I asked how she was, and she showed me by lifting her sunglasses. I saw her pretty face bruised and marred with a black shiner. She hugged me and said goodbye—she planned to leave the East Village for "home." I learned more when I bumped into Arnold, my acting teacher, and he said, "Suzie is everything a guy could ever want in a chick. Bostic is crazy. The fool bopped her one. Just once, and that's it—she packed up."

Marie and Suzie's troubles seemed like a warning signal, and I began to prepare for my own escape.

———

I needed to talk to someone I trusted, someone stable. At the end of the day in Mazaltov's studio, though we weren't supposed to make personal calls, I decided to reach out to Stan at his carting business. He answered, but some strain in his voice kept me from sharing my worries. Instead, I asked him what was wrong. He said they'd just received some bad news.

"Arthur's been arrested," he said. I thought, *Arthur? That quiet, studious, thoughtful guy?* It seemed inconceivable. Stan said no one saw it coming. He finally asked me why I'd called him. I answered vaguely. "Duffy? Are you all right?"

"Uh . . . not really. Someone broke in . . . and . . ." My voice broke.

Stan said, "Look, Duffy, can you get to Jamaica?"

———

"What's happening, Duffy?" Stan asked me as I sat by his desk that evening in Jamaica, but I wanted to hear about Arthur first. Stan looked down with pained eyes. "He was arrested for conspiracy to commit murder."

"No!" The whole gang felt shocked, Stan told me. "Who did Arthur want to kill?" I asked. "A racist, a cop, a Klansman?"

"No. I believe it was Bayard Rustin."

"That makes no sense," I said. I'd just read his article. Rustin was a Black organizer with Martin Luther King, a moderate.

Stan said Arthur believed Rustin was *too* moderate, a sell-out.

"Everything is getting insane."

We sat with that insanity for a grave moment. Then Stan asked about me. I stood up and paced, saying, "Yesterday in Tompkins Square Park I met a troubled friend, full of twisted ideas about love. Today I saw another friend who got punched by someone she loved." Stan listened, his eyebrows narrow. In a serious tone, he asked about the "break-in" I'd mentioned on the phone. I couldn't relive the scene with Andy. I said, "I should go home."

Stan asked, "Home to see your mother?" I said no and told him she would be no help. He said, "You'll talk to your father?" I told Stan that Dad was recovering from a heart attack and that I didn't even know where he lived. He asked, "What do you mean by *home* then?"

"I don't know," I said. "I meant I should go back to Third Street, to get myself together . . . but . . ."

"But what? You don't feel safe there?" I nodded. Stan said then I shouldn't go there. *Where else can I go?* I thought, *I have no alternative.* Stan was already making a call. When he laid the phone in the cradle he said, "Constance is glad to make up the extra bed for you."

Constance. Ain't this something? I thought, *Stan's wife, the model housewife, is prepared to put me up. She may not be his partner in the freedom movement, but the two of them do share a life—intimacy, children, and a home with a room to spare.* I said, "Thanks, but I'll just take the subway to the city."

Stan said that, if I insisted on being stubborn, he insisted on driving me to Third Street. In his Impala, I remarked how weird things have turned out since the time I first showed up at Freedom Place. He recalled that the previous September I was a freshman in college "coming to the ghetto to help Black people, like that evicted woman."

Ironic, I thought. *A year later, now this Black man is coming to a ghetto where I live to help me.* He said, "I see White folks aren't immune to trouble."

White folks. I squirmed every time he said it. I said, "Yeah, I guess trouble is an *equal opportunity* inflictor."

He asked if I still worked the art job uptown, and I nodded. He joked, "I wasn't sure—you were changing jobs every few weeks."

I had to laugh. I counted up the jobs I'd held since I knew Stan: Bill's, the bookstore, the office, the hospital, Hamburger Haven. I said, "The Madison Avenue job is my sixth job this year."

"What's Carmen's job?"

"He has no job." The car swerved slightly, and Stan's face tensed with disdain. He pressed his lips like he wanted to spit out a bad taste. We arrived in Alphabet City. I pointed out his windshield to Tompkins Square Park. Stan remembered it as the place that police raided on Memorial Day, an event that made the East Village famous. I said, "Then hippies poured in from all over."

"Oh, yes, the 'Summer of Love,'" Stan said, cynicism in his voice.

"The flower power and idealism pulled me in," I said. "At first." We passed the Real Great Society building where two of my paintings hung on display. "I left Queens to make this my home—for the artist's life, to be free."

Stan pulled his white Impala between two beat up cars with broken doors and missing tires and said, "Sounds like it didn't turn out the way you hoped." *No, it didn't.* Feeling foolish, I thanked him for the lift and said I'd walk from there. But he objected. "Duffy, I drove you this far, and now I'm going to make damn sure you get home safe by taking you all the way to your door."

Through the stale heat trapped between low-lying tenements, we walked in silence down bottle-strewn streets. Stan, upright in a sharp white shirt, caught the attention of bare-legged Puerto Rican girls straddled over stoop bannisters. With perspiration shimmering on their brown necks, they sung out to him, "*Hola.*" Shouting children, up too late, played in gushing waters of illegally opened fire hydrants. Stan maneuvered around the puddles with sure, heavy steps. But I stepped lightly, like a bug caught in a waterfall, ready to drown, fly, or be blown away.

———

At my pad on the fourth floor, I pulled out my key. I again thanked Stan and hoped he'd go—I didn't want him to see that inside we didn't even have working lights. But he couldn't miss the big hole over the door. Stan asked, "Is that where burglars broke in?" I nodded, and we stepped inside the dark, stale pad. No one home.

I lit some candles in the kitchen and slumped against the tub counter. I said, "I haven't seen Carmen in a couple days, since his sax was stolen."

Stan said, "Really? I have to say it angers me that you work and he doesn't. Duffy, do you think you can eliminate racism by supporting a Black fellow?" I had no answer. A bit softer, he said, "Another thing, you know, you don't end poverty by being poor yourself."

My gut rumbling, I imagined my insides like the interior of a demolished tenement building we'd passed: all rubble, broken glass and mirrors. I said, "Didn't you once tell me that I'd learn more about America on the streets—"

"You don't have to live on these streets." Standing tall, he looked around the place, then looked me in the eye, and said slowly, "Duffy, when I think of the fine person you are, when I think of *you*, I do not picture you *here*, in this place, living this way."

Feeling both flattered and flattened by his words, I fell silent, remembering how in the past he'd praised me (when he wasn't provoking me). He'd once said he wanted his sons to simply be in my presence to learn to see through my eyes; he'd called me a "jewel of youth."

I revealed that I had looked for other places but kept winding up back here because it was the only apartment I could afford. I felt like a loser. "Look," I said, "I'm sorry I dragged you into my personal mess. You need to go back to your community where people have real problems."

"Duffy, you think your problems are not *real*? Hell, your family broke up—that's a real problem, isn't it? And what did your folks do? They cut you and your little sister loose."

I didn't want to go there. "I told my parents I wanted to be on my own."

He got back to my current situation. "It's not just this place that's wrong for you."

He means that Carmen is wrong for me, I thought. I didn't tell Stan that I believed Carmen got hooked. Drugs were the wrecking ball of our once loving relationship, now crumbled like a demolished staircase. I felt discarded in love and foolishly lost in emotions. "Yeah," I said, "I once believed we were soulmates forever, but now I don't think we'll even last the summer."

Stan asked why I felt I couldn't turn to my mother for help, and I spilled out details: her foolish decisions, running away at eighteen with my dad, divorcing him, immediately remarrying. "That didn't even last the summer—"

I stopped— I'd just said the same thing about Carmen and me. Stan's eyes pierced me. I felt flustered but continued to say, "I finally rebelled against her impulsive decisions when she wanted to *remarry* my father."

"I see." After a pause, he asked, "Did your father ever remarry your mother?" I said he wouldn't commit to her. Stan asked me, "Will Carmen commit to you?" My head began spinning, but Stan kept on, like a Mack truck, headlights blazing. He said, "You told me your mother ran away with your father at eighteen." I nodded. "Duffy, what did *you* do when *you* turned eighteen?"

"I . . . uh . . . Oh, God." I had done the same damn thing—ran away with a guy. *Trying so hard not to act like my mother,* I thought, *I myself had acted foolish and impulsive.* Stan held me with his eyes. "I get it," I said. "It's not anyone else. *I* created my own problems."

He said gently and with certainty, "You painted yourself into a corner. You'll paint yourself out."

I thought, *If I could only see a bigger, better picture.*

Stan said that he admired that I tried not to repeat harmful family patterns and tried to break free. But the influence of families has deep roots. "It takes time," he said. "Look, Duffy, you've got the spirit of a rebel. I've watched you get knocked down over and over. You pick yourself up each time. It's like you're boxing with life, but you don't wear gloves. You keep getting back in the same ring for another round. It's time to stop getting punched and get out of the ring."

"I do feel like I'm swinging around, more like on a broken merry-go-round."

"Same idea," Stan said. "You gotta jump off." I felt plastered with confusion. He faced me and demanded my attention. "You can break free, Duffy. Do you *want* to?"

I held onto the counter, trying to balance myself. Embarrassed for being stuck and needy, I couldn't answer. Instead, I asked him, "Why are you here, Stan?" He, who usually commanded words easily, now had trouble answering. He gazed back at me. That's when I knew. I said to myself, *He's here because he loves me. And I love him. It's been that way since I felt a charge when we first met.* Everyone around us at Freedom Place—they all knew we shared feelings. Though we never did—and never could—touch, kiss, or even speak of love. To act on love would complicate our lives beyond repair. To act on love would destroy the integrity I most admired in him, and possibly push me over the edge.

"I think you know why I'm here, Duffy," Stan finally said, our eyes still locked.

"I do." My heart beating, I felt the desire for flight. I imagined wings emerging from my shoulder blades, thrashing, but too mashed to fly.

"Tell me, what do you want to do?" Stan asked, chest heaving.

"I *don't* want . . . to live like this." Once I spoke the truth, more words spilled out. "I *want* to do better." In a lighter tone, I said, "I want to do all the wonderful things my third grade teacher believed I could do."

He said, "Duffy, just remember, you don't have to do all the wonderful things in one year!" We laughed. He looked at my few belongings: some clothes, books, an easel and paint box. "I can squeeze it all in the trunk of my car. You could move out right now."

I agreed. "But not tonight."

Chapter 22
ESCAPE

I lay in bed the next morning in the steamy heat wearing only panties, my feet on the pillow. Alone and half-awake, I looked upside down out the window at the sky and dreamed of new places to go, people to meet, paintings to paint. I thought, *Tonight I'll be free*. I had agreed with Stan that at six o'clock that Thursday evening, after work, when I arrive back at Third Street, he'd pick me and my stuff up. I had to quickly decide what I'd keep and what I'd leave behind.

Footsteps in the hall distracted me. *If that's Carmen*, I thought, *what would I tell him about my packing*? But no key clicked in the door. I figured possibly a neighbor was picking through the discarded stuff I'd already left outside the door.

The alarm buzzed, and I jumped up. Yay! That meant the electricity finally was turned on, and I didn't have to run up to the roof to check the clock on the church bell tower. I passed the door, still hearing rummaging outside, and noticed that the night before I hadn't set the police lock properly. Fixing it required only a simple adjustment: temporarily unlock it, then lock it again. I lifted the pole to unlock . . . and, to my horror, saw the doorknob turn.

Someone was trying to get in! In panic, I leaned on the door and quickly stuck the pole back into locked position, just in time.

Heart pounding, I saw a hole in the door, where an old keyhole had never been covered and fixed. I looked out. Bloodshot eyes stared back at me! I felt invaded. I thought, *My God, whoever he is, he can see me here, half naked.* I leapt back.

The doorknob rattled, and a man's voice gurgled, "Open the door!"

I feared at first it could be Andy, the sculptor. But no, not his eyes or voice. I nervously looked up above at the space where a window had once been, now a gaping hole that more than one burglar had climbed through. I wanted to yell. But I remembered when that window had been smashed to smithereens not a soul appeared then to check out what caused the racket. Yelling now would be utterly pointless. I had no phone—I couldn't call the cops, or call Marie, who'd be useless anyway.

Anxiety gripped me. I focused on getting dressed and getting to work at Mazaltov's. I jerked a mini out of the closet and threw it on. With shaking hands, I tied my hair back with a paisley scarf and smeared on lipstick, now hearing scraping sounds in the hall. I wondered, *Is this man dragging boxes to stand on to get in through the hole? I need to get out of here before he breaks in. But how can I get past him?*

I knew only one way to escape. I grabbed my purse and wobbled in my heels over to the window and with trembling hands unlocked the black metal gate. I found the strength to heave up the heavy window, while feeling the intruder's eyes watching me through the keyhole. I crawled over the splintered windowsill out to the fire escape, afraid that, when I got down to the ground below, he'd be waiting in the yard to snag me.

Chapter 23
DAD

The light stabbed my eyeballs, and I quickly snapped them shut. I asked myself, *Where am I?* From somewhere above me I heard Nanny's Hungarian accent, recognizable even when she whispered. "She's been sleeping so long."

I heard Mom reply in a weak voice, "She was in a daze, totally exhausted." My head, resting on a soft pillow, felt like a bowling ball. I fluttered my eyelids half open to scan the space, and Janis Joplin came into focus. *Oh, the poster above Maureen's bed.* I understood I was occupying her room in Mom's apartment but not exactly how I got there. I recalled riding on the uptown subway on my way to Mazaltov's then, yearning for my mom, I switched lines to Queens. Right now, I wanted only to go back to sleep.

Distant voices piqued my ears. Nanny described her alarm when I'd showed up the previous morning at her home, asking for my mother. She told Mom, "Janet looked so thin. She asked for you, even though she knows you don't live with me, and you work during the day. Peculiar. Then I saw blood on her leg." I could picture Nanny clasping her hands, her thin lips stretched as she fretted that I "didn't seem to know" I'd cut myself or how. She told Mom I'd mumbled something about "a fire escape."

Fire escape. In a flash, I felt as if I were back there.

I'm on the fire escape, running away from a man trying to break into my pad. I climb down the black iron ladder, but it ends a full story above the backyard. I crouch in front of a window and look into a railroad flat and see someone familiar—the Ukrainian woman with her little white lap dog. I tap on her window, and she looks up, startled. Though I'm scared shitless, I act as if nothing is particularly peculiar about me, a stranger, standing out there on her fire escape in a mini dress and heels. I smile pleasantly and, as if it's an everyday request, I yell through the dark glass, "Would you please let me through your apartment?"

The lady frowns and points to her ear. *Oh, shit.* I figure she can't hear. Or doesn't speak English. The woman cocks her head and looks at me with curiosity. "I just need to get through to the stairs," I say, loudly, pointlessly. She shrugs her shoulders, raises her finger and disappears. My heart sinks. I can't go back up, and I can't get through; I have to jump off. I look down.

I'm pissed. I ask myself, *Why does the ladder of a fire escape end a full fucking story above ground? How stupid. Well, maybe not. If it was close to the ground, a robber or rapist could just walk up the fire escape and break in. But when there really is a fire or robber or rapist that people must escape—then what? Are we supposed to jump down a mile and risk breaking a fucking leg?*

The woman comes back. She scrutinizes me—my hair tied back with a paisley scarf similar to the one on her head—and probably decides I am not a robber or rapist. She holds up a key, takes forever fumbling to unlock the security gate and then gestures to me to lift the window. Grateful, I try. It's incredibly heavy. Straining, I heave it up just enough so I can squeeze through, and just as I lift my bare leg over the wooden ledge, her short husband charges into the room, his white hair flying. He yells, "No, no," followed by a rush of words I don't understand but sound like curses. He shoves me back out and barks at his wife. From his tone I figure he's saying, "You crazy woman, what the hell are you doing?"

Nanny's voice seemed closer. "She's pale and skinny as a ghost." Mom said, "I didn't know ghosts were skinny," joking like a child, which tickled me. I smiled as I fell back dreaming.

Floating back ten years to my beloved third grade teacher, I hear her say, as skinny ghosts fly around me, *"Nobody believed people could fly."* The beautiful Black face of Mrs. Rousson hovers over me, her cherry lips whisper to me, *"But now we can fly. You have so many gifts, you can do anything, nothing is impossible."* And I am flying, off a fire escape . . .

Nanny's voice rose in a low whine right above me. "She was always a good girl, a smart girl. What happened to my darling?" Mom didn't answer, her silence like ashes in a fading fire. I thought, *They're lamenting over me like I'm dying.* "Oh, no—Mom, Nanny—I am not dying," I wanted to say; "I am full of life." But my lips felt as cracked as desert flats. I sensed no saliva on my tongue. I asked, "Water, please."

I heard a quick inhale of breath, the rustling of clothes and slippers on the wood floor, and the faucet running. I imagined cool water pouring out like a waterfall. Nanny returned and raised my head off the pillow, caring for me as she had when, as a schoolgirl, I stayed home sick. Then and now she nursed me as if determined to ward off death, which had taken her own child, Pauline.

Mom, with nervous but gentle hands, helped me sit up and drink water. She combed my hair, as she did when I was little, making my scalp tingle. She asked me, "Janet, dear, your knee was bloody, and you were dazed. You talked to Nanny about a fire escape."

I nodded, thirst quenched, ready to sleep more.

"Did you fall off or jump?" Mom asked.

I recalled being on the fire escape, getting ready to jump off. But I slipped against the rail and fell. The old Ukrainian man must have seen me fall and changed his mind. In any case, he helped me in through his window and out through his door.

I just wanted to sleep, but I answered Mom, "I fell. I guess I got the cut on the fire escape.

Nanny whined, "Darling, what in the world were you doing on a fire escape?"

"Trying to . . . escape!"

Nanny held her hands in prayer and murmured, "My child . . ."

I closed my eyes and sensed Nanny thinking of her little Pauline. Images flashed in my mind of how her unnecessary and tragic death spread like fire through generations. Grief charred Nanny's heart so she couldn't dare love her surviving daughter, fueling Mom at a young age to seek love, and though she found passion with Dad, still craved attention from other men. Dad grew hot with jealousy, and our parents' arguments led to divorce and stoked desire in my sisters and me to break away too young. I turned my head to the wall and said, "Stop."

Mom heard and asked if I had pain. I shook my head. She examined my leg, smiled, and said, "Just scrapes, nothing broken." I thought, *The breaking had occurred inside me*. After many previous narrow escapes, the panicked fear I felt on the fire escape burned through me and left me craving the peaceful release of deep sleep.

With warm hands, Mom helped me sip cool water. I felt her love, unconditional love, and my heart softened. I thought, *She had a load to deal with—an emotionally damaged mother and an alcoholic husband, yet she's always made me feel loved.*

I thought, *Our family did share some happy times, too, didn't we?* Mom always tried to be cheerful. She loved fashion, and when my sisters and I were little, she dressed us in clothes that matched hers. Dad laughed at his own jokes. We girls loved watching them dance the Lindy Hop; all our friends said, "What a good-looking couple." And there were summer days at Jones

Beach and outings to church or to the city. I perked up and said to myself, *I am safe now, here with my mother and grandmother, whose love is lighting up the dark room. I am home, ready to wake up.*

———————

Maureen arrived home after school and further brightened my mood. She offered me Lipton tea and said, "Wow, Janet, you were totally zonked last night." I felt guilty I'd taken her bed, but she said, "No problem, I often prefer to stay at Aviva's home." Just then Aviva appeared, her wild hair hiding her pretty face.

She blurted out, "I'm sorry, I was wrong . . ."

I told her to forget it. I blamed Don, a man in his mid-twenties, for trying to seduce her, a child of fifteen. I said, "His idea of freedom is to screw as many girls as he can." The three of us agreed. "It was Don, not you."

"Yeah," Aviva said, then added, "It was a little me, too." We laughed again.

Barbara popped in for a surprise visit. I still felt weak but a full night's sleep in a safe place had done me wonders. Maureen shared that she was on track to graduate early, after the fall semester. In the spring, she'd turn eighteen, and, following the rebellious pattern of women in our family—Mom, Barbara, and me—she planned to immediately leave home.

I felt words of warning rising in my throat but getting stuck. Barbara also had concerns. She said, "I wouldn't marry right away, like I did." I asked about her husband, Maurice, a generation older than her. He became very jealous over nothing, Barbara said. "Like if I play Latin music on the radio, he accuses me of having a Latin lover."

After my sisters left, Mom brought me the phone to dial Penny. She was on her way to volunteer at the community center where she helped people fight eviction, but she decided instead to take the bus to visit me. Mom brought her to me, and Penny said, "Jan, I got your postcard when you were on the road with a guy." I told her that the guy, Carmen, had been on the anti-war march we attended with Martin Luther King Jr. to the United Nations for peace and freedom. And I said, "At art school we fell in love. But once Carmen and I set up in the East Village, the only freedom he desired was to play his music and get high."

Penny's lips curled at the thought of wasting time that could be used to work for change. She never smoked pot but did like smoking cigarettes and lit up. She asked what I'd seen in Carmen. I had to say that in the beginning we had loving times—I learned about jazz. And meditation—another thing she thought self-indulgent. She listened intensely to my stories of how it got tough when we ran out of money: searching for a place to lay our heads, panhandling for change to call about a job, trying to iron a skirt with a pot of boiling water. She said, "Sweetie, you experienced poverty firsthand. Most middle-class people have no idea how poor people struggle every damn day."

I told her our love was done when he got dragged into drugs. Penny rolled her eyes. "In the end," I said, "the most valuable thing I learned was how to survive."

In her wise and empathetic way, she said, "You were forced to find strengths you didn't know you had." She asked, now that I got that adventure out of my system, how I'd "get back on track." She reminded me it was not too late to register at City College. I thought about the Ivory Tower that I'd disdained. Now, after being on the streets, it seemed much more attractive.

Later, Mom came to sit with me. I asked her where Dad was living. She knew only where he was working—no longer in Jamaica or Bedford Stuyvesant. "He's not walking a beat anymore," she said. "He's been transferred to an NYPD office downtown, where he can't do much harm." *Harm?* I asked what Mom meant. In the past, Mom had rarely hesitated to lay on me the brutal truth about Dad, but now she avoided my question. "All I can say now is he's one lucky son-of-a-gun."

———

Feeling better on Saturday, I made the rounds of seeing friends while I was in Queens. The heat wave over, I rambled over to Bill's studio. I thought about how I loved Bill's humanity and how he found freedom by bucking conventions and finding his purpose in painting. Together, on a white wall, we'd flocked with magic blue dust, then painted in faces with bright oil colors, bringing forth an image of kindness. I kept his wise words with me every day. Bill taught me: "We need to hold the vision—and pass it on."

I hadn't expected to see Natasha at Bill's studio, but she appeared to fully belong. As she washed Bill's brushes like I did when *I* was a senior in high school, I thought, *She apparently found the guts to rebel against her strict parents' restrictions.* She packed chalk for flocking cartoons—Bill had a new commission to paint more murals. I noted the flowery Russian babushka around her head, and that she wore a more fitted dress over a slimmer figure.

"Bill's diet works," she said, smiling at him.

Bill asked me about college. I said I still wanted to study art. He said, "Your college in the city—doesn't it offer art courses?"

———

At Freedom Place, Socrates beamed, and the gang called out friendly hellos when they saw me. They'd gotten over their shock and disappointment over Arthur's arrest, and were busy debating details over a Great Society after-school program that would free kids from the temptations that come with too much unsupervised time.

Rudy introduced me to a Jewish girl, Rachel, who would teach arts and crafts. When they looked at each other, their faces erupted into smiles. He said, "We met at Queens College." Rudy had freed himself from the draft and now it looked like good things were developing for him all around.

Stan arrived with the usual delicious-smelling pepperoni pizza. When he saw me, he looked hurt. I asked him what was up. He said he'd shown up at six o'clock the previous Thursday, the day we'd agreed on, to move me out of Third Street. I apologized and told him about the intruder, my panicked flight down the fire escape, and making my way home to Mom's. His face softened. "The main thing, Duffy, is you got out of the ring. If you need me, you know how to reach me." I hoped we would stay in touch because we shared a commitment to the movement for national freedom. And I knew he wanted for his sons what I wanted: personal freedom.

On Sunday morning I walked to the Hollis Unitarian Church to worship and saw, hanging outside the modern box-shaped building, not a religious symbol, but a banner with the words, "Don't Buy Grapes." It showed support for increased wages for migrants working in California vineyards. I laughed, proud that our faith found spiritual fulfillment through social action.

One of Mom's artistic friends, Grace, who I'd last seen at Mom's wedding in New Jersey, came up to hug me and welcome me home. She recalled reading in our church newsletter my essay that, at the age of fifteen, I'd presented at a youth service—a monologue called "Who Am I?" I told Grace that I'd discovered many more facets of myself since then, but I still asked myself that same question. She said, "So do I," and we laughed. Then we cried together during the service, moved by singing a hymn I'd learned there in childhood, *"From all that dwell below the skies, / Let hymns of hope and faith arise; / Let peace, good will on Earth be sung, / Through every land, by every tongue."*

On Monday I fully expected Mazaltov to fire me, but because he'd been so kind, I wanted to show up in person. I expected I'd explain why I'd missed work, apologize, then leave jobless and broke. He looked at me with soft brown eyes and affirmed he'd received a call from my mother that explained my absence. He invited me, if I felt well enough, to get back to work. Grateful, I nodded and climbed upstairs to paint with Candy. At lunchtime I returned to thank him. Before I knew it, words popped out of my mouth announcing a plan not yet fully conscious in my own mind. "I've decided to go back to college in the fall."

A *mensch* to the end, Mazaltov told me that was a good decision. I gave notice, and he didn't even blink. He said, "If you want any freelance work, I'm keeping the door open."

Feeling free and energized, I sauntered through tree-lined paths in Central Park before taking the 8th Avenue subway to the Upper West Side near Columbia University. Vera, who cherished her freedom to study and was already ensconced at Vassar, had advised me to check out the neighborhood, not far from City College. She told me I'd find postings of rooms for rent on a bulletin board in a Jewish Deli. Eating a fresh knish, I looked at the notices. Most landlords charged about twenty dollars a week. On a public phone, a deep-throated woman answered my call and invited me right over to a building on 110th Street. A cool breeze from the Hudson River blew through the wide street, offering a refreshing preview of the fall season on its way.

My mind raced with questions as I rode up the elevator. After the diversity in the East Village, its kookiness and creativity, would I like uptown with its serious academic atmosphere? Would the neighborhood be too homogenous and predictable? I rang the bell and a black-haired woman flung open the door with a toothy smile. Wearing a rose in her hair, dangling earrings, and false eyelashes, she stood before a freely painted, colorful abstract painting. I felt right at home.

At the end of the day, running from the subway station to the police station, I could see the magnificent Brooklyn Bridge. I caught Dad just before his office doors closed. He wore a short-sleeved white shirt and red tie. Another police officer asked, "Ed, is this your daughter? A lovely girl." I hadn't expected the compliment and felt pleased when Dad said, "And she's smart, too," while smiling and placing his hand on my back like he was showing me off. *He sure is a good guy when he's sober*, I thought, and I hoped he would remain free of alcohol. "Let's go pick up a hot dog at the park," he said, "and take a look at the Statue of Liberty."

A great idea. We took the train down Broadway to Bowling Green and, amid the omnipresent noise of traffic, we headed toward the tip of Manhattan. I asked Dad how he liked his new job. He said, "I'm relieved to be off the streets. New York is a tinder box, just a match flick away from becoming Detroit." Dad walked gingerly and had to stop a couple times to calm the pain in his heart. I took his arm. When we heard the calls of the gulls and smelled the saltwater, I told him, "Dad, I'm going to get re-instated at City College."

He said, "That's good news." I informed him I planned to study art. "Art?" He advised me to get teaching credentials. He reminded me that teachers have steady jobs and summers off. "You'd be free to travel." I promised I'd think about it. He said, "You know, it's perfect, if in the future you ever want a family . . ."

"Dad, I don't know yet about any of that. All I know is, now, I love art." He acknowledged that art ran in the family, admittedly not on his side. I said, "No kidding. You got stuck at stick figures." He laughed his loud laugh, a sound so good to hear, I didn't care that people stared. Then I blurted out, "Listen, I'm leaving the East Village. I found a room on the Upper West Side."

"Good move," was all he ventured to say.

I told him the landlady charged twenty dollars a week. "Can you help me pay for it?" He grimaced, saying he wished he could help me out, but he was broke. I felt a zap of hurt. Sure, he was struggling to push up from rock bottom, but so was I. He did offer to pack his car and move my stuff, but said he had a limited budget. He asked if I knew he was retiring.

I did know. Mom had finally revealed what had happened with Dad. Cops she knew who'd worked with Dad told her different stories. One cop told her that Dad blacked out, fought with another cop and got arrested. Shocking. But another cop told her another story, that Dad had been drinking in a bar and took out his gun, held it to his own temple, and threatened to blow his head off. That broke my heart. It pained me to think how desperately unhappy he must have been. He swiftly faced consequences. He lost his beat and right to carry a gun. This humiliating incident occurred just months short of the twenty years he needed to serve on the police force to be eligible to receive his pension.

———————

Battery Park bloomed with summer-green trees. We walked past Castle Clinton, an old fort, renovated just last year, Dad informed me. I thought, *Only Dad knows these little facts*. I felt a tug on my heart, missing the long talks we used to have. On the riverside, I watched waves crash on small boats rocking in the wake of larger boats and invisible currents. I thought, *Our family breakup was a shipwreck—each of us scrambling to save ourselves— sink or swim*.

Dad almost lost it all, but the blue brotherhood took pity, Mom had told me. On condition that he stay sober, the police force employed him at an office to push paper until he reached the requirement for his pension. I asked Dad if he looked forward to retirement.

He said, "It's hard to imagine being free from work. I always wanted to travel," he said. "I will—if my heart holds up."

I felt a rush of sympathy. "Dad, for things I've said and things I did, I'm sorry if—"

"I know."

"I was foolish."

"Me, too," he said. "How about we put it behind us?"

He needed to sit. On a bench, we looked out on the sun-splashed river. He said, "New York boasts the safest harbor in the world."

We stared, transfixed by the glory of the Statue of Liberty. Proud that he'd taken his girls here, he asked what I remembered. The biggest thrill for my sisters and me was being allowed to climb toward the crown and the torch, way up high where birds flew in circles. We'd called out, "I lift my lamp to the golden door," the last line of "The New Colossus," the Emma Lazarus poem set on a bronze plaque in the pedestal of the statue, a poem that Dad had us learn by heart. He had pointed out the broken chains at Lady Liberty's feet, which most tourists missed, explaining that the French sculptor, Bartholdi, intended to celebrate the abolition of slavery in America.

I asked Dad if he remembered when, the prior Thanksgiving, we'd talked about the Black preachers who prayed under the statue for "sanity" in White America. He did. He sighed and said, "The movement for freedom cannot be stopped." He proclaimed that people from all over the world seek freedom in America, and he spoke of Nanny on her ship from the Old World heading toward Ellis Island, elated to be greeted by the Statue of Liberty. "When she arrived in a new world, she was just two years older than you are now," he said, giving me something to ponder. He said his ancestors had arrived a century ago, before France gave us the statue.

I said, "A lot of water has passed under the bridge since then."

Dad turned to me. "Okay, for your room, I can't afford twenty dollars a week," he said. "But I can pitch in fifteen." I suggested the landlady might accept eighteen. He said, "Okay. Seventeen." We laughed and shook on the deal.

A huge crowd of tourists caught our attention as they surged forward on the dock to board a ferry to Lady Liberty. Watching the parents, noisy kids, needy babies and elders hunched over on canes, I marveled at the variety of clothing styles, accents, languages, ethnicities, and skin colors. I said, "Visitors from all over America, and all over the world!"

Dad began to quote the Emma Lazarus lines in which the statue, "Mother of Exiles," beckons: *"Give me your tired, your poor, your huddled masses . . ."* Dad waved his hand over the crowd of tourists and, with a flash in his laughing Irish eyes, he joked, "Sure enough, they showed up—the 'huddled masses'!"

I finished the line, *"'. . . yearning to breathe free.'"*

The End

AFTERWORD

"The way to right wrongs is to turn
the light of truth upon them."

—Ida B. Wells-Barrett, an African American born
enslaved, an abolitionist, suffragist, and journalist
who campaigned against lynching in the 1890s.

Queens Village, which was all White when I grew up there, is now one of the more diverse neighborhoods in New York City and in the country. In another reversal, the tenements of the East Village have been renovated into homes that often sell for many millions of dollars.

In fall, 1967, I did take the apartment on the Upper West Side of Manhattan and waitressed after classes at City College. On New Year's Eve, gladly putting 1967 behind me, I painted myself, feeling determined to become the person I was meant to be. In January 1968, I transferred to the School of Visual Arts and moved to an apartment on East 25th Street with Maureen, who'd graduated high school early. Excited, newly in love, I allowed myself to be coaxed into taking a psychedelic, mescaline, and—after the stress of the previous year—I broke down.

Maureen turned eighteen in May 1968, flew to San Francisco, and returned in the fall to live with Ruthie on the Upper West Side while she attended City College. Aviva attended college in Madison, Wisconsin, earned a Master's in Social Work and worked as a middle school counselor in North Carolina. Ruth became a lawyer and raised a family in New York and New Jersey. Maureen moved to Florida, where our parents had relocated with their new spouses. Maureen became a highly successful massage therapist, earned a master's degree in mental health counseling, and lives a good single life as an ex-patriot in Ecuador.

Barbara divorced Maurice, returned to school, and earned a PhD, the only doctorate in the family. She married a wonderful man of Puerto Rican heritage, Spencer, and spends time with his son and family. As Dr. Duffy, she thrives as an author, speaker, management trainer, psychotherapist, and host of *Just Relationships*, a radio show on Long Island, New York.

Dad retired with a pension in 1968, married Carol, a mother of two children, and they took me in when I needed help. They moved to Florida and had a son—the year I turned twenty-one, I gained a brother. Soon afterwards, Dad gave up drinking, and I gave up resentments. He remained sober until his death—he died of a heart attack at age sixty-six in 1988. Today I enjoy a stepfamily of brothers, sisters, nieces, nephews, grandnieces, and grandnephews. I honor him for turning me on to literature, current events, and Unitarianism.

Mom re-married in 1968, and in 1970 she invited me to live with her after my breakdown so I could return to college. She divorced for the third time. In her sixties she became a senior model and married a man of means. Widowed, in 2001 she moved to an assisted living residence in Connecticut where she enjoyed a gentleman friend and special family occasions at my home. At Gibbs College, Norwalk, I arranged a one-person exhibit of her fashion art from the 1960s. She died the following year, 2008, at age eighty-two. She taught me love of beauty and art and how to explore emotions.

I earned a BA in fine art and a teaching certificate from Adelphi University, followed by a master's in art education from Queens College, City University of New York. I began my first job teaching in 1974, the same year I found my true love, Jim, an English teacher. We soon married and moved temporarily to

Switzerland, where our son was born. While abroad, I painted, and wrote the first draft of this memoir.

———

Nanny moved to a German Old Folks Home on Long Island, near Barbara and Spencer. Whenever my sisters or I visited her, she gave us whatever she could. She lived to see her great grandchild, my baby, David, before she died at age eighty-four in 1984. She taught me about unconditional love. Nanny's property on Long Lake in Rhinebeck, New York, passed through several owners and now serves as the home of Omega Institute for Holistic Studies.

———

Penny and I, in late 1967, celebrated the Supreme Court decision, Loving vs Virginia, which ruled that bans against interracial sex and marriage violated the Fourteenth Amendment of the

Constitution. She married a Haitian activist, and they had two children. She died of lung cancer in 2019. Her daughter followed her path of championing people's right to affordable housing. Penny's children, grandson, family, and friends will never forget her. Her passion for justice lives in me today.

————————

Vera and I continue "sharing our journeys." We met up in Paris and Geneva and lived near each other in Connecticut for thirty years. She picked up more languages and, as Professor Vera Schwarcz, she taught Chinese Studies at Wesleyan University and Hebrew University. She was awarded a Guggenheim Fellowship and authored nine scholarly and poetry books, including *Bridge Across Broken Time: Chinese and Jewish Cultural Memory* and *Colors of Veracity*. Widowed, she remarried and moved to Jerusalem. We correspond and manage an in-person visit about once a year, when she crosses the Atlantic to visit her three children and seven grandchildren.

Annie joined me in visiting Vera in 1969. That year, soon after Woodstock, she invited me to stay in her Manhattan apartment while I painted her portrait commissioned by her parents.

As she had dreamed, she did become a world-renowned writer, Ann Druyan. She penned several books and co-wrote *Cosmos: A Personal Voyage*, a spectacular TV series with the famed astrophysicist Carl Sagan, who became her husband. They had two children. After Carl died, Ann invited me to her new production at the opening of the Rose Center for Earth and Space at the American Museum of Natural History in New York City. We stay in touch sporadically online. In fall, 2020, I enthusiastically watched her production of her third Cosmos TV series, based on her marvelous book, *Cosmos: Possible Worlds*.

Stan visited me on the Upper West Side, and I sometimes visited Freedom Place in fall, 1967. In winter, 1968, he visited me on 25th Street. The last time I saw him was at Penny's apartment, a year after the assassination of Rev. Dr. Martin Luther King Jr.

I last visited Bill in 1972 when I graduated college. I heard he found a position teaching at a liberal arts college in New Jersey but could not locate him.

Rudy and I stayed in touch. I visited him and his girlfriend in the Bronx, and he visited me on Long Island where we bicycled to a Quaker meeting. I regret that we lost contact when Jim and I moved abroad in 1978.

Jim and I are going strong after forty-five years, both writing books, enjoying friends, and hiking out West when we visit our son, David, our daughter-in-law, Meghan, and our beloved granddaughter. I pray that all children (who go forth, stumble, and pick themselves up) be blessed with equal opportunity and healthy, creative, prosperous lives.

———————

The Unitarian Universalist faith that urged me as a child to "go forth," still nourishes my spirit and values. We act on our beliefs and support Black Lives Matter as the civil rights movement of our times. Our faith is building a beloved community for racial justice, gender equity, and a more perfect democracy, similar to the rebellious movement I joined in 1967.

CREDITS

All the works of art are by author, Janet Luongo. Photographs are by the author, or a friend, family member, or someone unknown. Known photographers are credited below.

Photographers

Front Cover: Janet in 1967. Photographer unknown.

Chapter 4: Demonstrators-Harlem-1964. Photo File URL: https://upload.wikimedia.org/wikipedia/commons/c/c8/ Demonstrators-Harlem-1964.jpg Attribution: Dick DeMarsico, New York World Telegraph & Sun / Public domain

Chapter 6: Vera and Janet. Photo by Ann Druyan

Chapter 11: Rev. Dr. Martin Luther King Jr. marching with Dr. Spock in NYC in April, 1967. Photo: Benedict J. Fernandez (Nat'l Portrait Gallery, Smithsonian Inst., gift of Eastman Kodak Prof. Photog. Div., the Engl Trust and Benedict J. Fernandez). Photo: public domain.

Chapter 14: NYPD arrests on Memorial Day, Tompkins Square Park, Photo by Wes Waites, *The East Village Other*, a counter-culture newspaper, 1965-72. Volume 2, issue 14, June 15—July 1, 1967. Source: Independent Voices, an Open Access Collection of an Alternative Press

Afterword: Janet and Jim's wedding, 1976; photo by Nicholas DeCandia.

Ann Druyan at NYU, 1966, printed by permission.

Poetry, Songs, Lyrics

Poems selected are in the public domain.

Song titles are not granted copyright.

Lines of literature quoted are short and within limits of fair use.

ACKNOWLEDGMENTS

My loving husband Jim, over decades, offered generous support that allowed room for me to pursue creative projects. I am forever grateful.

Editors and teachers: Writing group leader, Patrick McCord at *Write Yourself Free*, brilliantly perceived my underlying themes before I did. Carol Dannhauser, author, journalist, editor, and co-founder with Tessa Smith McGovern of Fairfield County Writers' Studio (FCWS), urged me to dive deep. Sophfronia Scott, author and teacher at FCWS, inspired me with powerful essays, her perspective on issues of race, and her life as a successful author.

She Writes Press, an award-winning Indie publisher, the first and only one to which I applied, is the partner I hoped for. I am grateful for publisher Brooke Warner, an invaluable and accessible guide; Laura Matthews and Megan Hannum, sensitive proofreaders; and Samantha Strom, who managed my project to completion.

Early readers gave perceptive and honest feedback: Denise Page, Director and Facilitator of Racial Justice at Ubuntu

Storytellers; Roz McCarthy, journalist and former English teacher; Marina Thomas, social worker and therapist; and Jamie Forbes, former Family Faith Formation Director at the Unitarian Church in Westport.

Supporters: Colleagues at the National Speakers Association offered opportunities to present. Jan Yager at Hannacroix Creek Books, Inc., invited me to publish. Sharon Crain invited me to China to speak on creativity. Writers and directors at the Westport Art Center: Gina and Chris Tracey, Gabi Coatsworth, and Ina Chadwick offered me a stage for my play and stories. At the Norwalk Public Library, librarians Cynde Lahey and Sally Nacker provide several platforms to speak about writing and Indie publishing.

Justice partners: Arnela Ten Meer, LGBTQ+ activist; Dr. Amanda Kemp, author and facilitator of interracial conversations; and Sonja Ahuja, co-leader of Eliminating Racism, shared their insights and friendship at the Unitarian Church, Westport, Connecticut.

Unitarian Universalists and kindred spirits: Rev. Frank Hall, Rev. John Morehouse, Ed Thompson, David Vita, Nate Pawleck, Rev. Barbara Fast, Rev. Debra Haffner, Rev. Jim Francek, Pat Francek, Cheryl Dixon Paul, Sudha Sankar, Beth Cliff, Sari Bodi, Dan Iacovella, Ellie Grosso, Shanonda Nelson, and my entire beloved community who inspire, connect, and act on our values of peace and unity. Yogi Hari, Shanti Mission, Muktinath, and Self Realization Fellowship offer me treasured spiritual insights.

ABOUT THE AUTHOR

Janet Luongo creates stories and art, gives speeches and workshops, and works for racial and gender justice. Her book, *365 Daily Affirmation for Creativity*, with a foreword by Jack Canfield, was published in five countries and led to bookings as far away as Xian, China. Janet served as president of the New York Metro chapter of the National Speakers Association. She taught art to students from college to kindergarten; exhibited paintings in New York, Geneva, and Paris; and designed diversity programs in Connecticut museums for underserved students, programs that garnered awards and media. She founded a nonprofit for feminist artists in Connecticut, a chapter of Women's Caucus for Art, and in fifteen years, they mounted forty exhibits and produced *Women Make Art*, a film screened at a UNIFEM festival.

Born in New York City, Janet lived in Switzerland for eight years and moved to Connecticut in 1986. She returned to the faith of her childhood in joining the Westport Unitarian Universalist congregation, who honored her in 2020 as a Leading Light for her lay ministry and activism for democracy. She resides in Norwalk with her husband Jim, also a writer, and their cat Lucky. They enjoy yoga and hiking with their son and his family in the Rockies.

Engage with Janet at www.janetluongo.com.

SELECTED TITLES FROM SHE WRITES PRESS

She Writes Press is an independent publishing
company founded to serve women writers everywhere.
Visit us at www.shewritespress.com.

The Outskirts of Hope: A Memoir by Jo Ivester. $16.95, 978-1-63152-964-1. A moving, inspirational memoir about how living and working in an all-black town during the height of the civil rights movement profoundly affected the author's entire family—and how they in turn impacted the community.

You Can't Buy Love Like That: Growing Up Gay in the Sixties by Carol E. Anderson. $16.95, 978-1631523144. A young lesbian girl grows beyond fear to fearlessness as she comes of age in the '60s amid religious, social, and legal barriers.

Home Free: Adventures of a Child of the Sixties by Rifka Kreiter. $16.95, 978-1-63152-176-8. A memoir of a young woman's passionate quest for liberation—one that leads her out of the darkness of a fraught childhood and through Manhattan nightclubs, broken love affairs, and virtually all the political and spiritual movements of the sixties.

Hippie Chick: Coming of Age in the '60s by Ilene English. $16.95, 978-1-63152-586-5. After sixteen-year-old Ilene English, the youngest of six, finds her mother dead in the bathroom, she flies alone from New Jersey to San Francisco, embarking upon a journey that takes her through the earliest days of the counterculture, psychedelics, and free love, on into single parenthood, and eventually to a place of fully owning her own strengths and abilities.

All the Ghosts Dance Free: A Memoir by Terry Cameron Baldwin. $16.95, 978-1-63152-822-4. A poetic memoir that explores the legacy of alcoholiwsm and teen suicide in one woman's life—and her efforts to create an authentic existence in the face of that legacy.